INTELLIGENT TESTING: INTEGRATING PSYCHOLOGICAL THEORY AND CLINICAL PRACTICE

The field of intelligence testing has been revolutionized by Alan S. Kaufman. He developed the Wechsler Intelligence Scale for Children – Revised (WISC-R) with David Wechsler, and his best-selling book, *Intelligent Testing with the WISC-R*, introduced the phrase "intelligent testing." Kaufman, with his wife, Nadeen, then created his own series of tests: the Kaufman Assessment Battery for Children (K-ABC), the Kaufman Test of Educational Achievement (K-TEA), the Kaufman Brief Intelligence Test (K-BIT), and many others. The K-ABC, the first major intelligence test to challenge the Wechsler, helped raise the bar for future tests. This book is a celebration of Kaufman's life, and work, with contributions by a who's who in IQ testing, including Bruce A. Bracken, Dawn P. Flanagan, Elaine Fletcher-Janzen, Randy W. Kamphaus, Nancy Mather, R. Steve McCallum, Jack A. Naglieri, Thomas Oakland, Cecil R. Reynolds, and Robert J. Sternberg. The book, edited by his son James, features essays from former students and colleagues expanding on Kaufman's work and ideas.

James C. Kaufman, PhD, is an associate professor at the California State University at San Bernardino, where he directs the Learning Research Institute. Dr. Kaufman's research focuses on the nurturance, structure, and assessment of creativity. Kaufman is the author or editor of 15 books either published or in press. These include *Essentials of Creativity Assessment* (with Jonathan Plucker and John Baer; 2008), *International Handbook of Creativity* (with Robert J. Sternberg; Cambridge, 2006), and *Applied Intelligence* (with Robert J. Sternberg and Elena Grigorenko; Cambridge, 2008). His research has been featured on CNN, NPR, and the BBC and in the *New York Times*. Kaufman is a founding coeditor of the official journal for APA's Division 10, *Psychology, Aesthetics, and the Arts*. He is also the associate editor of *Journal of Creative Behavior* and *Psychological Assessment* and the new editor of *International Journal of Creativity and Problem Solving* and the series editor of the Psych 101 series. He received the 2003 Daniel E. Berlyne Award from APA's Division 10 and the 2008 E. Paul Torrance Award from NAGC's Creativity Division.

Intelligent Testing

INTEGRATING PSYCHOLOGICAL THEORY AND CLINICAL PRACTICE

Edited by

James C. Kaufman

California State University at San Bernadino

CAMBRIDGE UNIVERSITY PRESS

Cambridge, New York, Melbourne, Madrid, Cape Town, Singapore, São Paulo, Delhi

Cambridge University Press

32 Avenue of the Americas, New York, NY 10013-2473, USA

www.cambridge.org

Information on this title: www.cambridge.org/9780521861212

First published 2009

Printed in the United States of America

A catalog record for this publication is available from the British Library.

Library of Congress Cataloging in Publication Data

Intelligent testing: integrating psychological theory and clinical
practice / edited by James C. Kaufman.
p. cm.
Includes bibliographical references and index.
ISBN 978-0-521-86121-2 (hardback)
1. Intelligence tests. 2. Kaufman, Alan S., 1944– I. Kaufman, James C.
II. Title.

BF431.S565 2009
153.9′3–dc22   2008043033

ISBN 978-0-521-86121-2 hardback

This book is about Alan S. Kaufman, the psychologist.
My dedication is to Alan S. Kaufman the man –
my father and my friend and an integral part of everything I am.
I love you, Dad.

CONTENTS

vii

ACKNOWLEDGMENTS

Thanks to Phil Laughlin, Jeanie Lee, Eric Schwartz, and Simina Calin for their help in shepherding this book to press and to David Loomis and Royah Peterson for editorial assistance.

ALPHABETICAL LIST OF AUTHORS AND AFFILIATIONS

JAN ALM
Uppsala University, Sweden

KYLE BASSETT
School Board of Hillsborough County, Florida

BRUCE A. BRACKEN
The College of William and Mary

MICHÈLE CARLIER
Aix Marseille University and CNRS
University Institute of France

JASON C. COLE
Institute of Consulting Measurement Group

CLAIRE ÉNÉA-DRAPEAU
Aix Marseille University and CNRS
University Institute of France

DAWN P. FLANAGAN
St. John's University

ELAINE FLETCHER-JANZEN
University of Northern Colorado

TOSHINORI ISHIKUMA
University of Tsukuba

RANDY W. KAMPHAUS
Georgia State University

JAMES C. KAUFMAN
California State University at San Bernardino

NADEEN L. KAUFMAN
Yale University School of Medicine

ELIZABETH O. LICHTENBERGER
Alliant University (San Diego)

NANCY MATHER
University of Arizona

R. STEVE MCCALLUM
University of Tennessee, Knoxville

JACK A. NAGLIERI
George Mason University

THOMAS OAKLAND
University of Florida

SAMUEL O. ORTIZ
St. John's University

CECIL R. REYNOLDS
Texas A&M University

JENNIE KAUFMAN SINGER
California State University at Sacramento

ROBERT J. STERNBERG
Tufts University

PART ONE

THOSE WHO KNOW HIM

1

Alan S. Kaufman's Contributions

NADEEN L. KAUFMAN
Yale University School of Medicine

JAMES C. KAUFMAN
California State University at San Bernardino

The field of intelligence testing has been revolutionized by the work of Alan S. Kaufman. As the project manager for the Wechsler Intelligence Scale for Children – Revised (WISC-R), he worked directly with David Wechsler. His best-selling book, *Intelligent Testing with the WISC-R*, introduced and popularized the phrase "intelligent testing," an idea that stressed the psychologist's theoretical knowledge and experience as the primary ingredient for meaningful and appropriate testing to occur. Single numbers, or scores, mean little by themselves; the key to functionality is the score within a broad, yet individualized, context. The test examiner is expected to apply her integrated and internalized training and bring her own clinical experience to the testing session. In this way, the examiner can best help the child or adult being evaluated by understanding and interpreting a wide range of behaviors, and making direct inferences about observed problem solving strategies, to answer pertinent referral questions. Every aspect of psychology is brought into play to interpret a set of scores in the context of accumulated research. This kind of assessment is far more likely to change lives than the narrow, test-centered intelligence testing more typical of the decade of the 1970s, when Kaufman was venturing farther away from his "pure" measurement background and feeling the needs of clinicians.

Kaufman, with Nadeen, then created his own series of tests: the Kaufman Assessment Battery for Children (K-ABC), the Kaufman Test of Educational Achievement (K-TEA), the Kaufman Brief Intelligence Test (K-BIT), the Kaufman Adult and Adolescent Intelligence Test (KAIT), and many other instruments. The K-ABC, the first major intelligence test to

3

challenge the Wechsler, was known for its top-notch standardization process and accompanying validity research studies, raising the bar for future tests. Kaufman's measurement and statistics background (he received his PhD from Columbia under Robert L. Thorndike) helped develop a new level of sophisticated test interpretation. The K-ABC was also the first test to integrate theoretical cognitive psychology into testing, using the ideas of Luria and Sperry in its conception. The Kaufmans have also written the K-CLASSIC, a computerized test of cognitive ability, for ECPA, a French publisher, and have revised the K-ABC, K-TEA, and the K-BIT.

Alan Kaufman, with Nadeen, has edited a series of *Essentials of Assessment* books that explain different testing tools in an easy-to-understand manner. Kaufman continues to be an active test author (completely revised second editions of the K-ABC and K-TEA appeared in April 2004, and new tests, books, and other projects will be coming out shortly) and research psychologist. He was been a coeditor of the journal *Research in the Schools* from 1992 to 2003, served on the board of five professional journals and has published 18 books and more than 200 articles, reviews, and chapters in professional journals and books in the fields of school psychology, special education, clinical psychology, neuropsychology, and educational psychology. Among Alan Kaufman's books are *Intelligent Testing with the WISC-R* (1979), *Intelligent Testing with the WISC-III* (1994), *Assessing Adolescent and Adult Intelligence* (1990; 3rd ed. with Liz Lichtenberger, 2006), and several that he has coauthored for the *Essentials* series, such as *Essentials of WISC-IV Assessment* (with Dawn Flanagan, 2004).

Alan Kaufman is a fellow of four divisions of the American Psychological Association (APA) and of the American Psychological Society, and is a recipient of several awards, including the Mensa Education and Research Foundation Award for Excellence and APA's Senior Scientist Award from Division 16 (School Psychology).

In addition, Alan S. Kaufman has served as a mentor to a whole new generation of intelligence test authors and users. From 1974 to 1997, Nadeen and Alan Kaufman trained school psychologists and clinical psychologists, and supervised graduate-student research at the University of Georgia, the National College of Education in Evanston, Illinois, the California School of Professional Psychology, San Diego campus, and the University of Alabama. These students, such as Jack Naglieri, Bruce Bracken, Cecil Reynolds, Randy Kamphaus, and Steve McCallum, have further changed the field that Kaufman helped establish.

2

Who Is Alan S. Kaufman?

ELIZABETH O. LICHTENBERGER
Alliant University (San Diego)

Alan S. Kaufman needs little introduction to those in the field of psychological assessment, as he has been well known for his strong influence on the field for nearly four decades. The qualities that have made Kaufman such an influential person in his field are personal as well as professional. The impressive and immense list of articles, chapters, books, presentations, and assessment tools that Kaufman has on his vita clearly demonstrates his impact as a professional. However, who Kaufman is personally – a kind, generous, insightful, and strong man – is just as important to understanding how his influence has reached so far.

Working with Kaufman can be, at first, intimidating. However, despite that fact that he is a larger-than-life figure in the field, Kaufman possesses the ability to make you feel as important as he is, by revealing his humanity and kindness through sharing many anecdotes about his work and his life. He is truly one of the best story-tellers I know, and has a memory for details that is keener than most. A typical meeting with Kaufman is over a late breakfast or dinner, with his wife and work colleague, Nadeen, at his side. The meeting may proceed with Kaufman sharing an anecdote about his work on the WISC-R with the late David Wechsler. Perhaps he may tell the story of when he tried to convince Wechsler to get rid of the WISC item "Why should women and children be saved first in a shipwreck," which ends with a red-faced Wechsler exclaiming, "Chivalry may be dying. Chivalry may be dead. But it will not die on the WISC." Or perhaps he may share the story of how he first started his higher education as a medical student, but luckily ended up instead as a psychology doctoral student specializing in psychometrics under Robert L. Thorndike at Columbia. If you are a baseball fan, he may reel off an impressive list of memorized baseball statistics for you. No matter what the story, smoothly delivered with his dry sense of humor, Kaufman has the ability to engage you and simply put you at ease.

Once Kaufman has shared bits and pieces of himself through his very entertaining anecdotes, then he gracefully slides from the casual conversation into the business portion of the meal without even skipping a breath. During the business part of the conversation, the manner in which he suggests that you should undertake a new project is subtle, but always persuasive. Kaufman has an uncanny ability to make you believe that you are the perfect man or woman for the job (and truthfully, his insight into people's own capabilities is often better than their own). His words of persuasion typically begin with something like, "I would like it if you wrote this article" or "I would like it if you coauthored this book with me." Not a more direct, "You should do this or that" but, "I would like it if . . ." Because of his engaging personality and subtle ability to persuade, Kaufman has planted many seeds of greatness and has cultivated a field of leading experts in assessment.

Part of what has made Kaufman's reach in the field so broad is his eye for spotting the potential greatness in those around him, and fostering excellence in those that he believes has potential. He has taught and worked with many individuals who have gone on to become well recognized test authors, prolific researchers and writers, and professors. The list of professionals that Kaufman has mentored and taught includes Cecil Reynolds, Randy Kamphaus, Bruce Bracken, Steve McCallum, Jack Naglieri, and Patti Harrison, just to name a few. Through coauthorships and his editorial roles, he continues to shape, teach, and encourage professionals, such as myself and Dawn Flanagan. Thus, his reach in the field has extended well-beyond his own professional works.

By setting the stage with an understanding of who Kaufman is as a person and how his influence has broadly affected many in the field, his professional achievements are even more awe-inspiring. The field of intelligence testing has been revolutionized by Kaufman's work. As project manager for the Wechsler Intelligence Scale for Children – Revised (WISC-R), he worked directly with David Wechsler. His best-selling book, *Intelligent Testing with the WISC-R,* introduced and popularized the phrase "intelligent testing," an idea that stressed the psychologist's theoretical knowledge and experience as the primary ingredient for meaningful and appropriate testing to occur. Single numbers, or scores, mean little by themselves; the key to functionality is the score within a broad, yet individualized, context. The test examiner is expected to apply her integrated and internalized training and bring her own clinical experience to the testing session. In this way, the examiner can best help the child or adult being evaluated by understanding and interpreting a wide range of behaviors, and making direct inferences about observed problem solving strategies, to answer pertinent referral questions. Every aspect of psychology is brought into play to interpret a set of scores in the context of accumulated research. This kind of assessment is far more likely to change lives than the narrow, test-centered intelligence testing more typical of the decade of the 1970s, when Kaufman was venturing farther away from his "pure" measurement background and feeling the needs of clinicians.

As a psychologist, researcher, and author, Kaufman has never been afraid to stand up for what he believed was true. Even when working with his well-respected mentor, Wechsler, he was compelled (albeit, at times, a bit hesitantly) to say what needed to be changed on the WISC. In the early 1980s, Kaufman broke from the Wechsler tradition when he and Nadeen created their own intelligence test: the Kaufman Assessment Battery for Children (K-ABC). As the first major intelligence test to challenge the Wechsler, the K-ABC was known for its top-notch standardization process and accompanying validity research studies, raising the bar for future tests. Kaufman's measurement and statistics background helped develop a new level of sophisticated test interpretation. The K-ABC was also the first test to integrate theoretical cognitive psychology into testing, using the ideas of Luria and Sperry in its conception. When the K-ABC was published, the Kaufmans received a lot of feedback, and the test itself became very controversial. However, the Kaufmans did not shy away from the controversy, instead they took the positive and negative feedback to develop the second edition of the test – the KABC-II. In their desire to advance the science and quality of psychological assessment, together the Kaufmans have published eleven cognitive, achievement, and neuropsychological tests, including the popular first and second editions of the K-ABC, K-TEA, and K-BIT.

The significant contribution that Kaufman has made to the field with the publication of his numerous tests has had an effect not just in the United States, but worldwide. In fact, a psychologist in Germany (and a friend of Kaufman's), Dr. Peter Melchers, once reminded Kaufman, "Don't forget that the K-ABC is influential worldwide ... You have a responsibility, not just to the U.S., but to the K-ABC worldwide." Kaufman has taken that responsibility seriously, and now his K-ABC has been translated, adapted, and standardized in more than fifteen countries. The Kaufman tests in the United States and worldwide are just the tip of the iceberg in terms of how Kaufman's professional work has influenced and continues to shape the fields of clinical assessment, school psychology, and neuropsychology. He has authored or coauthored 17 texts and more than 150 articles in peer-reviewed professional journals, many of which continue to impact how and why professionals interpret various tests of cognitive ability the way they do.

It is difficult, if not impossible, to concisely summarize what Kaufman means to the fields of psychology, school psychology, and neuropsychology. His life and work have touched and continue to touch so many – some through his inspiring professional talks and insightful writing, others through his shaping of their professional lives as their teacher or mentor, and for most through his tests and related texts, which articulate his continually evolving conceptualizations of how to best understand assessment data as an "intelligent tester." As a person on whom Kaufman's influence has reached, I feel fortunate.

3

Alan S. Kaufman: The Man and the Professional

JENNIE KAUFMAN SINGER
California State University at Sacramento

Growing up as somebody's daughter, it is sometimes hard to observe who your parent is, as a person in the world. However, as you grow up, and become an adult yourself, one can reflect back and see a more balanced picture of the person who raised you. My father is someone dedicated to his profession, to his students, to the idea that he could make a difference in the world. He was able to look at theories, statistical tables, and formulas, and to study children with learning disorders, and then somehow evaluate and synthesize the information in a unique way so that the field of intelligence would be forever enriched and changed for his having entered it.

He is a man capable of great love. He met his wife, Nadeen, when they were both teenagers. Their love would solidify over the years and transcend a number of life events that might have separated many others. They provided comfort to each other as life partners and intellectual collaboration as working partners. Their specialties and thought processes intertwined to create the long list of tests enumerated in this book. Nadeen worked with him and they processed their thoughts and ideas 24/7 in a thriving atmosphere for their creative and brilliant minds.

The idea of what is just, or justice, has been an important idea for my father. This idea, combined with the knowledge he has gained and synthesized in the field of IQ has led to many important accomplishments in the field of intelligence. He has brought the idea of theory, and in particular, of neuropsychological theory, to the field of intelligence testing. He has made the point that it is the clinician's judgment, and not a number, that should help define an individual's true potential. He has brought logic and statistical knowledge into the field so that random error, statistical error, and behavioral observations can carry the appropriate weight in assessing a person's abilities. His methods of analyzing subtest scatter along with clinical observations and other test information make sense both logically

9

and clinically. Mainly, when using his methodology, a clinician is taught to consider all variables including culture and immediate environment, which might impact a fair and appropriate assessment of the client's intelligence level.

Mentoring others has always been important for my father. He has spent many hours working with all levels of graduate students over the years. It has been his mission to help as many as possible complete their doctoral dissertations, and he has been instrumental in aiding many (including me) to getting their dissertations finally done. He has helped others to publish their work, and to develop their own ideas. He has been influential in training a new generation of test authors, such as some of the highly esteemed authors in this book. The act of teaching and helping someone to learn a concept has always given him satisfaction. Regardless of all of the tests and books that are an immense credit to him, the amount of teaching that he himself has done, along with the amount of learning he has facilitated through his many books, such as his "Intelligent Testing with the WISC" series, is one of his biggest accomplishments.

MY FATHER'S INFLUENCE ON ME

I always knew that my father was well-known in certain circles, but as a child I was not sure which circles those were. Certainly, he was not a television or movie star. When I entered graduate school to get my PhD in clinical psychology, I found out. I took a course in intelligence testing my second semester. Two of the three texts required were written by Alan S. Kaufman. My fellow students, who had already been in class with me for a semester, started asking me, "Hey, are you related to this guy?" When I replied that my father had written both the texts *Intelligent Testing with the WISC-R* and *Assessing Adolescent and Adult Intelligence*, the jig was up. All of my classmates looked at me with new eyes that belied the awe that a reference to my father would bring up. I would see that look in the years to come in conferences and at lectures.

For now, it meant that I had to read a few chapters ahead in the books and sometimes field questions on the phone: "What did your dad mean by this or that in Chapter 10?" I would be asked. I would tell the caller that I would think about it and then get back to them. I would put in a call to my father. "What did you mean by this or that in Chapter 10?" He always made time for me, even if he was famously writing a chapter in his head (he would see the entire chapter appear in his head and then would have to quickly get to a computer to type it out). He explained the concept in detail, and I would call my friend back, and would explain it to them, word for word.

When it came time for me to write my dissertation, my father's advice kept me on track: Pick a topic that you can do quickly so that you can finish, analyze your data, and be done. He went through the huge, over 200-page document with a red pen. I have never known anyone, before or since, who has a better grasp of American Psychological Association (APA) style, grammar, or the best way to state something. He spent hours and hours helping me with what has to be the most painful rite of passage.

I went into clinical practice, but my father's passion for teaching and research had an influence on my idea of an "ideal career." I am now a university professor, and I teach and work on research projects. My field of criminal justice and forensic psychology is different than his, but I have given many of my father's (and mother's) tests, and have read and studied his books and methods. I have had the opportunity and luck to be able to discuss and debate his methodology with him personally, and can say that I have had personal tutoring by Dr. Alan Kaufman in the best way to give and interpret intelligence tests. I have taken full advantage of the opportunity of being the daughter of Alan S. Kaufman.

PART 2

INTELLIGENT TESTING

4

Intelligent Testing: Bridging the Gap between Classical and Romantic Science in Assessment

ELAINE FLETCHER-JANZEN
University of Northern Colorado

INTRODUCTION

One of the many contributions made by Alan Kaufman to the field of psychology in the past 30 years, *Intelligent Testing*, became the gold standard for psychometric test interpretation and clinical assessment. It was an interpretive system developed by Kaufman (1979, 1994; Kaufman & Lichtenberger, 2004, 2006) during the revisions of the Wechsler scales (Wechsler, 1949, 1974, 1981) and introduced the notion that appropriate use of information gained from any IQ test used in a comprehensive assessment was guided by various clinical principles that incorporated both quantitative and qualitative analyses.

The development of this system was probably a natural response on the part of Kaufman and many others to calm the controversy surrounding the measurement of intelligence in the latter part of the twentieth century. Metatheoretical principles for clinical assessment were needed in the 1970s because impassioned arguments against the misuse of IQ scores were frequent, and, sadly, evidence of misuse was replete (Berninger & O'Donnell, 2005; Fletcher & Reschly, 2005; Prifitera, Weiss, Saklosfse & Rolfus, 2005).

The intelligent testing philosophy was essentially the first system of test interpretation that followed scientific principles and at the same time overtly sought to reduce inappropriate use of obtained test scores. Intelligent testing moved emphasis away from pure psychometric and reductionistic comparisons of test scores and demanded incorporation of a contextual analysis of the test subject and interventions that had ecological validity. This demand was reflective of a broader history of romantic science from the nineteenth century and early twentieth century where scientists explored consciousness from a pragmatic point of view and used narrative techniques to "expand the often impoverished repertoire of scientific language" (Halliwell, 1999, p. 238). Intelligent testing challenged the status quo by placing the onus of test interpretation squarely on the shoulders of the clinician and it demanded a very high standard of clinical expertise. Indeed, Anne Anastasi (1988) remarked:

> The basic approach describe by Kaufman undoubtedly represents a major contribution to the clinical use of intelligence tests. Nevertheless, it should be recognized that its implementation requires a sophisticated clinician who is well informed in several fields of psychology (p. 484).

This article speaks about the efforts of Alan Kaufman to unify the disparate forces in the field of psychometrics that have placed principles of assessment at the center of controversy. All great systems in psychology are born of circumstances that reflect history, survive controversy, maintain parsimony, are flexible and metaanalytical in nature, and have clinical utility. Kaufman's intelligent testing is no exception to this trend.

HISTORICAL CONTEXT OF INTELLIGENT TESTING

The intelligent testing philosophy was reflective of an older and broader struggle within the field of psychology as modern theories and applications melded with the zeitgeist of the times throughout the nineteenth and twentieth centuries. Divisions between science, ethics, and esthetics evolved into polemic debates about the inadequacies of objective science in capturing the elusive qualities of the human subject (Halliwell, 1999). On the other hand, at the turn of the twentieth century, most writings on psychology were bound up in an examination of the possible nature of psychology even being a science. Wilhelm Wundt, known as the father of experimental psychology (Cole, 1990), forcefully argued that the study of culture must be an integral part of psychology, in fact, a full half of its enterprise (Cole, 1990). Wundt called the first half "physiological psychology" and it was designed to analyze the contents of individual consciousness into its constituent elements so that universal laws that combined the elements could be illuminated (Cole, 1990). The other half of Wundt's theory was the "Volkerpsychologie," which was a historical and descriptive science. It included the study of higher psychological functions such as processes of reasoning and human language that extended beyond the individual consciousness (Blumenthal, 2001; Cole, 1990).

In terms of romantic science, Wundt was in good company. The current of romantic perspectives stayed steady with researchers and authors such as William James, Otto Rank, Heinz Werner, Ludwig

Binswanger, Erik Erikson, Alexander Luria, and Oliver Sacks, to name just a few, all of whom rejected dualism and encouraged pragmatics, holism, and research (in any area of psychology) that preserved nature and experience as one (Wilson, 2001).

In terms of intelligence per se, classical influences were emboldened with the establishment of psychometric methods, especially in North America (Tupper, 1999). The development of intelligence tests was prodded by exploration in empiricism and by society-driven variables (Kaufman, 2000). Sir Francis Galton, in England, pursued the assessment of giftedness and came to social policy conclusions (Nichols & Jarvis, 2006). Terman, Otis, and Yerkes, in America, assisted in personnel selection for the armed forces during wartime and also furthered psychometric design (Kaufman, 2000), and in France, formal measurement of intelligence emerged as a response to compulsory education for children and was lead by Alfred Binet (Das, 2004). Binet was interested in studying intelligence and how individuals differed from each other, especially individuals from different economic and ethnic backgrounds. Das (2004) suggests that Binet's aim was to

> determine qualitatively the mental level at which a child functioned, rather than to give the child a number, such as mental age. Thus he would have thought the use of his tasks to determine a strictly quantitative score, such as IQ, a betrayal of the tests' objective (p. 6).

Binet's concerns about differential impact of his tests did not appear to carry through to North American practice. The leading text on the Stanford-Binet battery was written by McNemar in 1942 and took a purely classical and psychometric perspective on interpretation (Kaufman, 2000). Indeed, this perspective continued with "a general compulsion toward psychometrically sound, data-driven quantitative research and assessment procedures" (Reynolds & French, 2005).

In Russia at this time, A.R. Luria was fully engaged in what ended up being a long journey of neuropsychological scientific inquiry that attempted to push the limits of brain–behavior knowledge and also meld romantic and classical research methods. Luria initially called the melding of the two approaches "the combined motor method" (Cole, 1990). This approach was based in the hope that Freud's clinical assessment methods could be positioned to experimentation. While the method did not eventually hold up to long-term use, Luria did experience progression of his ideas and came firmly to believe that "[t]he structure of the organism presupposes not an accidental mosaic, but a complex organization of separate systems... (that) unite as very definite parts into an integrated functional structure" (Cole, 1990, p. 15).

Luria, along with his colleagues, came to believe that the understanding of the sociohistorical context of a given patient directly led to diagnosis and intervention. Indeed, Luria later lamented that most twentieth century science was reductionistic and had lost the very reality of the patient that it sought to examine because the field had reduced all behavior to constituent parts, thereby losing the romantic whole (Sacks, 1990). He believed that thinkers who used observational and descriptive methods had declined in number and that the new science, which used technology and formal tests frequently, led the clinician to "overlook reality" (Sacks, 1990). He also believed that romantic science would "preserve the wealth of living reality" (Wasserstein, 1988, p. 440).

Oliver Sacks (1990) suggests that a characteristic of genius is to "contain great contradiction and richness, but at the deepest level resolve these into an ultimate unity" (p. 186). Luria struggled with this great contradiction and steadfastly remained an advocate of romantic science his attempts to resolve the ultimate unity in many of his later writings had the characteristics of elaborate case studies. Luria's romantic appreciation also culminated in a theory of brain functioning that (a) was developed without the benefit of modern imaging technology, (b) remains essentially unchallenged to this day (Golden, 1997; Tupper, 1999), (c) is responsible for the theoretical basis of newer intelligence tests and interventions (Kaufman & Kaufman, 1983, 2004; Angler & Das, 1996; Tupper, 1999), and (d) is currently leaving the confines of neuropsychology and infiltrating the practice of clinical and school-based clinicians (D'Amato, Fletcher-Janzen, & Reynolds, 2005; Angler & Dash, 1997; Hale & Fiorello, 2004; Kaufman & Kaufman, 1983; 2004; Miller, 2007; Prifitera et al., 2005; Reynolds & Fletcher-Janzen, 2007).

Probably the most salient point that can be made about these early and mid-twentieth century researchers is that as romantic scientists, they inherited from the nineteenth century romantics an emphasis on subjectivity but avoided a "transcendental idealism that enchewed empiricism" (Halliwell, 1999). At no time were any of these researchers seduced into reductionistic practice where the context of the individual patient was lost to quantitative analyses. Nor did they descend into specious subjectivity that lost what objectivity could be mustered through scientific methods. All were bound by an attempt to find unifying constructs that provided metatheoretical and metaanalytic explanations of cognitive functions.

DEVELOPMENT OF THE INTELLIGENT TESTING MODEL

In the 1960s, the zeitgeist of the times in cognitive assessment melded with the growth of the learning disabilities movement and the need for multiple indexes of abilities that would highlight cognitive strengths and weaknesses emerged. David Wechsler's answer to this movement was the development of the Wechsler scales and so began a directive for clinical as well as psychometric interpretative techniques (Kaufman, 2000; Kaufman & Lichenberger, 2006; Prifitera, Weiss, Sakalofske, & Rolfus, 2005).

One of the major influences on Kaufman that shaped the development and creation of the intelligent testing interpretive model was his relationship with David Wechsler. Kaufman speaks very fondly of his opportunity to work with Dr. Wechsler during the revision of the Wechsler Intelligence Scale for Children (Kaufman, 1994). He describes his mentor as being very perceptive and a gifted clinician more interested in the clinical (and romantic) applications of test items than psychometric qualities of item statistics, item bias, and factor analysis. Although Wechsler had studied with Charles Spearman and Karl Pearson and was fully capable of carrying out the sophisticated statistical analyses required, he maintained that he was just a clinician (Kaufman, 1994). Kaufman remarked on Wechsler's views about quantitative and qualitative analyses:

> Dr. Wechsler also wouldn't have been too pleased with the elimination of *beer-wine* in Similarities or of *knife and gamble* in Vocabulary – all potent clinical stimuli. He never worried much about a person missing an item or two or three because of its clinical content. More than once, he'd chide me, until it finally sunk in, "First and foremost, the Wechsler scales are clinical tests – not psychometric tests but clinical tests." That was why he got so upset when someone complained about the unfairness of this or that item. What's a couple of items to a good clinician? He never could really accept that stupid way so many people interpreted his tests, with formulas, and cut-off points, and the like: it's not what he had ever planned for his clinical Wechsler scales." (p. xv)

In the late 1970s, as demands for a coherent and parsimonious system of interpretation reached a peak, Kaufman unveiled the intelligent testing philosophy (Kaufman, 1979). The idea for the intelligent testing approach was sparked by Wesman's (1968) observations that intelligence tests of that time period basically measured what an individual had learned. Wesman's ideas also included arguments against the zeitgeist of the times (that intelligence tests measured an innate and immutable latent trait) and suggested that the separation of intelligence, ability, and achievement measures was more artificial than real (Kamphaus, 2001). Kaufman also negatively reacted to the common practice of overinterpreting single subtest point differences or low subtests scores from a psychoanalytical point of view (Kaufman, 2000). He built upon some of Wesman's ideas, continued ideas introduced to him by his mentor R.L. Thorndike, assimilated information about ipsative measurement from his wife and colleague, Nadeen Kaufman (Kaufman, 2000) and developed a system of principles of test interpretation that continues to include five guiding tenets of assessment (Kaufman, 1979; 1994; Kaufman & Lichtenberger, 2006).

CONTROVERSY ABOUT INTELLIGENT TESTING

The intelligent testing principles became very popular and, for many, the sina qua non of interpretation systems. The principles provided a reassuring directive for a clinician to present a sociohistorical and contextual picture of a patient so that appropriate interventions could directly lead from the assessment. Intelligent testing was, above all, a flexible, dynamic, and fluid system that was designed to bend to clinical judgment (Kaufman, 1994). In this sense, romantic and classical aspects of assessment were both respected and included. However, notwithstanding Kaufman's clear directive to keep a synthetic understanding of the system in mind, some researchers in the field criticized certain aspects of the intelligent testing method from a rigid psychometric point of view (e.g., McDermott, Fantuzzo, & Glutting, 1990; Reschly 1997; Watkins & Baggley, 1990; Watkins & Kush, 1994; Witt & Gresham, 1985) and Kaufman (1994) rebutted these claims many times and in many different ways but essentially believed that

> Those who have criticized the WISC-III, other intelligence tests, or the "Kaufman method" on empirical grounds have continually stressed the child's obtained scores, not an intelligent interpretation of them. They have focused on the specific theory a test was designed to measure, not on the multiplicity of theories that might offer alternate views of the scores, and they have usually argued their positions from the vantage point of group data. In short, they have abandoned the fundamental principles that were set forth to make IQ testing intelligent. (p. 25)

The flexibility of the system was to be steered by the expertise of the examiner and suited to the referral question at hand. Implicit in the intelligent testing model was the assumption that constituent parts of an assessment such as theories of intelligence, obtained test scores and the like, would be examined in detail, but at all times be used in an ecologically and clinically valid manner. Kaufman defended attempts to reduce the intelligent testing system to its constituent parts by repeatedly and carefully explaining the five tenets upon which it rested and stressing the interrelationships between the tenets (Kaufman, 1979, 1994, 2004, 2006). Each one of the tenets exemplifies the melding of qualitative and quantitative data and, in more historically broader terms, the merging of classical and romantic science. It is very difficult to determine from any of Kaufman's explanations of these tenets (Kaufman, 1979, 1994, Kaufman & Lichtenberger, 2004, 2006) that interpretation was based solely on quantitative analyses of scores. The irony, of course, is that the critics of intelligent testing ignored its metaanalytic nature and rested their rejection of the system on quantitative arguments. Indeed, Kaufman (1994) vividly describes the actions of the critics in the following passage:

> I came to the inescapable conclusion that my method of Wechsler test interpretation is sound and defensible, and that those researchers simply do not (or do not choose to) understand it. They have extracted from the system the few empirical steps that were imposed primarily to keep clinicians "honest" – the practice had long existed within the field of clinical assessment to interpret as meaningful small differences between subtests or IQs. But they missed the crux of the book, the part that outlined a method of intelligent assessment that encourages examiners not to interpret subtest profiles or IQ discrepancies in isolation. To prove their point that the ipsative approach should be punished painfully, they stripped the method of all dignity. They gutted it of its heart and soul, and lopped off the skull of a skeleton. (p. 5)

Steven Brecker (2006), the executive director for science of the American Psychological Association, recently suggested that reductionism has always been a central concern in psychology, that as new information about complex systems emerges so does the danger of individuals examining only the components of the system also emerge. This sole focus on components usually comes at the expense of understanding of how the components fit into the whole system. Brecker concludes that

> Complex systems – such as human behavior and cognition – are better understood through careful analysis of their components. This is just good science. The risk, of course, is equating our understanding of the components with the understanding of the complex system itself. (p. 23)

Perhaps criticism of intelligent testing was representative of naturalistic tendencies for the field of psychometrics to focus on advances of certain aspects of measurement rather than placing those advances within the context of clinical practice. Perhaps North American scientists were giddy with the exploration and momentum of quantitative analysis and the behavioral theory gains in the research literature. Perhaps the criticisms of intelligent testing were reflective of the vitriolic social arguments surrounding the practice of intelligence testing per se, and from a macro perspective, were an unrelenting continuation of the controversy that has plagued intelligence testing for the past century (Kaufman, 2000; Reynolds, 2007; Reynolds & French, 2005).

Much of the current controversy surrounding intelligence tests has localized to educational applications. Since learning disability (LD) discrepancy models were initiated and used in the past 30 years, the singular IQ score became overused or magnified as a central marker of intelligence (Berninger & O'Donnell, 2005). The full-scale scores were most certainly viewed as representing an individual's total intellectual capacity. This singular view translated into a parsimonious description of learning disabilities and transformed into the LD discrepancy model of learning disability identification. For many years, educational professionals were confined to strict eligibility guidelines set forth by federal and state agencies that demanded narrow statistical formulae using obtained IQ scores while ignoring psychometric principles such as measurement error (Berninger & O'Donnell, 2005; Reynolds, 2007). These constraints led to relatively easy placement decisions but poor intervention choices and program outcomes (Fletcher et al., 2002; Fletcher, Lyon, Fuchs, & Barnes, 2007). The latter, along with inappropriate expectations of treatment validity rising from single scores (Witt & Gresham, 1985), eventually led to the demise of the LD discrepancy model as its inadequacy was easily demonstrated (e.g., Fletcher, et al 2002; Fletcher & Reschly, 2005). Kaufman repeatedly traversed the LD discrepancy model by maintaining that "[t]he global IQ on any test, no matter how comprehensive, does not equal a person's total capacity for intellectual accomplishment" (Kaufman & Lichtenberger, 2006 p. 20). He also maintained that overinterpretation of global IQ scores was inappropriate and clinically unsound (Kaufman, 1994).

Regardless of the learning disability identification debate, Kaufman maintained a broader perspective for clinical practice, suggesting that the demise of the discrepancy model need not necessarily mean the demise of assessment of cognitive strengths and weaknesses (Hale, Naglieri, Kaufman, & Kavale, 2004). After all, the intent of the intelligent testing model was and remains to "bring together empirical data, psychometrics, clinical acumen, psychological theory, and careful reasoning to build an assessment of an individual leading to the derivation of an intervention to improve the life circumstances of the subject" (Reynolds, 2007, p. 1133).

Just as intelligent testing held the line for clinical standards of assessment during these years, advocates of reductionistic views on mental measurement certainly maintained a strong and influential course as well. For example, political and scientific advocates of the reauthorization of the Individuals with Disabilities Education Act (2004) suggested a model of assessment of children with severe learning problems and mental retardation that do not include norm referenced tests of cognitive ability (e.g. Fletcher & Reschly, 2005; McDermott, Fantuzzo, & Glutting, 1990; Reschly, 1997; Ikeda & Gustafson, 2002; Siegel, 1988; Witt & Gresham, 1985). This "RTI only" approach clearly displays an extreme, classical, behavioral, and reductionistic ideology that ignores the rich and valuable contribution of newer psychometric design and contributions about brain–behavior relationships furnished by newer cognitive ability tests (Berninger, Dunn, Alper, 2005; Fuchs & Young, 2006; Hale, Naglieri, Kaufman & Kavale, 2004; McCloskey & Maerlender, 2005). It is not surprising, therefore, to find Alan Kaufman once again voicing the tenets of intelligent testing to balance extremist views and bring back a unifying structure that tolerates diverse ideas about psychological assessment of children in educational settings (Hale, et al., 2004; Hale, Kaufman, Naglieri, & Kavale, 2007) He is joined by others in suggesting that the solution is not to throw out IQ tests but to "use the IQ test results in more intelligent and flexible ways" (Berninger & O'Donnell, 2005, p. 228 and e.g., Flanagan, Ortiz, Alfonso, & Dynda, 2006; Hale, 2006; Hale, Naglieri, Kaufman & Kavale, 2004; Naglieri & Paolitto, 2005; Schrank, Miller, Caterino, & Desrochers, 2006; Wodrich, Spencer, & Daley, 2006).

Kaufman makes the argument that environment versus heredity debates are applicable to policy decisions about group intelligence data but lose power when applied to finding out what an individual has learned from his or her life experiences (Kaufman & Lichtenberger, 2006). Group data describing general characteristics and general observations are appropriate in many cases, but group data has also, in the past, translated into policies and generalizations about intelligence being an immutable construct. However, individuals present a unique and singular life. It has been found that the brain has millions of cells that are genetically programmed to unfold and then are pruned and paired. These periods of growth and pruning are also filtered by environmental factors that influence which cells live and which cells die. Experiences change brain structure and vice versa (e.g., Perry, 2002; Perry & Pollard, 1997). Therefore, cognitive neuroscience has started to illuminate how "nurture" interacts with "nature" and vice versa. At the individual level, intelligent testing suggests that the clinician must try to determine the cognitive neuroscience involved with each subject in terms of cognitive strengths and weaknesses and then how the patterns evidence in everyday activities:

> The goal of the intelligent tester is to deduce when one or more subtests may be an invalid measure of a person's intellectual functioning for more subtle reasons: distractibility, poor arithmetic achievement in school, subcultural differences in language or custom, emotional content of the items, suspected or known lesions in specific regions of the brain, fatigue, boredom, extreme shyness, bizarre thought processes, inconsistent effort and the like.
>
> (Kaufman & Lichetenberger, p. 21).

Today, clinicians cite purposes of measuring potential of capacity, obtaining clinically relevant information, and assessing functional integrity of the brain, as the most important reasons for administering intelligence tests (Kaufman & Lichtenberger, 2006). Practitioners, regardless of political changes being forced into everyday practice by a few classical scientists or determination models, are therefore still interested in neuropsychological and clinical information that proves to be relevant to the referral question. Indeed, Reynolds and French (2005, p. 109) suggest that future efforts to elaborate and discover the mechanisms of biological intelligence will "likely fall to the neuropsychologist and behavioral neurochemist for resolution." Others (e.g., Yun Dai, 2005) maintain that future views on intelligence should include reductionistic and emergentist approaches.

THE FUTURE OF INTELLIGENT TESTING

Scientific inquiry into the workings of the brain and mind has a long history. Controversy about ways to assess the workings of the brain has accompanied that inquiry and will probably continue. There are many in the extremist behavioral camp insisting upon the total demise of norm-reference tests of cognitive processes and abilities. However, there is no reason to suppose that they will get their wish. Controversy will continue to surround these issues as long as classical and romantic perspectives remain embedded in the zeitgeist of the times. Human beings adore the mental exercise of bouncing between polar opposites, perhaps it is just too much fun not to do it. However, when the natural constraints of the scientific method draw the field of measurement too far into reductionism, thereby leaving practicality, ecological validity, and the reality of the patient behind, someone or something has to pull the field back to the everyday. Someone or something has to remind us that constituent parts need a cohesive and binding agent to make sense of collected data. That something could be a theory, or it could be a set of principles that guide practice, or both. In the case of psychological assessment, that something is intelligent testing.

Intelligent testing ascends to the concrete where all deductive and inductive judgments are guided by theory, translated by the clinician, and synthesized into an elegant whole. It takes us on a journey of analysis of the tiny details of history, culture, theory of mental measurement, test behavior, test results, context, and ecological validity. It then demands that we tell a story about an individual in the hope that the story makes sense and leads to an improvement of quality of his or her life. Kennedy and Turkstra (2006) summarize this point with a statement about clinical judgment:

> As researchers and clinicians, we recognize that even the most carefully designed, well-controlled study will never be sufficient to determine the best clinical practice for an individual client. This requires clinical judgment, which in some circles has taken on a pejorative connotation. Clinical judgment does not mean "anything goes if it seems reasonable." Rather, it is the skilled use of logical reasoning, knowledge, and experience to make decisions. The challenge for researchers and clinicians is to generate good judgments, avoid judgments that will not benefit the client, and learn to recognize the difference. (p. 158)

It is also supported by Prifitera et al, (2005):

> Test scores in and of themselves are not sufficient for a proper psychological assessment. Scores should be interpreted in the context of other relevant information, all of which may not be clear and objective but relies in part on the integrative skills and professional expertise of the evaluator. (p. 28)

The central point of intelligent testing is that the clinician's judgment regarding the patient is the central point. Insisting on a human element across all of the tenets of intelligent testing places Alan Kaufman as a romantic and classical scientist (among other honors). We live in an age of technology and computers that are not romantic in the least and will most assuredly play a large part of the future in testing (Kaufman, 2000; Lichtenberger, 2006). However, this does not shake Kaufman's insistence on clinical judgment being the single-most important factor in future assessment practice (Kaufman, 2000)

When Oliver Sacks (1990) was describing Luria's struggle to unify experiences, he suggested that a characteristic of genius is to "contain great contradiction and richness, but at the deepest level resolve these into an ultimate unity" (p. 186). This could very easily be applied to Kaufman's sustained efforts for balance through the teachings of intelligent testing. He has had the genius to observe and remark on the metatheoretical and metaanalytical aspects of mental measurement and the rare ability to resolve its contrasts into a unity of guiding principles. He has been constant in his vigilance to keep the balance between classical and romantic science and to defend against reductionistic practices that would drag clinical practice products down to simple and soulless sets of crunched numbers. Kaufman's vigilance has opened him up to severe and tiresome criticism over the years, however, criticism is the price of moving the field forward or even holding it constant. It is the price of sustaining prudence and reason, and it is the price of accepting romantic science. Alan Kaufman fortunately does have company – and what company! The history of melding romantic and classical science is littered with genius that struggled and fought for unifying concepts. A difficult task indeed, but one that remains, at heart, in the best interests of those it serves.

REFERENCES

Anastasi, A. (1988). Intelligent testing. Psychological Testing (6th ed.). New York: Macmillan.

Bayliss, Donna M.; Jarrold, Christopher; Gunn, Deborah M.; Baddeley, & Alan D. (2003). Do children's attention processes mediate the link between family predictors and school readiness? *Developmental Psychology* 39(3), 581–593.

Bernard, H.R. (1994). *Research Methods in Anthropology*, (2nd ed.). Thousand Oaks, CA: Sage.

Berninger, V.W., & O' Donnell, L. (2005). Research-supported differential diagnosis of specific learning disabilities. In A. Prifitera, D.H. Saklofske, & L.G. Weiss (Eds.), *WISC-IV Clinical Use and Interpretation* (pp. 189–229). Burlington, MA: Elsevier.

Berninger, V.W., Dunn, A., & Alper, T. (2005). Integrated multilevel model for branching assessment, instructional assessment, and profile assessment. In A. Prifitera, D.H. Saklofske, & L.G. Weiss (Eds.), *WISC-IV Clinical Use and Interpretation* (pp. 151–185). Burlington, MA: Elsevier.

Blumenthal, A.L. (2001). A Wundt primer: The operating characteristics of consciousness. In R.W. Reiber, & D.K. Robinson, (Eds.), *Wilhelm Wundt in History: The Making of a Scientific Psychology*. Dordrecht: Kluwer Academic.

Brecker, S.J. (2006). The newest age of reductionism. *APA Monitor on Psychology*, 37, 23.

Cole, M. (1990). Alexandr Romanovich Luria: cultural psychologist. In E. Goldberg (Ed.), *Contemporary Neuropsychology and the Legacy of Luria* (pp. 11–28). Hillsdale, NJ: Erlbaum.

D'Amato, R.C., Fletcher-Janze, E., & Reynolds, C.R. (2005). *The Handbook of School Neuropsychology*. New York: Wiley.

Das, J.P. (2004). Theories of intelligence: Issues and applications. In G. Goldstein, and S.R. Beers (Eds.), *Comprehensive Handbook of Psychological Assessment* (pp. 5–25). New York: Wiley.

Flanagan, D.P., Ortiz, S.O., Alfonso, V.C., & Dynda, A.M. (2006). Integration of response to intervention and norm-referenced tests in learning disability identification: Learning from the Tower of Babel. *Psychology in the Schools*, 43, 807–824.

Fletcher, J.M., Foorman, B.R., Boudousquie, A.B., & Barnes, M.A., Schatschneider, C., & Francis, D.J. (2002). Assessment of reading and learning disabilities: A research-based, intervention-oriented approach. *Journal of School Psychology*, 40, 27–63.

Fletcher, J.M., Lyon, G.R., Fuchs, L.S., & Barnes, M.A. (2007). *Learning Disabilities from Identification to Intervention*. New York: Guildford.

Fletcher, J.M., & Reschly, D.J. (2005). Changing procedures for identifying learning disabilities: The danger of perpetuating old ideas. *The School Psychologist*, 59, 1, 10–15.

Fuchs, D., & Young, C.L. (2006). On the irrelevance of intelligence in predicting responsiveness to reading instruction. *Exceptional Children*, 73, 8–30.

Golden, C.J. (1997). The Nebraska Neuropsychological Children's Battery. In C.R. Reynolds & E. Fletcher-Janzen (Eds.), *Handbook of Clinical Child Neuropsychology*, (2nd ed., pp. 237–251). New York: Plenum/Kluwer.

Hale, J.B. (November, 2006). Implementing IDEA 2004 with a three-tier model that includes response to intervention and cognitive assessment methods. *School Psychology Forum: Research in Practice*, 1, 16–27.

Hale, J.B., & Fiorello, C. (2004). *School Neuropsychology: A Practitioner's Handbook*. New York: Guilford.

Hale, J.B., Naglieri, J.A., Kaufman, A.S., & Kavale, K.A. (2004). Specific learning disabilities classification in the new Individuals with Disabilities Education Act: The danger of good ideas. *The School Psychologist*. Winter, 6–13.

Hale, J.B., Kaufman, A.S., Naglieri, J.A., & Kavale, K.A., (2007). Implementation of IDEA: Integrating response to intervention and cognitive assessment methods. *Psychology in the Schools*, XLIII, 753–770.

Halliwell, M. (1999). *Romantic Science and the Experience of the Self: Trans-atlantic Crosscurrents from William James to Oliver Sacks*. Aldershot, England: Brookfield.

Individuals with Disabilities Education Act (2004). 20, U.S.C. 1400–1419.

Ikeda, M.J., & Gustafson, J.K. (2002). Heartland AEA 11's problem solving process: Impact on issues related to special education (Research Report No. 2002–01). Available from authors at Heartland Area Education Agency 11, 6500 Corporate Dr., Johnston, IA 50131.

Kamphaus, R.W. (2001). *Clinical Assessment of Child and Adolescent Intelligence* (2nd ed.). Needham Heights, MA: Allyn & Bacon.

Kaufman, A.S. (1979). *Intelligent Testing with the WISC-R*. New York: Wiley.

Kaufman, A.S. (1994). *Intelligent Testing with The WISC-III*. New York: Wiley.

Kaufman, A.S. (2000). Intelligence tests and school psychology: Predicting the future by studying the past. *Psychology in the Schools*, 37, 1, 7–16.

Kaufman, A.S., & Kaufman, N.L. (1983). *The Kaufman Assessment Battery for Children (K-ABC)*. Circle Pines, MN: AGS.

Kaufman, A.S., & Kaufman, N.L. (2004). *The Kaufman Assessment Battery for Children*, second edition (KABC-II). Minneapolis, MN: Pearson.

Kaufman, A.S., & Lichtenberger, E.O., (2004, 2006). *Assessing Adolescent and Adult Intelligence* (3rd ed.) New York: Wiley.

Kennedy, M.R.T., & Turkstra, L. (2006). Group intervention studies in the cognitive rehabilitation of individuals with traumatic brain injury. *Neuropsychology Review*, 16, 151–159.

Lichtenberger, E.O. (2006). Computer utilization and clinical judgment in psychological assessment reports. *Journal of Clinical Psychology*, 62, 19–32.

McCloskey, G., & Maerlender, A. (2005). The WISC-IV integrated. In A. Prifitera, D.H. Sakalofske, & L.G. Weiss (Eds.), *WISC-IV Clinical Use and Interpretation* (pp. 101–149). Burlington, MA: Elsevier.

McDermott, P.A., Fantuzzo, J.W., & Gluttting, J.J. (1990). Just say no to subtest analysis: A critique on Wechsler theory and practice. *Journal of Psychoeducational Assessment*, 8, 290–302.

Miller, D. (2007). *Essentials of School Neuropsychological Assessment*. New York: Wiley.

Naglieri, J.A., & Das, J.P. (1997). *Cognitive Assessment System*. Chicago. IL: Riverside.

Naglieri, J.A., & Paolitto, A.W. (2005). Ipsative comparisons of WISC-IV index scores. *Applied Neuropsychology*, 12, 208–211.

Perry, B.D., & Pollard, D. (1997). Altered brain development following global neglect in early childhood. Society for Neuroscience: Proceedings from Annual Meeting, New Orleans, 1997.

Perry, B.D. (2002). Childhood experience and the expression of genetic potential: what childhood neglect tells us about nature and nurture. *Brain and Mind* 3: 79–100.

Prifitera, A., Weiss, L.G., Saklofske, D.H., & Rolfhus, E. (2005). The WISC-IV in the clinical assessment context. In A. Prifitera, D.H. Saklofske, & L.G. Weiss (Eds.), *WISC-IV Clinical Use and Interpretation* (pp. 3–28). Burlington, MA: Elsevier.

Reschley, D.J. (1997). Diagnostic and treatment utility of intelligence tests. In D.P. Flanagan, J.L. Genshaft, & P.L. Harrison (Eds.), *Contemporary Intellectual Assessment: Theories, Tests, and Issues* (pp. 437–456). New York: Guilford.

Reynolds, C.R. (2007). Intelligent testing. In C.R. Reynolds & E. Fletcher-Janzen (Eds.), *Encyclopedia of Special Education* (3rd ed; pp. 1132–1135). Hoboken, NJ: Wiley.

Reynolds, C.R., & Fletcher-Janzen, E. (2007). *Encyclopedia of Special Education* (3rd ed.). Hoboken, NJ: Wiley.

Reynolds, C.R., & French, C.L. (2005). The brain as a dynamic organ of information processing and learning. In R.C. D'Amato, E. Fletcher-Janzen, & C.R.

Reynolds (Eds.), *The Handbook of School Neuropsychology* (pp. 86–119). Hoboken, NJ: Wiley.

Sacks, O. (1990). Luria and "romantic science." In Goldberg, E. (Ed.), *Contemporary Neuropsychology and the Legacy of Luria* (pp. 181–194). Hillsdale, NJ: Erlbaum.

Schrank, F.A., Miller, J.A., Caterino, L.C., & Desrochers, J. (2006). American Academy of School Psychology survey on the independent educational evaluation for a specific learning disability: results and discussion. *Psychology in the Schools*, 48, 771–780.

Siegel, L.S. (1988). IQ is irrelevant to the definition of learning disabilities. *Journal of Learning Disabilities*, 22, 469–478, 486.

Tupper, D.E. (1999). Introduction: Alexander Luria's continuing influence on worldwide neuropsychology. *Neuropsychology Review*, 9, 1–7.

Wasserstein, A.G. (1988). Towards a romantic science: The work of Oliver Sacks. *Annals of Internal Medicine*, 109, 440–444.

Watkins, M.W., & Kush, J.C. (1994). Wechsler subtest analysis: The right way, the wrong way, or no way? *School Psychology Review*, 23, 640–651.

Wechsler, D. (1949). *Wechsler Intelligence Scale for Children (WISC)*. San Antonio, TX: The Psychological Corporation.

Wechsler, D. (1974). *Wechsler Intelligence Scale for Children-Revised*. (WISC-R). San Antonio, TX: The Psychological Corporation.

Wechsler, D. (1981). *Wechsler Adult Intelligence Scale (WAIS)*. San Antonio, TX: The Psychological Corporation.

Werner, H. (1937). Process and achievement: A basic problem of education and developmental psychology. *Harvard Educational Review*, 7, 353–368.

Wilson, E. (2001). Romantic science and the experience of the self: Book review. *Journal of the History of Science in Society* 92, 189.

Witt, J.C., & Gresham, F.M. (1985). Review of the Wechsler intelligence scale for children-revised. In J.V. Mitchell (Ed.), *Ninth Mental Measurements Yearbook* (pp. 1716–1719). Lincoln, NE: University of Nebraska Press.

Wodrich, D.L., Spencer, M.L.S., & Daley, K.B. (2006). Combining RTI and psychoeducational assessment: What we must assume to do otherwise. *Psychology in the Schools*. 43, 797–806.

Yun Dai, D. (2005). Reductionism versus emergentism: A framework for understanding conceptions of giftedness. *Roeper Review*, 27, 144–151.

5

The Intelligent Testing of Children with Specific Learning Disabilities

NANCY MATHER

University of Arizona

INTRODUCTION

The category of specific learning disabilities (SLD) encompasses a heterogeneous group of disorders that adversely impacts the development of some aspect of academic functioning and proficiency. Although few doubt the existence of SLD, a lack of consensus regarding definition, as well as a failure to resolve various identification and treatment issues, has plagued the field since its inception. One major area of controversy is the use of intelligence tests for the identification of individuals with SLD (Kaufman & Kaufman, 2001). During the last four decades, the work and writings of Dr. Alan Kaufman, in association with his wife, Dr. Nadeen Kaufman, have helped to clarify, refine, and substantiate the most efficacious ways intelligence tests can and should be used with individuals having or suspected of having SLD. The purpose of this chapter is to discuss various aspects of their contributions that have had particular relevance to and impact on the field of learning disabilities through my own perspective. The chapter includes discussion of several issues that have affected SLD identification and assessment procedures, as well as consideration of the most pragmatic and valid processes and procedures for diagnosing SLD.

DEFINITION OF SPECIFIC LEARNING DISABILITIES

One component of the controversy surrounding intelligent testing of individuals with SLD has been agreeing upon the fundamental characteristics of these disorders. To identify a disorder accurately, one must first define and delineate the characteristics that typify the problem. In essence, the basic component of nearly all SLD definitions is that learning disabilities comprise a category of specific disorders in one or more of the basic psychological processes involved in learning. Because development is uneven with some abilities being far more advanced than others, a discrepancy exists between a set of intact cognitive processes and one or more disordered processes (Hale, Naglieri, Kaufman, & Kavale, 2004; Kaufman, 2004). These weaknesses in the basic psychological processing or intracognitive discrepancies are considered to be the hallmark of SLD (Kaufman & Kaufman, 2001; Kavale, Kaufman, Naglieri, & Hale, 2005). Thus, to fulfill the requirement of the SLD definition, it is necessary to document cognitive integrities and one or more disorders within the basic psychological processes that are linked to academic difficulties (Hale et al., 2004; Kaufman, 2004).

Within both school and clinical settings, a major purpose of cognitive assessment is then to describe the fundamental disorder or disorders that have affected some, but not all aspects, of cognitive and academic performance. Unfortunately, the recent IDEA 2004 reauthorization does not realign identification procedures with the definition, and contributes further to a disconnection between the SLD definition and the selected assessment methodology. The reauthorization maintains the original definition of learning disabilities but does not provide a methodology for diagnosing SLD or make specific recommendations regarding how to identify and document the spared and disordered processes (Kaufman, Lichtenberger, Fletcher-Janzen, & Kaufman, 2005). In essence, the definition of SLD demands the identification of a processing disorder because identification is the central characteristic and defining feature of the disability (Kaufman, 2004) but the law does not specify how this should be accomplished.

During a class seminar on learning disabilities, the late Dr. Samuel A. Kirk proffered that "... a learning disability is like pornography; it's hard to define but you know it when you see it" (personal communication, September, 1981). The analogy holds true because most skilled psychologists, diagnosticians, and special education teachers recognize various types of learning disabilities when they encounter them. These seasoned professionals are guided, however, by clinical impressions and experience, rather than by legalistic constraints that have been imposed by rigid interpretation of the law. For example, after years of remediation to improve accuracy, a person with a reading disability may obtain a score in the average range on a measure of reading decoding (i.e., standard score of 90), but their scores on measures of processing speed and reading speed still remain well below average. In school districts that demand strict adherence to a legalistic criterion, slow processing speed and reading speed by themselves may not be considered sufficient to document the existence of a reading disability. The skilled evaluator will make an accurate diagnosis based upon a review of background information, as well as the functional limitation that results from slow reading speed on timed tests. Thus, an accurate diagnosis adheres to the definition, but must be multidimensional in nature.

ABILITY–ACHIEVEMENT DISCREPANCIES VERSUS CLINICAL TRADITION

For the last three decades, the field of SLD has been dominated by pre-occupation with mathematical formulas for identification of SLD despite the fact that intelligence tests were not originally built or designed to be used in mathematical formulas (Kaufman & Kaufman, 2001). After the passage of PL 94-142, most states and school districts based documentation of SLD on the existence of an ability–achievement discrepancy, rather than documentation of unusual variability among an individual's cognitive, perceptual, linguistic, and academic abilities. In fact, it appears that the biggest discrepancy that existed was between the SLD definition and then how this definition was operationalized (Hale et al., 2004; Kavale et al., 2005). Systems of educational classification were based upon special claims that intelligent quotients (IQs) actually measured a person's intellectual potential, a belief that was neither conceptually nor psychometrically jus-tifiable (Kaufman, 1979; Stanovich, 1999). This misplaced emphasis resulted in increased attention to test scores, and decreased attention to the meaning and inferences that could be derived from a careful analysis of the results.

The many limitations inherent with the use of an ability–achievement discrepancy procedure have been enumerated repeatedly (e.g., Aaron, 1997; Berninger, 2001; Fletcher et al., 1998; Fuchs, Mock, Morgan, & Young, 2003; Lyon, 1995; Mather & Healey, 1990). Bateman (1992) observed that the problems with the use of a formula for SLD identification are "... many, serious, and too often disregarded" (p. 32). To further complicate matters, state and school district guidelines have varied in regard to the specific method used to quantify a discrepancy, as well as to the magnitude of the discrepancy that is needed to qualify for services. Therefore, a child may be identified as having a learning disability in one school district, but then denied services in another, depending upon the state and the local criteria or the personal philosophy of an independent evaluator (Berninger, 1996).

In many school settings, unrealistic rules, which overemphasized the value and role of the obtained test scores, governed the eligibility decisions

(Kaufman, Harrison, & Ittenbach, 1990). Some school psychologists were even required to employ a specific formula to establish the existence of a significant discrepancy because of a misguided belief that this simplistic procedure was tantamount to legal compliance. Because of these state and district mandates, the focus became more upon compliance with eligibility policy, rather than on thoughtful clinical interpretation of multiple sources of information. The real problem was not, however, the clinicians, but rather the state guidelines that mandated the use of these formulas (Kaufman & Kaufman, 2001). This is not meant to imply that the test themselves were not useful. It was just that their diagnostic and clinical utility was lost because of a narrow focus upon just a few broad-based scores. As aptly noted by Willis and Dumont (2002), the determination of a disability should be more than "an exercise in arithmetic" (p. 173) and students who truly have SLD should not be denied services "simply because of the results of a statistical exercise" (Dumont, Willis, & McBride, 2001, p. 13).

Thus, in some districts, school psychologists became viewed as "gatekeepers" who held the mechanism for providing or denying special education services to students. One puzzling aspect regarding this whole process was that qualification for services was not based upon a need for help or even the level of severity of the problem, but rather upon the existence of a discrepancy between the scores from some selected intelligence test and some achievement battery. Children with low intelligence were usually not classified as students with SLD and rarely received the help that they needed (Siegel, 1989). Common sense dictates that mathematical formula should not be used to deny services to students who truly require a program of special education or to falsely "label" a student who does (Willis & Dumont, 2002). Clearly, unfairness and bias exist in a legal system that requires categorization and placement in services before students can receive help that is obviously needed, but these are different issues; unfair guidelines do not negate the fact that SLD is a meaningful category (Kaufman & Kaufman, 2001).

In spite of these constraints, well-trained clinicians have always used test instruments wisely. The beliefs of those who adhere to the clinical tradition have forever been at odds with the rigid ways in which local, state, and federal agencies enforced requirements for diagnostic and placement decisions (Kaufman, 2000). Sole reliance on a quantitative procedure clearly abdicates common sense. In fact, the use of formulae is the complete opposite of what skilled evaluators are trained to do. One may even assert that the identification of an ability–achievement discrepancy in a rigid, quantitative fashion has no meaningful role in SLD identification (Kavale et al., 2005).

In fact, the ability–achievement discrepancy procedure was never a good idea from the start because plugging the most global score into a formula was just "plain dumb" (Kaufman, 2004). Kaufman further observed that elimination of the discrepancy requirement from IDEA 2004 frees school psychologists from the shackles of the past. Kaufman and Kaufman (2001) reiterated that: "The time has come to release professionals from the burden of using psychometric instruments for purposes that the test authors never intended, and in ways (e.g., plugging obtained scores into uncompromising formulas) that defy a common-sense understanding of psychometrics" (p. 450). To be an intelligent evaluator, psychologists must go beyond mere score generation (Kaufman & Harrison, 1991) and translate psychoeducational data into educational action (Kaufman & Kaufman, 1983b).

PROBLEMS WITH FULL-SCALE INTELLIGENCE TEST SCORES

Strict adherence to a formula for the diagnosis of SLD resulted in an overreliance on global or full-scale scores that did not convey useful information for educational planning. When considering the diagnostic and clinical implications of cognitive assessment results, the least useful score is the broad-based, full-scale IQ score. The concept of general intelligence or *g* does little to assist with the identification or diagnosis of individuals with SLD. In fact, it is antithetical to most modern theories of intelligence (Kaufman, 2004).

Stanovich (1999) aptly defined intelligence as "... the statistical amalgamation of a panoply of different cognitive processes" (p. 352). A full-scale IQ score simply represents the individual's relative standing compared to the norm group, based on their aggregate performance at a specific point in time on a specific set of tasks that are designed to measure the test authors' conceptualization of intelligence (Mather & Wendling, 2005). As early as 1938, Stern reflected upon the limited value of global IQ scores, stating: "To be sure there has been and there still is exaggerated faith in the power of numbers. For example, 'an intelligence quotient' may be of provisional value as a first crude approximation when the mental level of an individual is sought; but whoever imagines that in determining this quantity he has summed up 'the intelligence' of an individual once and for all, so that he may dispense with the more intensive qualitative study, leaves off where psychology should begin" (p. 60).

Furthermore, all broad-based or composite scores mask the contribution made by reading-related cognitive abilities, so for individuals with specific reading disabilities the results must be interpreted with caution (Vellutino, 2001). Orton (1925) cautioned that for individuals with reading problems, full-scale scores tend to provide an entirely erroneous estimate of intellectual capabilities. Similarly, Kaufman (1979) advised that intelligence tests can underestimate a child's intellectual functioning and without careful interpretation, the results are unfair, and even "hazardous" to the child's welfare.

In addition, because the existence of SLD can impact and lower the full-scale score, definitions of SLD that require normal intelligence as part of the identification criteria are also suspect (Kaufman et al., 1990). A low intelligence score does not rule out the possible existence of a learning disability; the evaluator has to examine and consider the reasons for the low score. In addition, superior intelligence does not rule out the possibility of a learning disability. The evaluator has to consider all facets of performance. A learning disability can exist in people of any age who are at any level of intellectual functioning (Cruickshank, 1983; Shaywitz, 2003).

IMPACT OF PROCESSING AND LINGUISTIC DEFICITS

Processing deficits are as likely to impair performance on intelligence tests as on measures of academic performance (Kaufman & Kaufman, 2001). In addition, limited school achievement impairs performance on fact-oriented items and when communication problems occur, a child's intelligence test scores undoubtedly suffer (Kaufman, 1994). Similarly, Fletcher et al. (1998) observed that: "To the extent that the child who reads poorly has a significant language disorder, scores on a language-based IQ test will underestimate the child's aptitude for learning in other areas" (p. 200).

For individuals with SLD, as well as those with language impairments, certain subtests measure the weak cognitive and linguistic processes that can be the defining characteristics of the disorder, thus reducing the full scale score. These tests can be primarily linguistic in nature (e.g., low vocabulary), providing supportive information for a language impairment, or perceptual in nature (e.g., slow processing speed or poor memory span), providing supportive information for SLD. When examining an individual's performance on a subset of tests, the evaluator must consider how certain factors or abilities are suppressing the more global, broad-based scores. In these instances, an explanation must be provided regarding how one or more specific abilities are impacting linguistic or academic development.

For example, on many intelligence tests, considerable emphasis is placed on measures of acquired knowledge or crystallized intelligence and as a result, the low scores can be either the cause or the effect of the disorder (Kaufman, 1979). Because depressed performance may be the result of poor school achievement and limited learning opportunities, the obtained results may not provide an accurate estimate of learning potential. In addition, research supports the conclusion that verbal abilities for SLD samples decrease over time, demonstrating the gradual impact of the learning disability upon subsequent linguistic and academic performance and development (Kaufman, 1994). Kaufman and Harrison (1991) stated: "Thus, performance on an intelligence test may misrepresent the potential ability of individuals, which is less immune to the effects of culture and past learning, because the test is measuring an achievement-like component" (p. 100). In some instances, nonverbal tests provide a more accurate measure of general ability for children with SLD (Kaufman & McLean, 1986). Even with nonverbal measures, however, the evaluator must take care to acknowledge the potential impact of low specific abilities that are typically classified as nonverbal in nature (e.g., processing speed, visual-motor, visual-spatial thinking, etc.) on the broad-based score.

DISTINCTION BETWEEN INTELLIGENCE AND ACHIEVEMENT TESTS

With regard to the use of an ability–achievement discrepancy as the main criterion for SLD identification, one flaw was related to the proposed distinction between the contents of intelligence and achievement tests. If an individual's scores on the two different measures were to be used to document SLD, then the measures should be relatively independent and distinct from each other. A clear distinction does not always exist, however, between the contents of intelligence and achievement tests. Each can measure aspects of the same underlying ability. For example, if a vocabulary test requires oral questions and responses, it would be included as part of an intelligence test battery. If, on the other hand, the test requires reading words and providing oral or written responses, the test would be included as part of an achievement battery. If a person does not have difficulty with reading or writing, the same underlying ability, that is knowledge of word meanings, is being measured.

Kaufman (1984) contended that the large, unrotated first factor (*g*) of many cognitive tests may actually be better described as a measure of general achievement rather than as general intelligence. If many of the tests (cognitive and achievement) load on the same factor, then the examiner may actually be comparing two aspects of a person's performance on the same underlying mental construct (Kaufman & O'Neal, 1988). We now know that many valid measures of school achievement have high *g* loadings, thus the somewhat mired distinction between the content of these test batteries makes comparisons between a single ability and achievement score artificial at best (Kaufman & O'Neal, 1988). Fortunately, the mandatory discrepancy requirement has been removed from the reauthorization of IDEA 2004, providing increased flexibility in identification procedures, but conceivably, creating a new set of issues and concerns regarding SLD identification procedures. As noted before, the reauthorization does not provide clear guidance regarding how to operationalize the definition, or how to develop uniform criteria that can be applied from state to state, or even school district to district.

RESPONSE TO INTERVENTION AS A METHOD FOR SLD IDENTIFICATION

As specified in the IDEA 2004 reauthorization, states may permit a process that examines whether or not a student responds to scientific, research-based intervention as *part* of the learning disability evaluation procedure. This process of data collection is often referred to as response to intervention (RTI). Although RTI may be used as part of the process, it is not clear how big that part is, or how and when that part is integrated into the diagnostic assessment process.

Many states have been implementing or are planning to implement some form of RTI with the hopes of (a) reducing the number of students referred for evaluations, (b) providing early intervention to children in a more timely fashion, (c) providing targeted assistance to all children who need help, and (d) increasing the validity of actual placement decisions. Clearly, efficient progress monitoring and early intervention can provide benefits to and help improve the quality of instruction to all children. It seems, however, that RTI can be viewed most accurately as a prereferral intervention rather than a proxy for SLD.

Limited response to a treatment does not confirm or negate the existence of SLD (Kavale et al., 2005; Kavale, Kauffman, Bachmeier, & LeFever, 2008). The primary concern of RTI is not valid SLD identification and its use as an identification procedure perverts the SLD category, making it into a convenient home for any student who otherwise might be left behind (Kavale et al., 2008). A failure to respond to treatment only indicates that a student is having problems achieving at a certain rate or level with a selected intervention as compared to his or her peers. Numerous reasons exist for why a student would not fully respond to a certain intervention, only one of which is a learning disability. Some of the reasons for low achievement are extrinsic, whereas others would be considered intrinsic.

Examples of extrinsic factors that could affect responsiveness to an intervention would include an ineffective methodology, improper implementation of an intervention, or poor school attendance. In addition to SLD, examples of other intrinsic factors that could influence responsiveness to treatment would include: attention problems, oral language impairments, behavior disorders, and cultural and linguistic differences. All low-achieving students should not be lumped into a single package (Kaufman & Kaufman, 2001). Different treatments, as well as alterations in the rate and mode of presentation of materials, will be effective with different learners (Kaufman & Kaufman, 1983b).

In fact, it seems somewhat inexplicable that RTI has only been recommended as a procedure for SLD identification, when it may be equally, if not more, effective for helping to substantiate other types of disabilities, such as behavior disorders or mild mental retardation. If a child with behavioral problems showed a poor response to increasingly structured reinforcements and behavior management techniques, this information certainly has direct relevance to the evaluation and identification procedure. In other words, a failure to respond to treatment (or more accurately a limited or insufficient response to a selected treatment) does not provide any type of unique information that is only applicable to the category of SLD. The removal of cognitive processing measures is likely to increase classification errors, as there are multiple causes of low achievement, other than SLD (Hale et al., 2004). In addition, increasing the breadth of the category to all students with low achievement is likely to increase the number of students being identified as needing special education services.

In essence, various forms of RTI have always been practiced by good psychologists and teachers. Zach (2005) provided an interesting reflection regarding this fact: "When I was working as a school psychologist some 50 years ago and received a referral from a teacher about a child who was having trouble learning, the very first thing I did was to visit the teacher to inquire about the problem. I wanted to know what the child was having trouble with. I wanted to know what the teacher had tried that did not work and most importantly, I wanted to know what had been done that had worked. At that time I had never heard of Response to Intervention (RTI) and I certainly would not have predicted that there were going to be initials to describe what has always been good practice, as a 'new' procedure" (p. 151).

Furthermore, RTI does not provide the field with a consistent means of determining responsiveness, and the application of different methods results in different prevalence rates and different subsets of unresponsive children (Fuchs, Fuchs, & Compton, 2004; Reynolds, 2005). Essentially RTI is based on a discrepancy from grade level, making it a special case of severe discrepancy analysis that assumes everyone is of equal ability or possesses similar academic aptitude (Reynolds, 2005).

Consider the case of Jason, a fourth-grade student who has been identified as having SLD (poor short-term memory), fetal alcohol syndrome (diagnosed at birth), and attention-deficit hyperactivity disorder (ADHD) (diagnosed in preschool). Upon a premature birth, he was addicted to both cocaine and heroin and his birth weight was below 2 pounds. He has received special services since preschool with small group instruction from a special education teacher daily for 45 minutes. His adoptive parents have provided him with private tutoring for one hour three times weekly from a learning disability specialist since first grade. In addition, he has attended summer school every year. Although Jason is doing quite well considering the complex nature of his attention and learning problems, he is still not achieving at grade level in any area except verbal knowledge. School personnel have suggested retention as an option, but even then, his academic performance would still lag behind his peers in reading, writing, and mathematics. Jason has challenges that other children do not have to face; he also provides his teachers with special challenges in adapting and modifying the curriculum so that he can learn and succeed.

Nearly every classroom in the country has one or more students with needs as intensive as Jason's. From years of research on developmental differences, it is apparent that fundamental differences exist in human abilities. Over eight decades ago, Caldwell and Courtis (1924) explained that educational psychology and measurement have accumulated a mass of data that demonstrates that the most constant trait about human nature is its variability. People differ and different standards are necessary to accommodate these differences. Larson (2005) admonished promotion of a uniform criteria for all children, stating: "It is time to resolve the convoluted thinking that mandates the 'same" high ('rigorous') grade-level standards for all. One of the things that we know for sure in special education is that one size does not fit all, and that the same standards, rigorous or not, will not result in the same outcomes" (p. 248).

Thus, RTI is really subject to the major criticism that was made against the use of an ability–achievement discrepancy as a method of SLD identification: the unreliability of the diagnostic criterion (Fuchs et al., 2004). In addition, RTI only addresses the achievement criterion of the SLD definition. To help resolve these critical issues, Hale, Kaufman, Naglieri, and Kavale (2006) suggested that a multitiered approach to serving children with learning problems be used, one that begins with RTI, but then provides for a comprehensive evaluation of cognitive processes when RTI methods are unsuccessful in resolving a student's learning difficulties. RTI procedures should be combined with psychometric testing, including cognitive ability testing, which provides both diagnostic and instructional data (Kavale et al., 2008). If a child fails to respond to intervention, then the results of a comprehensive evaluation indicate that the child has a processing deficit that impacts academic performance; both the definitional criteria for SLD and the limited response to evidence-based instruction as part of the SLD eligibility criteria have been addressed, resulting in a balanced model that promotes diagnostic accuracy (Hale et al., 2006).

CLINICAL ASSESSMENT OF STRENGTHS AND WEAKNESSES

Kaufman (2000) credits Dr. David Wechsler for converting intellectual assessment from a "psychometric exercise to a clinical art" (p. 10). The major purpose of the use of intelligence tests on individuals with SLD is to identify a person's specific strengths and weaknesses. In fact, an understanding of this comprehensive profile is the key to interpretation (Kaufman, Kaufman, & Shaughnessy, 2007). The findings are then critical to determining appropriate accommodations and interventions. The evaluator hypothesizes the nature of the problem through careful analysis of an individual's profile of scores. In the past, the various problems associated with interpreting individual differences through profile analysis of the Wechsler scales were discussed (e.g., Glutting, McDermott, & Konold, 1997). One must consider, however, that these studies were performed using tests that lacked specificity or were mixed measures of cognitive abilities, rather than using more psychometrically defensible and discrete factors, such as defined by the Cattell–Horn–Carroll (CHC) theory (Carroll, 1993; Horn & Cattell, 1966).

Profile interpretation for individuals suspected of having SLD can lead to insights regarding the child's relative strengths and weaknesses, as well as suggesting the need for differentiated educational materials (Kaufman, 1976a; Kaufman, 1979). In fact, the documentation of significant variability among a person's abilities is precisely how intelligence tests contribute to SLD determination and educational planning (Mather & Wendling, 2005). Prudent subtest analysis can hold the key to understanding a child's unique profile (Kaufman, 1982).

Intelligent testing requires that the evaluator use test instruments as tools for helping to understand an individual's strong and weak areas and then finding and confirming the hypothesis or hypotheses that explain the pattern of scores through multiple sources of information (Kaufman, 1979; Kaufman & Lictenberger, 1998). In addition to measuring the weak or problems areas, an evaluator should also administer cognitive tests that circumvent the deficiency to document the person's spared or intact neuropsychological assets (Kaufman, 1979; Kaufman & Kaufman, 2001). Individuals with SLD typically present an uneven profile of abilities demonstrating difficulty with some types of learning, but ease with others.

For example, one consistent finding across Wechsler Intelligence Test for Children – Revised (WISC-R; Wechsler, 1974) studies was that children with SLD exhibited high scores on spatial abilities or the perceptual organization subtests, average scores on verbal comprehension subtests, but consistently lower scores on the Arithmetic, Coding, Information, and Digit Span subtests, or what has been referred to as the ACID (Arithmetic, Coding, Information, and Digit) profile (Kaufman, 1981; Kaufman et al., 1990). In fact, it appears that for students with SLD, Coding and Arithmetic are the two most difficult subtests, followed by Digit Span (Kaufman et al., 1990). Thus, the intent of a comprehensive evaluation is to reveal the profile of an individual's unique learning abilities.

As noted, individuals with superior cognitive abilities can have SLD. Because these individuals may have average scores on achievement measures (despite advanced verbal and reasoning abilities), their difficulties can only be identified through an evaluation of strengths and weaknesses and consideration of background information and educational history. After examining the strengths and weaknesses of children of superior intelligence as well as SLD on the WISC-R, Schiff, Kaufman, and Kaufman (1981) concluded that the group of children exhibited advanced verbal comprehension and oral expression skills, but weaknesses on the Arithmetic, Coding, and Digit Span subtests, as well as in emotional and motor development.

In essence, many individuals with SLD have intact verbal or oral language abilities and obtain scores in the average to above average range in many linguistic abilities (with the exception of areas like phonological awareness and verbal short-term memory). These students can orally verify and clarify knowledge with ease, but their performance falters when they have to read or write the answers to test questions. In essence, assessment of their subject-area knowledge is compromised by their reading and/or writing disabilities, and a written examination assesses the disability, rather than their actual level of understanding. Such practice results in a very biased and highly inaccurate measure of their actual knowledge.

In analyzing performance, an evaluator should consider both ipsative (within-child) strengths and weaknesses, as well as normative, standard score indexes greater than 115 and less than 85 (Kaufman et al., 2005). The noted discrepancies within performance must constitute statistically significant deviations that are unusual in the normative population. Before interpreting the amount of scatter that exists within a person's profile, one must first consider what normal fluctuations are and what constitutes atypical scatter (Anderson, Kaufman, & Kaufman, 1976; Kaufman, 1976a; McLean, Reynolds, & Kaufman, 1990). After reanalysis of the WISC-R standardization sample, Kaufman (1976b) cautioned that one must be wary of interpreting test scatter because normally achieving children also exhibited numerous significant differences between pairs of test scores.

Furthermore, one must consider the difference between what is "normal" or in the average range as is statistically defined (between 85 and 115) and what is average or typical as compared to peers. For example, a child whose test score is better than 17% of their peers (standard score of 87) would be defined as obtaining a score within the statistically normal range. This child's performance, however, is below average in terms of age cohorts, and the measured ability may be considered a significant weakness in light of additional quantitative information and qualitative observations. The point being that within any given categorization scheme, considerable variability in actual performance still exists. Test authors in the past have attempted to clarify and refine this classification system by referring to the standard score range between 80 and 89 as below average (Kaufman & Kaufman, 1983a) or low average (Woodcock, McGrew, & Mather, 2001).

Intelligence tests have multiple applications for SLD evaluations, including documenting the intact abilities, uncovering the processing deficits that lead to academic problems, understanding a person's unique profile, and developing recommendations for educational intervention

(Kaufman & Kaufman, 2001). Thus, the ipsative assessment approach can be used to hypothesize strengths and weaknesses within a profile but then the observed pattern must be supported or negated by additional relevant information (Kaufman, Lichtenberger, & Naglieri, 1999; Lichtenberger, Mather, Kaufman, & Kaufman, 2004). These practical applications are best accomplished using tests that are well designed and theory-based. When combined with behavioral observations and background information, understanding of diverse theoretical perspectives allows for interpretation of an individual's test score profile in a unique way (Kaufman, 2000).

IMPORTANCE OF THEORETICAL FRAMEWORKS FOR
TEST INTERPRETATION

In the early years of test development, theory was subservient to practice in determining what tests were developed and used (Kaufman, 2000). Kaufman (1981) insisted that the application of theory to test interpretation fostered a more process-oriented treatment of the strengths and weaknesses of children with SLD, which then would translate more readily into appropriate educational interventions. Throughout the last several decades, the Kaufmans have focused upon enhancing test interpretation by building a rich theoretical and clinical base that placed emphasis on the role of and importance of cognitive and neuropsychological theory to test development. By studying and understanding various cognitive theories, practitioners are better equipped with an understanding of the educational implications (Kaufman & Kaufman, 1983b). If practitioners are familiar with a variety of theoretical models, they can select the particular framework that provides the most insight into an individual's cognitive structure (Kaufman, 1982).

Although the Wechsler scales were not developed from a specific theory, the scales have advanced theory and have been studied and interpreted from a variety of different theoretical perspectives (Kaufman, 2000). In summarizing research findings related to SLD assessment, Kaufman (1981) explored the usefulness of the WISC-R and concluded that: (a) little practical value existed for discrepancies between Wechsler's verbal-performance dichotomy as a marker for SLD; (b) children with SLD obtained consistently low scores on the Arithmetic, Digit Span, and Coding subtests; (c) Bannatyne's four-category approach of (1) verbal conceptualization (Similarities, Vocabulary, Comprehension), (2) spatial (Picture Completion, Block Design, Object Assembly), (3) sequencing (Arithmetic, Digit Span, Coding), and (4) acquired knowledge (Information,

Arithmetic, Vocabulary) had better clinical utility and led to more process-oriented treatment than any WISC-R two- or even three-factor solution; and (d) future research should attempt to clarify what the specific factors mean in either a clinical or theoretical sense. Thus, the specific factors that are measured by tests should provide meaningful information and treatment validity. In addition, tests that provide a multiple factor approach to interpretation provide richer information than those with only a two- or three-factor solution.

Fortunately, over the past 20 years, theory has become paramount in the construction and interpretation of tests (e.g., Das, Naglieri, & Kirby, 1994; Kaufman, 2000; Kaufman et al., 2007; Naglieri, 2001; Woodcock et al., 2001). Emphasis has shifted to a qualitative approach in which cognitive theories have played an important role (Gunnison, Kaufman, & Kaufman, 1982). The original Kaufman Assessment Battery for Children (K-ABC; Kaufman & Kaufman, 1983a) was built on a blend of theories: the integration of psychological cerebral specialization theory (Sperry, 1968), Luria' s (1966, 1980) neuropsychological theory, and Horn's and Cattell's (1966) distinction between fluid and crystallized intelligence.

The K-ABC was predicated on the distinction between problem-solving abilities and factual knowledge (Kaufman et al., 1999). The K-ABC also provided measures of two types of processing: sequential and simultaneous. These two types of information processing relate to how children solve problems, rather than the types of problems they are asked to solve (Kaufman & Lictenberger, 1998). Sequential processing refers to problems that need to be solved in a serial order or where stimuli are processed one by one or in some kind of linear arrangement, whereas simultaneous involves problems requiring gestalt-like, holistic integration of data (Gunnison et al., 1992). One common finding has been that children with reading disabilities tend to have average performance in simultaneous processing but weaknesses in sequential processing, which is related to problems in decoding, spelling, and memorization (Gunnison et al., 1982; Kaufman, 1982; Kaufman & Kaufman, 1983). Thus, the theoretical rationale provided by the K-ABC made it particularly appropriate for neuropsychological evaluations and the assessment of children suspected of having SLD (Kaufman & Harrison, 1991).

The Kaufman Adolescent & Adult Intelligence Test (KAIT; Kaufman & Kaufman, 1993) was also based on theoretical constructs, including Horn and Cattell, as well as Luria's (1980) concept of planning ability and Piaget's (1972) formal operational theory. Within the KAIT framework, tasks measure the retrieval and application of general knowledge, as well as problem-solving tasks that measure the ability to learn and to solve novel problems that are less dependent on prior experience and acquired knowledge (Kaufman et al., 1999).

More recently, the KABC-II (Kaufman & Kaufman, 2004) has continued the use of two modern theoretical models: the CHC model of broad and narrow abilities, and Luria's neuropsychological processing theory. Using a subset of subtests from the KABC-II, the evaluator can interpret the test results from two different, but complementary perspectives (Kaufman & Kaufman, 2004). CHC theory places emphasis on the interpretation of specific cognitive abilities and understanding how these abilities are related to performance, whereas Luria's neuropsychological theory emphasizes the way children process information when solving problems.

When considering the assessment of individuals suspected of having SLD, both approaches are useful for different types of referral questions. In clinical cases that involve the role of language as a factor affecting performance, application of the Luria framework deemphasizes the role and importance of factual knowledge and allows the evaluator to consider mental processing while reducing the impact of low language performance. The authors state the following fundamental principle for understanding when to include or exclude measures of acquired knowledge (*Gc*) from an evaluation: "measures of *Gc* should be excluded from any score that purports to measure a person's intelligence or overall cognitive ability whenever the measure of *Gc* is not likely to reflect that person's level of ability" (p. 4). In most instances, when assessing individuals suspected of having SLD, the authors recommend use of the CHC model over the Luria model because *Gc* is an important aspect of cognitive performance (Kaufman & Kaufman, 2004) and this factor is often a relative strength for individuals with SLD. Results from the KAIT and KABC-II can help identify an individual's strengths and weaknesses in cognitive ability and mental processing, making them valuable tools for identifying strengths in processing, as well as basic psychological processing disorders, a key aspect of SLD definitions (Kaufman & Kaufman, 2004).

ROLE OF COMPREHENSIVE EVALUATIONS

Although school districts may become immersed in the use of RTI as part of the evaluation procedure, elimination of the discrepancy requirement and use of RTI as part of the evaluation process do not diminish the need for comprehensive evaluations or lead to the demise of clinical assessments. Although the conflict between intelligent testing and "stupid decision-making procedures" may not be resolved soon, individual clinical tests of intelligence will always survive because of their diagnostic utility (Kaufman, 2000). These evaluations focus upon problem solving for an individual. When conducted by a skilled clinician who integrates actual classroom performance, educational history, and behavioral observations, comprehensive evaluations provide important information to help explain the nature and severity of a learning disability, as well as the various treatment options.

A comprehensive, individualized assessment includes an assessment of cognitive processes, academic performance, social-emotional functioning, and the environmental factors affecting performance (Kavale et al., 2005). Kaufman et al. (2005) outlined the three phases involved in a comprehensive evaluation. In the first phase, emotional, cultural, social, or physical factors related to the learning difficulty are ruled out; in the second phase, the cognitive and processing strengths and weaknesses of the individual are identified; and in the third phase, evidence-based interventions directly related to the child's strengths and weaknesses are prescribed. Based upon the diagnostic conclusions, the evaluator selects specific interventions to meet the identified needs. For students with SLD, differential instruction that addresses the source of the problem is far more effective than global, generalized approaches that do not (Aaron, 1997; Gunnison et al., 1982; Kavale et al., 2005; Mather & Jaffe, 2002). In addition, taking full advantage of identified cognitive strengths such as strong verbal comprehension can help to justify critical accommodations and support and clarify the mode and methods of instructional intervention.

As noted, one facet of comprehensive, clinical evaluations is that all conclusions from the test profiles are supported with data from multiple sources (Kaufman, 1994). The evaluator relates observations of behavior to the test profile and integrates information from a variety of instruments and observations to support or clarify the diagnostic hypotheses (Kaufman et al., 1999; Lichtenberger et al., 2004). Because the obtained scores may not have a unitary explanation and children can obtain low scores for a variety of reasons, an evaluator must corroborate information with a "judicious selection" of other tests and then integrate the referral information, clinical observations of test-taking behaviors, detailed analysis of errors, and an analysis of the profile fluctuations (Kaufman, 1994).

As a case example, results from an intelligence test indicated that Michael, a fourth-grade boy, had advanced reasoning abilities and acquired knowledge, but slow performance on all timed tasks. During testing, he worked slowly on a task where he was asked to match symbols quickly and on tasks involving the rapid naming of objects, digits, and letters. His general education teacher reported that Michael did not have behavioral, emotional, or social problems, but that he did have a slow reading rate, as well as difficulty completing most assignments in a timely manner. Additional academic testing substantiated Michael's slow reading rate.

In consideration of his strengths in reasoning and knowledge contrasted with his slow rate of performance and production, the evaluator made recommendations for accommodations that included shortened assignments and extended time on tests, as well as recommendations for the implementation of instructional methods designed to increase reading rate and fluency. In addition, a recommendation was made for supplemental testing in the form of oral follow-up for missed or unfinished items on examinations to ensure that his less efficient reading skills did not affect comprehension of the question(s) even though extended time was granted. All pieces of information were used to construct a diagnostic hypothesis, confirm it, and then select appropriate accommodations and interventions. In addition, the intact cognitive and linguistic abilities, the processing weakness, and the slow reading speed, all supported the diagnosis of a specific reading disability.

CONCLUSION

Some professionals have suggested that intelligence tests are outdated and are no longer needed in the field of SLD because the results have limited value (e.g., Gresham, Restori, & Cook, 2008). Siegel (1989) described the intelligence test as a "sacred cow that the LD field is not willing to abandon" (p. 518). More recently, Reschly (2005) maintained that the focus should be solely on intervention and not on ". . . internal child attributes that rarely have significant implications for special education interventions" (p. 512). Sole use of RTI is focused on the identification of weaknesses, and not, as a good cognitive assessment does, on the documentation of strengths as well. In this regard, an "intrinsic" child characteristic such as above-average verbal abilities has significant educational relevance. Yet if only RTI methods were used, the need and justification for emphasizing verbal methods of instruction and providing oral testing on classroom assessments of subject-area knowledge might be deemphasized or overlooked. To think that you can diagnose SLD from RTI is just simply wrong (Kaufman et al., 2007).

The history of the SLD field and the present suggest that we should challenge practices, but not the SLD construct (Hale et al., 2006). The definition of SLD requires the identification of a processing deficit which is the key aspect of contemporary SLD assessment (Kaufman et al., 2007). For accurate SLD identification, cognitive testing is a necessary and productive part of a comprehensive evaluation. Intelligence tests can also be used to help increase understanding and inform intervention when emphasis is placed on understanding the educational implications (Kaufman & Kaufman, 1983b; Mather & Jaffe, 2002; Naglieri & Pickering, 2003). Even in light of new regulations, it is highly unlikely that the demand for evaluations will diminish. If school districts cut back on evaluations, the practice of private clinicians will flourish. Kaufman et al. (2005) noted: "... there is a demand for the comprehensive assessment to drive intervention. This is the way it has always been, and this is the way it will always be because the referral questions for children with SLD have always asked, What is wrong? And how can we help? These questions demand differential diagnosis, a large part of which is determined by the cognitive abilities present in the individual child" (p. 211). We must also ask: What is right? And how can we use the spared and intact cognitive abilities to help (Kaufman et al., 2005)? Assessments can aid us in understanding a person's information-processing capabilities, including the factors that facilitate performance. Gardner (1999) clearly made this point when he suggested, "We shouldn't ask how smart you are, but rather how are you smart?"

Thus, the goals of intelligent testing for individuals suspected of having SLD are to identify a person's strengths and weaknesses, attempt to understand the relationship among these abilities, and then translate these findings into meaningful intervention plans. Within these plans, instruction is individualized; different approaches are used for different people; strengths and weaknesses are considered in selecting accommodations and methodologies; and the effectiveness of the accommodations and instruction is evaluated frequently and altered as needed. The examiner is intimately involved and an integral part of all facets of the test administration and interpretation process (Kaufman, 2000). The central goal of intelligent testing of individuals with SLD is not, however, eligibility, but rather using the results to help a person improve his or her educational and life outcomes (Kaufman, 1981; Kaufman, 2000; Kaufman et al., 2007). As Kaufman (1979) stated: "The focus is the child ..." (p. 1). After all, that is what it's all about.

ACKNOWLEDGMENT

The author wishes to express her gratitude to Dr. Michael E. Gerner for editorial suggestions on the first draft of this chapter.

REFERENCES

Aaron, P.G. (1997). The impending demise of the discrepancy formula. *Review of Educational Research*, 67, 461–502.

Anderson, M., Kaufman, A.S., & Kaufman, N.L. (1976). Use of the WISC-R with a learning disabled population: Some diagnostic implications. *Psychology in the Schools*, 13, 381–386.

Bateman, B. (1992). Learning disabilities: The changing landscape. *Journal of Learning Disabilities*, 25, 29–36.

Berninger, V.W. (1996). *Reading and Writing Acquisition: A Developmental Neuropsychological Perspective*. Boulder, CO: Westview Press.

Berninger, V.W. (2001). Understanding the 'lexia' in dyslexia: A multidisciplinary team approach to learning disabilities. *Annals of Dyslexia*, 51, 23–48.

Caldwell, O.W. & Courtis, S.A. (1924). *Then and now in education, 1845–1923*. Yonkers-on-Hudson, NY: World Book.

Carroll, J.B. (1993). *Human Cognitive Abilities: A Survey of Factor-Analytic Studies*. Cambridge, England: Cambridge University Press.

Cruickshank, W.M. (1983). Learning disabilities: A neurophysiological dysfunction. *Journal of Learning Disabilities*, 16, 27–29.

Das, J.P., Naglieri, J.A., & Kirby, J.R. (1994). *The Assessment of Cognitive Processes: The PASS Theory of Intelligence*. Boston, MA: Allyn & Bacon.

Dumont, R., Willis, J., & McBride, G. (2001). Yes, Virginia, there is a severe discrepancy clause, but is it too much ado about something? *The School Psychologist, APA Division of School Psychology*, 55(1), 1, 4–13, 15.

Fletcher, J.M., Francis, D.J., Shaywitz, S.E., Lyon, G.R., Foorman, B.R., Stuebing, K.K., & Shaywitz, B.A. (1998). Intelligent testing and the discrepancy model for children with learning disabilities. *Learning Disabilities Research & Practice*, 13, 186–203.

Fuchs, D., Fuchs, L., & Compton, D. (2004). Identifying reading disabilities by responsiveness-to-instruction: Specifying measures and criteria. *Learning Disability Quarterly*, 27, 216–227.

Fuchs, D., Mock, D., Morgan, P., & Young, C. (2003). Responsiveness to intervention: Definitions, evidence, and implications for the learning disabilities construct. *Learning Disabilities Research & Practice*, 18, 157–171.

Gardner, H. (1999). *Reframing Intelligence*. New York: Basic Books.

Glutting, J.J., McDermott, P.A., & Konold, T.R. (1997). Ontology, structure, and diagnostic benefits of a normative subtest taxonomy from the WISC-III standardization sample. In D.P. Flanagan, J.L. Genshaft, & P. L Harrison (Eds.). *Contemporary Intellectual Assessment: Theories, Tests, and Issues* (pp. 349–372). New York: Guilford Publications.

Gresham, F.M., Restori, A.F., & Cook, C.R. (2008). To test or not to test: Issues pertaining to response to intervention and cognitive testing. *NASP Communique*, 37, 5–7.

Gunnison, J., Kaufman, N.L., & Kaufman, A.S. (1982). Reading redemption based on sequential and simultaneous processing. *Academic Therapy*, 17, 297–307.

Hale, J.B., Kaufman, A.S., Naglieri, J.A., & Kavale, K.A. (2006). Implementation of IDEA: Response to intervention and cognitive assessment methods. *Psychology in the Schools*, 43, 753–770.

Hale, J.B., Naglieri, J.A., Kaufman, A.S., & Kavale, K.A. (2004). Specific learning disability classifications in the new Individuals with Disabilities Education Act: The danger of good ideas. *The School Psychologist*, 58(1), 6–29.

Horn, J.L., & Cattell, R.B. (1966). Refinement and test of the theory of fluid and crystallized intelligence. *Journal of Educational Psychology*, 57, 253–270.

Individuals with Disabilities Education Improvement Act (IDEA) of 2004, PL 108–446, 20 U.S.C. §§ 1400 et seq.

Kaufman, A.S. (1976a). Do normal children have "flat" ability profiles? *Psychology in the Schools*, 13, 284–285.

Kaufman, A.S. (1976b). A new approach to the interpretation of test scatter on the WISC-R. *Journal of Learning Disabilities*, 9, 160–168.

Kaufman, A.S. (1979). *Intelligent Testing with the WISC-R*. New York: John Wiley & Sons.

Kaufman, A.S. (1981). The WISC-R and learning disabilities assessment: State of the art. *Journal of Learning Disabilities*, 14, 520–526.

Kaufman, A.S. (1982). The impact of WISC-R research for school psychologists. In C.R. Reynolds & T.B. Gutkin (Eds.), *A Handbook for School Psychology* (pp. 156–177). New York: Wiley.

Kaufman, A.S. (1984). K-ABC and controversy. *Journal of Special Education*, 18, 409–444.

Kaufman, A.S. (1994). *Intelligent Testing with the WISC-III*. New York: Wiley.

Kaufman, A.S. (2000). Intelligence tests and school psychology: Predicting the future by studying the past. *Psychology in the Schools*, 37, 7–16.

Kaufman, A.S. (2004). Standardized cognitive assessment and the new IDEA guidelines- Fit or misfit? Presentation at the National Association of School Psychologists Annual Convention, April 1, Dallas, TX.

Kaufman, A.S., & Harrison, P.L. (1991). Individual intellectual assessment. In C.E. Walker (Ed.), *Clinical Psychology: Historical and Research Foundations* (pp. 91–119). New York: Plenum.

Kaufman, A.S., Harrison, P.L., & Ittenbach, R.F. (1990). Intelligence testing in the schools. In T. Gutkin & C.R. Reynolds (Eds.), *The Handbook of School Psychology* (2nd ed., pp. 289–327). New York: Wiley.

Kaufman, A.S., & Kaufman, N.L. (1983a). *K-ABC Interpretive Manual*. Circle Pines, MN: American Guidance Service.

Kaufman, N.L., & Kaufman, A.S. (1983b). Remedial intervention in education. In G.W. Hynd (Ed.), *The School Psychologist* (pp. 293–322). Syracuse N.Y.: Syracuse University Press.

Kaufman, A.S., & Kaufman, N.L. (1993). *Manual for Kaufman Adolescent & Adult Intelligence Test*. Circle Pines, MN: American Guidance Service.

Kaufman, A.S., & Kaufman, N.L. (2001). Assessment of specific learning disabilities in the new millennium: Issues, conflicts, and controversies. In A.S. Kaufman & N.L. Kaufman (Eds.), *Specific Learning Disabilities: Psychological Assessment and Evaluation* (pp. 433–461). Cambridge Monographs in Child and Adolescent Psychiatry. Cambridge, England: Cambridge University Press.

Kaufman, A.S., & Kaufman, N.L. (2004). *Kaufman Assessment Battery for Children* (2nd ed.). Circle Pines, MN: American Guidance Service.

Kaufman, A.S., Kaufman, N.L., & Shaughnessy, M.F. (2007). An interview with Alan and Nadeen Kaufman. *North American Journal of Psychology*, 9, 611–626.

Kaufman, A.S., & Lichtenberger, E.O. (1998). Intellectual assessment. In A.S. Bellack. & M. Hersen. (Series Eds.) & C.R. Reynolds. (Vol. Ed.), *Comprehensive Clinical Psychology, Volume 4: Assessment* (pp. 203–238). Oxford, England: Elsevier Science.

Kaufman, A.S., Lichtenberger, E.O., Fletcher-Janzen, E., & Kaufman, N.L. (2005). *Essentials of the K-ABC-II Assessment*. New York: John Wiley & Sons.

Kaufman, A.S., Lichtenberger, E.O., Naglieri, J.A. (1999). Intelligence testing in the schools. In C.R. Reynolds & T. Gutkin (Eds.), *The Handbook of School Psychology* (3rd ed.) (pp. 307–349). New York: Wiley.

Kaufman, A.S., & McLean, J.E. (1986). K-ABC/WISC-R factor analysis for a learning disabled population. *Journal of Learning Disabilities*, 19, 145–153.

Kaufman, A.S., & O'Neal, M.R. (1988). Analysis of the cognitive, achievement, and general factors underlying the Woodcock-Johnson Psycho-Educational Battery. *Journal of Clinical Child Psychology*, 17, 143–151.

Kavale, K.A., Kaufman, A.S., Naglieri, J.A., & Hale, J. (2005). Changing procedures for identifying learning disabilities: The danger of poorly supported ideas. *The School Psychologist*, 59, 16–25.

Kavale, K.A., Kauffman, J.M., Bachmeier, R.J., & LeFever, G.B. (2008). Response-to-intervention: Separating the rhetoric of self-congratulation from the reality of specific learning disability identification. *Learning Disability Quarterly*, 31, 135–150.

Larson, N.W. (2005). "The time has come," the Walrus said, "to speak of many things!" *Learning Disability Quarterly*, 28, 247–248.

Lichtenberger, E.O., Mather, N., Kaufman, N.L., & Kaufman, A.S. (2004). *Essentials of Assessment Report Writing*. New York: Wiley.

Luria, A.R. (1966). *Higher Cortical Functions in Man*. New York: Basic Books.

Luria, A.R. (1980). *Higher Cortical Functions in Man* (2nd ed.). New York: Basic Books.

Lyon, G.R. (1995). Toward a definition of dyslexia. *Annals of Dyslexia*, 45, 3–27.

Mather, N. & Healey, W.C. (1990). Deposing aptitude-achievement discrepancy as the imperial criterion for learning disabilities. *Learning Disabilities: A Multidisciplinary Journal*, 1(2), 40–48.

Mather, N., & Jaffe, L. (2002). *Woodcock-Johnson III: Recommendations, Reports, and Strategies*. New York: Wiley.

Mather, N., & Wendling, B. (2005). Linking cognitive assessment results to academic interventions for students with learning disabilities. In D.P. Flanagan & P.L. Harrison (Eds.), *Contemporary Intellectual Assessment: Theories, Tests, and Issues* (2nd ed., pp. 269–294). New York: Guilford Publications.

McLean, J.E., Reynolds, C.R., & Kaufman, A.S. (1990). WAIS-R subtest scatter using the profile variability index. *Psychological Assessment: The Journal of Consulting and Clinical Psychology*, 2, 289–292.

Naglieri, J.A. (2001). Cognitive Assessment System: A test built from the PASS theory. In A.S. Kaufman & N.L. Kaufman (Eds.), *Learning Disabilities: Psychological Assessment and Evaluation* (pp. 141–177), Cambridge, England: Cambridge University Press.

Naglieri, J.A., & Pickering, E. (2003). *Helping Children Learn: Intervention Handouts for Use in School and at Home.* Baltimore, MD: Brookes.

Orton, S.T. (1925). Word-blindness in school children. *Archives of Neurology and Psychiatry*, 14, 581–615.

Piaget, J. (1972). Intellectual evolution from adolescence to adulthood. *Human Development*, 15, 1–12.

Reschly, D.J. (2005). Learning disabilities identification: Primary intervention, secondary intervention, and then what? *Journal of Learning Disabilities*, 38, 510–515.

Reynolds, C.R. (2005, August). Considerations in RTI as a method of diagnosis of learning disabilities. Paper presented at the Annual Institute for Psychology in the Schools of the American Psychological Association, Washington DC.

Schiff, M.M., Kaufman, A.S., & Kaufman, N.L. (1981). Scatter analysis of WISC-R profiles for learning disabled children with superior intelligence. *Journal of Learning Disabilities*, 14, 400–404.

Shaywitz, S. (2003). *Overcoming Dyslexia: A New and Complete Science-based Program for Overcoming Reading Problems at Any Level.* New York: Alfred Knopf.

Siegel, L.S. (1989). Why we do not need intelligence test scores in the definition and analyses of learning disabilities? *Journal of Learning Disabilities*, 22, 514–518.

Sperry, R.W. (1968). Hemisphere deconnection and unity in conscious awareness. *American Psychologist*, 23, 723–733.

Stanovich, K.E. (1999). The sociopsychometrics of learning disabilities. *Journal of Learning Disabilities*, 32, 350–361.

Stern, W. (1938). *General Psychology from the Personalistic Standpoint.* New York: Macmillan Company.

Vellutino, F.R. (2001). Further analysis of the relationship between reading achievement and intelligence: A response to Naglieri. *Journal of Learning Disabilities*, 34, 306–310.

Wechsler, D. (1974). *Wechsler Intelligence Scale for Children – Revised.* San Antonio: Psychological Corporation.

Willis, J.O., & Dumont, R.P. (2002). *Guide to Identification of Learning Disabilities* (3rd ed.). Peterborough, NH: authors. Available from authors: print copy from johnzerowillis@yahoo.com or CD from dumont @fdu.edu

Woodcock, R.W., McGrew, K., & Mather, N. (2001). *Woodcock-Johnson Tests of Cognitive Abilities and Tests of Achievement* (3rd ed.). Rolling Meadows, IL: Riverside Publishing.

Zach, L.J. (2005). Déjà vu all over again: The current controversy over the identification of learning disability. *The School Psychologist*, 59, 151–155.

6

Temperament Preferences for Children Ages 8 Through 17 in a Nationally Represented Sample

KYLE BASSETT[1]

School Board of Hillsborough County, Florida

THOMAS OAKLAND

University of Florida

This chapter describes the prevailing temperament qualities in a representative sample of children and youth, ages 8 to 17, in the United States. This may be the first reported study with a national scope. Age and gender differences also are described. Information on children's temperament is discussed in light of broader literature on child and adolescent development.

The topic of temperament is viewed as suitable and important for this book, as it recognizes the contributions of Dr. Alan Kaufman. Temperament characterizes important and enduring qualities displayed by children, youth, and adults – a life span age range consistent with Dr. Kaufman's commitment to research-based scholarship that addresses important issues for persons of all ages (e.g., Kaufman, 1979, 1994). The availability of reliable measures of temperament for children and youth facilitates its assessment and provides nationally representative data on children. Additionally, the topic of temperament is consistent with Dr. Kaufman's commitment to a fundamental principle that professional services in psychology and education rest first and foremost on an accurate description of enduring traits.

Temperament constructs constitute enduring traits. Moreover, an understanding of the impact of temperament on behavior is fundamental to an understanding of children. This understanding complements the many methods developed by Dr. Kaufman to describe cognitive development. The authors hope this discussion will encourage others to routinely assess children's temperament and thereby identify some of their strengths

---

[1] Dr. Bassett currently is employed by the School Board of Hillsborough County, Florida.

that, when properly utilized, have the potential to foster academic, social, emotional, and vocational development.

The chapter discusses background information on temperament and the data base used to describe children's temperament and then reports temperament data in light of four bipolar styles: extroversion–introversion, practical–imaginative, thinking–feeling, and organized–flexible. This information is discussed in a broader developmental literature perspective.

Interest in temperament may be as old as humankind. Hippocrates reportedly recorded the first notions about temperament around 350 B.C. in his *On the Nature of Man*. Notions about differences in temperament are also found in the writings of philosophers, including Plato, Aristotle, Galen, Bruno, Hume, Voltaire, Rousseau, Locke, and Kant (Roback, 1927; Kagan, 1989, 1994a, b; Keirsey, 1998; Strelau, 1998).

Contemporary research generally characterizes temperament as stylistic and relatively stable traits that subsume intrinsic tendencies to act and react in somewhat predictable ways to people, events, and stimuli (Teglasi, 1998a,b). Temperament traits generally are characterized as predispositions to display behaviors, or their blueprint, with no assurance that people, events, and stimuli will always elicit the same temperament behaviors. Given its early appearance in life (e.g., Thomas, Chess, & Birch, 1968; Goldsmith, et al., 1987), psychologists assume that temperament has a biological origin, tempered both by an individual's environment as well as personal choice (Keogh, 2003; Goldsmith, et al., 1987). Age and gender also are assumed to influence temperament.

Rothbart's (1989) extensive review of the literature reported the developmental sequence of temperament from the newborn period through childhood. In summary, the newborn period is marked by the emergence of individual differences in negative emotionality (i.e., reactivity), activity level, distractibility, attention span (i.e., task persistence), and approach-withdrawal. Early infancy is associated with all components of newborn temperament and the emergence of individual differences in positive emotionality (i.e., reactivity). The period of late infancy is associated with all components observed in earlier periods as well as the emergence of inhibition of approach, sociability (i.e., introversion–extraversion), and self-regulation (i.e., effortful control). During the preschool to late adolescent years, temperaments are refined through experience and practice and help form the adult personality.

A model of temperament proposed by Jung (1921/1971, 1953) and modified and applied by Myers and Briggs (i.e., the Myers–Briggs Type Indicator [MBTI], 1980; Myers, et al., 1998) has been used to examine temperament qualities in both adults (Hammer, 1996) and children

(Oakland, Glutting, & Horton, 1996). The model includes four bipolar dimensions[2]: extroversion–introversion, practical–imaginative, thinking–feeling, and organized–practical temperament preferences. Prior studies found these constructs to be stable for males and females (Stafford & Oakland, 1996a) and for blacks and whites (Stafford & Oakland, 1996b), and children from various countries display similar temperament constructs (Benson et al, in press). Temperament accounts for significant variance associated with vocational interests in children as young as age 8 (Oakland, et al., 2001) and may distinguish gifted children from children not so gifted (Oakland, et al., 2000), sighted and nonsighted children (Oakland, Banner, & Livingston, 2000), and those who display conduct and oppositional defiant disorders (Joyce & Oakland, 2005). Thus, this temperament model, used to assess temperament in children (i.e., Student Styles Questionnaire, Oakland, et al., 1996), shows promise for use in understanding the impact of temperament on children's behaviors.

The following description of children's temperament is derived from the standardization sample of the Student Styles Questionnaire (SSQ).[3] The data from 7,902 children are representative of the 1990 U.S. census data with reference to four categories within each of the ten age groups (i.e., 8–17 years): gender (50% males), race/ethnicity (70% whites, 15% blacks, 11% Hispanics, and 4% other), geographic region (Northeast, North Central, South, and West; from 29 states and Puerto Rico), and school type (public and private) (Oakland et al., 1996).

The SSQ measures four bipolar temperament styles: extroversion–introversion, practical–imaginative, thinking–feeling, and organized–flexible. A brief description of these styles is provided in this chapter and are described in greater detail elsewhere (Oakland, et al. 1996; Horton & Oakland, 1996).

EXTROVERSION–INTROVERSION STYLES

Information on extroversion–introversion styles helps define the sources from which individuals derive energy. Children with a preference for an extroverted style are inclined to derive energy from being with others, need

---

[2] Terms used to describe the same temperament qualities may differ. For example, the SSQ uses the terms *practical* and *imaginative* while the MBTI used the terms *sensing* and *intuitive*. Additionally, the SSQ uses the terms *organized* and *flexible* while the MBTI uses the terms *judging* and *perceiving*.

[3] Readers are encouraged to see Bassett (2004) for a more complete description of the methods and results of this study.

considerable affirmation and encouragement from others, prefer to have many friends, and tend to take on the characteristics of those around them. They often learn best through talking and cooperative group activities.

In contrast, children with a preference for an introverted style are inclined to derive their energy from themselves. They generally prefer to have a few close friends, have a few well-developed interests, and enjoy spending time alone. They are more hesitant to share their ideas with others. They appreciate acknowledgement of their careful work and reflection. They learn best by having time to think about and reflect upon what they have learned (Myers & Myers, 1980; Keirsey, 1998; Oakland, Glutting, & Horton, 1996).

Children ages 8–17 generally are more likely to prefer an extroverted (55%) to and introverted (45%) style. Although these figures generally are comparable for males and females (Table 6.1), a preference for extroversion tends to be higher for males than females at ages 8, 9, and 17 and lower at age 13. An age by gender interaction effect is evident (Figure 6.1). Temperament changes are represented by two nonparallel lines with intersecting and somewhat concave curves, one for each gender, with both female and male preferences for an extroverted style increasing between ages 8 and 13 and decreasing thereafter. When children from contiguous age groups are compared, significant differences are apparent between ages 9–10, 11–12, 12–13, 13–14, and 16–17.

Thus, preferences for extroversion and introversion styles are impacted both by age and gender. Of the two, age clearly is the overriding quality.

The initial preferences for a somewhat balanced preference for extroversion and introversion styles seen at the age 8 gives way to a significant shift toward a higher preference for an extroverted style that asymptotes for both males and females at age 13, and then declines marginally thereafter. This finding is consistent with research that characterizes older children and young adolescents as increasingly seeking peers as a significant source of energy and direction, at least during the beginning of puberty.

Children generally are considered to be well functioning and normal when they are eager to invest their energy with others in active exploration of their immediate physical and social environment (Matas, Arend, & Sroufe, 1978). Western families generally expect children to become increasingly physically and psychologically separated from parents (Steinberg & Silverberg, 1986), thus encourage them to acquire a repertoire of social skills, to experiment with interpersonal relationships, to assume new behaviors, and to engage in new experiences (Higgins & Parsons, 1983). Moreover, the role of parents is not necessarily replaced by a peer system

TABLE 6.1. *Percent of temperament style preferences for children by age and gender*

	(N)	E	I	P	M	T	F	O	L
Male 8	(265)	49	51	47	53	75	25	88	12
Female 8	(266)	38	62	51	49	42	58	93	7
Total 8	(531)	44	56	49	51	59	41	90	10
Male 9	(324)	52	48	44	56	74	26	77	23
Female 9	(324)	40	60	38	62	33	67	90	10
Total 9	(648)	46	54	41	59	54	46	84	16
Male 10	(466)	52	48	36	64	75	25	74	26
Female 10	(466)	50	50	39	61	32	68	89	11
Total 10	(932)	51	49	37	63	54	46	82	18
Male 11	(587)	54	46	39	61	73	27	71	29
Female 11	(587)	53	47	43	57	33	67	82	18
Total 11	(1174)	54	46	41	59	53	47	77	23
Male 12	(560)	58	42	43	57	72	28	60	40
Female 12	(559)	58	42	39	61	33	67	77	23
Total 12	(1119)	58	42	41	59	53	47	68	32
Male 13	(581)	62	38	44	56	75	25	58	42
Female 13	(581)	66	34	37	63	28	72	70	30
Total 13	(1162)	64	36	41	59	52	48	64	36
Male 14	(460)	57	43	47	53	77	23	54	46
Female 14	(461)	59	41	43	57	29	71	63	37
Total 14	(921)	58	42	45	55	52	48	59	41
Male 15	(319)	57	43	47	53	74	26	46	54
Female 15	(320)	56	44	46	54	27	73	60	40
Total 15	(639)	56	44	46	54	50	50	53	47
Male 16	(204)	52	48	46	54	69	31	44	56
Female 16	(205)	57	43	38	62	22	78	65	35
Total 16	(409)	54	46	42	58	45	55	55	45
Male 17	(184)	54	46	35	65	66	34	54	46
Female 17	(183)	40	60	45	55	19	81	72	28
Total 17	(367)	47	53	40	60	42	58	63	37
Male	(3950)	56	44	43	57	74	26	63	37
Female	(3952)	54	46	41	59	30	70	77	23
Total	(7902)	55	45	42	58	52	48	70	30

Note: N = Sample Size, E = Extroverted, I = Introverted, P = Practical, M = Imaginative, T = Thinking, F = Feeling, O = Organized, L = Flexible.

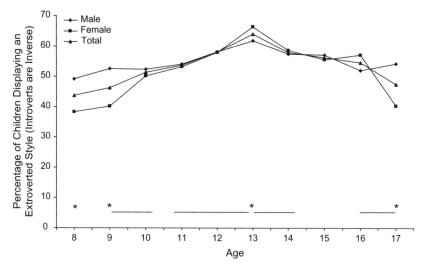

FIGURE 6.1. Percentage of children who display an extroverted style across ten age groups. Age differences are signified by solid lines. Gender differences are signified by an asterisk.

during this period; rather, the child may move quite comfortably between their parents and peers (Brown, Mounts, Lamborn, & Steinberg, 1993).

Early adolescence (e.g., between ages 12 and 14) may initiate another stage in life, when an understanding of family becomes established and an understanding of peers becomes better rooted, thus requiring more peer interaction. An expanding social network marks the periods of later childhood and early adolescence. Both the number of peers and time spent interacting with them typically increase during childhood and adolescence. Some report a linear increase in social contact with peers between early and middle childhood (Feiring & Lewis, 1989).

The possible restructuring of one's peer network to include a larger number of peers and more frequent interactions with them also may provide a functional value in school settings. As children transition from elementary to middle schools, they typically move from self-contained classrooms to larger, constantly shifting classes with many classmates they have not seen before (Brown, 1989). To the extent that peers provide mutual support and guidance (Moran & Eckenrode, 1991), increased interaction with peers in different groups may help them navigate these changes. Indeed, for many, being a member of a group is more important in early and middle adolescence (i.e., seventh through tenth grades) than at prior or later ages (Furman, 1989).

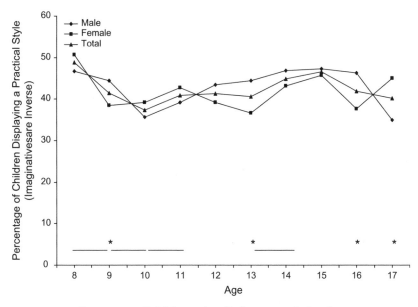

FIGURE 6.2. Percentage of children who display a practical style across ten age groups. Age differences are signified by solid lines. Gender differences are signified by an asterisk.

PRACTICAL–IMAGINATIVE STYLES

Information on practical–imaginative styles helps define how individuals see the world and their lives in it. Children with a preference for a practical style tend to focus their attention on what is seen, heard, or experienced through their senses. Children with this preference often base their decisions on facts and personal experience. They often learn best using step-by-step approaches, are provided with many examples and hands-on experience, and view what they are learning as applicable to their lives. They become discouraged when work seems too theoretical or complex.

In contrast, children with a preference for an imaginative style are more inclined to prefer theories and thus to focus their attention on generalizations and global concepts. They often base their decisions on intuitive hunches and may overlook details when learning and working. They learn best when given opportunities to use their imagination and to contribute their unique ideas. They appreciate others who value and praise their creativity (Myers & Myers, 1980; Keirsey, 1998; Oakland, et al. 1996).

The general prevalence for an imaginative style (58%) is higher in children ages 8–17 than for a practical style (42%). Although these figures generally are comparable for males and females, gender differences appear (Table 6.1). In contrast to males, female preference for an imaginative style is higher at ages 9, 13, and 16 and lower at age 17. When children from contiguous age groups are compared, significant differences are apparent between ages 8–9, 9–10, 10–11, and 13–14 (Figure 6.2).

Development trends, although present, are of short duration and non-linear. A significant shift from a somewhat balanced perspective toward a more imaginative style is found between ages 8 and 10 and then returns toward a more balanced style between ages 10 and 15. Finally, another shift toward an imaginative style is found between ages 15 and 17. The brevity and nonlinearity of these trends suggest that children, as a group, display considerable consistency in their preferences for practical and imaginative styles. Moreover, the preference for a practical style seen in adults (Hammer & Mitchell, 1996) is not apparent in these data.

THINKING–FEELING STYLES

Information on thinking and feeling styles helps define how people make decisions. Children with a preference for a thinking style rely on objective and logical standards when making decisions. They want to be treated fairly and desire truth to be told accurately. Further, because they highly value truth, they may express unpleasant comments and ideas in a blunt fashion, thus hurting others' feelings. They may praise others infrequently and may be uncomfortable openly expressing their emotions or feelings. These children tend to enjoy competitive activities and learn best when information presented is logically organized.

In contrast, children with a feeling style tend to rely on their feelings and own subjective standards when making decisions. They generally are compassionate and sensitive to the feelings of others and value harmony. Children with a feeling style tend to learn best when engaged in cooperative activities that help personalize their learning (Myers & Myers, 1980; Keirsey, 1998; Oakland, et al, 1996).

The general prevalence of thinking style (52%) in children ages 8–17 is slightly higher than of feeling style (48%) (Table 6.1). However, these figures are misleading in that sizable gender differences are found at each age (Figure 6.3). Males (74%) generally express a preference for a thinking style, and females (70%) generally express a preference for a feeling style. The two declining nonparallel lines (Figure 6.3), one for each gender, show preferences for a thinking style decline more rapidly for females than

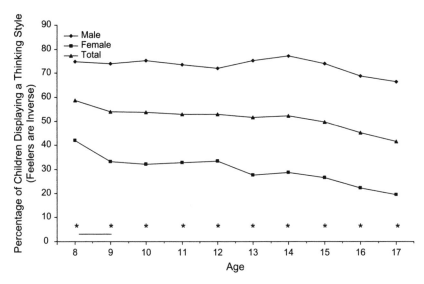

FIGURE 6.3. Percentage of children who display a thinking style across ten age groups. Age differences are signified by solid lines. Gender differences are signified by an asterisk.

males. When children from contiguous age groups are compared, significant differences are apparent only between ages 8 and 9.

Preferences for thinking and feeling styles are strongly impacted by gender and to a lesser extent by age. The prevalence of a thinking style among males generally is stable between ages 8 and 17. In contrast, the prevalence of a feeling style among females generally increases with age. For example, among females, 58% prefer a feeling style at age 8 and 81% at age 17. These data are consistent with research findings that characterize men as more objective and tough-minded and women as more subjective and caring.

These results also are congruent with cross-national findings of a preference for a thinking style more commonly among males and feeling styles more commonly among females in Australia (Oakland, Faulkner, & Bassett, 2005), Costa Rica, (Oakland, & Mata, 2007), Greece (Hatzichristou & Oakland, in press), Nigeria (Oakland, Mogaji, & Dempsey, 2006), South Africa (Oakland, Pretorius, & Lee, in press), Romania (Oakland et al, under review), and Venezuela (León, Oakland, Wei, & Berrios, in press) as well as in adults (Hammer & Mitchell, 1996).

Biological factors may explain these preferences. For example, genetic coding, with males displaying greater relative physical strength and lung capacity, may make them better suited for competitive struggles to obtain resources necessary for survival. In contrast, females, with childbearing and lactating capacities, may be predisposed to nurturing roles (Whyte, 1998).

Brain differences also may help explain these gender differences. The ability of women to better verbally express emotions may be explained by brain-related differences. In contrast to males, the right hemispheres of females, which control emotions, generally are better connected to the left side of the brain, which controls verbal expression (Moir & Jessel, 1989). The greater reliance of females on their feelings may have helped develop this hemispheric difference. Differences in emotional reactions of men and women also may be attributable to differential hormonal responses (Fischer, 1998).

Sociobiologists are likely to acknowledge environmental factors also may help explain these behavioral differences among males and females (Whyte, 1998). Indeed, psychoanalytic and socialization perspectives provide an interesting forum for explaining these gender preferences. According to Freud (1958), the establishment of gender identity is a major developmental milestone in early childhood. By age 3, almost all children identify themselves as either a boy or a girl (Pogrebin, 1980: Thompson, 1975) and begin to develop organized beliefs regarding qualities that constitute femaleness and maleness (Bem, 1981). In Western cultures, masculinity is characterized as assigned attributes of competitiveness and self-reliance. Femininity is assigned attributes of emotional expression, sensitivity, and nurturing (Ruble, 1983). These and other gender-related beliefs may strengthen as children evaluate their adequacy based on conformity to culturally defined role requirements regarding the way they should think and behave (Bem, 1983). The development of this dichotomous arrangement in gender-related beliefs and behavior also is evident in Western countries with more liberal attitudes (Goldman & Goldman, 1982).

Research in child-rearing practices suggests that preferences for a thinking or a feeling style may be learned. According to a feminist version of psychoanalysis, mothers relate to their sons and daughters differently (Chodorow, 1999). While fusing identities with their daughters, mothers relate to their sons as being separate and distinct. Consequently, young males and females are described as approaching relationships differently: girls are described as being more inclined to adopt styles marked by connectedness while boys are said to prefer independence and autonomy.

Mothers talk more about emotions and a greater variety of emotions with daughters than sons. Moreover, girls talk more about emotion and about a greater variety of emotions than do boys. Additionally, girls initiate more emotion-related discussions than do boys (Kuebli, Butler, & Fivush, 1995). Similarly, adolescent boys have fewer intimate relationships than do girls (Berndt, 1999; Youniss & Smollar, 1985).

Social learning and behavioral theories suggest that gender-related personality styles develop as result of social reinforcement (Bandura & Walters, 1963). Parents encourage children to engage in activities considered sex appropriate (Lytton & Romney, 1991). In Western cultures, girls generally receive praise and attention for their interest in feminine toys or activities while boys are positively reinforced for their interest in masculine toys or activities (Fagot & Hagan, 1991; Lytton & Romney, 1991).

Adult females tend to be more expressive, emotionally oriented, and nurturing while adult males tend to be more self-reliant, emotionally detached, and competitive. One large study of college students from 30 countries found that men consistently are described as adventurous, strong, dominant, assertive, task-oriented, aggressive, enterprising, and independent. In contrast, women are consistently described as sensitive, gentle, dependent, emotional, sentimental, weak, submissive, and people-oriented (Williams & Best, 1990). Women's social relationships are more dyadic and intimate while men's friendships tend to focus on activities of an emotionally detached nature such as sports or the completion of a task (Parker & de Vries, 1993; Wright, 1982). Women are more empathetic toward others (Eisenberg & Lennon, 1983), are more willing to discuss their emotional experiences with others (Dindia & Allen, 1992), and do so more overtly and with more confidence (Fischer, 1998).

ORGANIZED–FLEXIBLE STYLES

Information on organized and flexible styles helps to explain when an individual prefers to make decisions. Children who prefer an organized style like to make decisions as soon as possible and prefer structure and organization. They do not cope well with surprises or changes to their routine. They like to rely on lists and are likely to respond well to a more structured and organized setting. What is expected of them should be communicated clearly and schedules clearly established and followed. Children with this style like to do things the right way (e.g., that follow rules) and enjoy receiving praise for completing work in a timely manner.

In contrast, children who prefer a flexible style delay decision-making as long as possible and feel that they never have sufficient information to make decisions. They prefer a flexible and open schedule, enjoy surprises,

Kyle Bassett and Thomas Oakland

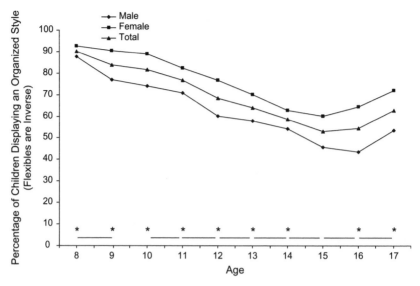

FIGURE 6.4. Percentage of children who display an organized style across ten age groups. Age differences are signified by solid lines. Gender differences are signified by an asterisk.

and adapt well to new situations. They may not respond well to externally imposed rules and regulations. The manner in which they learn best is somewhat complex. They are most highly motivated when given some flexibility in their assignments and are able to turn work into play. However, teachers and parents may have to provide structure and assist them in other ways to complete assignments on time (Myers & Myers, 1980; Keirsey, 1998; Oakland, et al, 1996).

The general prevalence of an organized style (70%) is considerably higher in children ages 8–17 years than a flexible style (30%), with both males (63%) and females (77%) generally preferring an organized style (Table 1). The fact that the majority of children prefer an organized style is noteworthy. These findings are consistent with adult data (Hammer & Mitchell, 1996).

Age differences are discernable (Figure 6.4), with a declining preference for organized and an inclining preference for flexible styles between ages 8 and 15, at which age 15, both males and females express an inclining preference for an organized style. Gender differences are apparent at all ages, with males more likely than females to prefer a flexible style and females more likely than males to prefer an organized style.

Culture-based factors may help explain a strong preference for an organized style. From a historical perspective, evidence suggests that a preference for an organized style, characterized by a strong work ethic and achievement, is valued in U.S. society. Almost from the beginning, settlers in America believed that hard work and education pay rich dividends. For example, John Wesley, who founded the Methodist church, exalted entrepreneurial success and urged his followers "to gain all they can, and to save all they can; that is, in effect, to grow rich" (Weber, 1904/1958, p. 175). The "pursuit of individual salvation through hard work, thrift, and competitive struggle" (Whyte, 1956, p. 4) has been described as the American dream.

This achievement orientation also was evident on the western frontier. While land was inexpensive, the lack of a division of labor forced people to be self-reliant (Potter, 1970). Francis J. Grund, an Austrian-born journalist working in the United States, noted "there is probably no people on earth with whom business constitutes pleasure, and industry amusement, in an equal degree with the inhabitants of the United States of America" (Grund, 1971, p. 1).

A strong organized work ethic remains a central feature of American character. A dominant view held among Americans is that leisure time ought to be used in a productive manner (Yankelovich, 1994). The United States consistently ranks as one of the most task-oriented nations in the world (Trompenaars, & Hampden-Turner, 1997). Americans work longer hours than their European and Japanese counterparts (Economist, 1994a; Bell & Freeman, 1994) and, in contrast to Europe, where status often is attributed to birth, gender, or age, Americans are more likely to approve merit-based reward systems (Trompenaars & Hampden-Turner, 1997).

An achievement orientation also is reflected in the value Americans place on education for success. In contrast to European culture, where welfare and other public policies are more widely accepted as means for helping the less affluent, Americans place greater emphasis on achieving social mobility through investment in education (Lipset, 1996). The United States generally spends more of its gross domestic product on education than the spending of countries in the European Union or Japan (*Economist*, 1994b). The United States historically leads the world in the proportion of young people attending elementary school, high school, and college (Lipset, 1996). The proportion of 20- to 24-year-olds in higher education in the United States has been almost double that of Japan and the most affluent European countries (Hampden-Turner & Trompenaars, 1993).

Child-rearing practices may play a role in preferences for an organized style. In Western cultures, parents admire children when achievement is attained by one's own effort (Hofstede, 1980; Triandis, 1995). Such ideology likely perpetuates an achievement orientation from one generation to the next.

As noted previously, adolescents display a significant and gradual shift toward a preference for a more flexible style between the ages 8 and 15. Similar results have been reported in cross-national research. For example, Australian and Chinese adolescents increasingly show a stronger preference for a flexible style between the ages 9 and 15 (Oakland, Faulkner, & Bassett, 2005; Oakland & Lu, 2006).

Developmental and psychoanalytic perspectives may be useful in explaining this trend. During preadolescence, when an organized style is most pronounced, children are most likely to accept parental views because they are viewed as most knowledgeable and dependable (Kaplan, 1991; Selman, 1980; Smollar & Youniss, 1989; Weissman, Cohen, Boxer, & Cohler, 1989). Deference to authority during this stage may be adaptive. An incentive for children to learn to behave in ways that ensure parental affection is strong (Sullivan, 1953). Children may experience feelings of love and acceptance when parental values are internalized. Consequently, they strive to correct tendencies or impulses that would incur disapproval or abandonment (Sullivan, 1953).

However, beginning in middle childhood, changes occur in children's susceptibility to parental influence (Berndt, 1979). Whether prompted by parents' attitudes suggesting that they become more autonomous in functioning (Baltes & Silverberg, 1994; Baumrind, 1971; Maccoby & Martin, 1983; Steinberg & Silverberg, 1986), by psychosocial goals of detaching from parental ties (Erikson, 1968; Freud, 1958; Sullivan, 1953), or the onset of the realization of the fallibility of parents (Steinberg & Silverberg, 1986), increasing opposition to adult authority marks the period between childhood and adolescence (Kearney, 1998). Indeed, the middle adolescent period has been characterized as a time of acting out and experimenting with different forms of subjectivity (Kearney, 1998). Adolescents often characterize their subordinate position in the family and adult control over their activities as restrictive and irksome (Mayall, 1999). Beginning around ages 11 or 12, issues such as choice or timing of activities often generate conflict. Children often demand more negotiation and flexibility in their approach to matters rather than simply accepting the absolute authority of their parents (Ambert, 1997).

Some congruence exists between when adolescents show the greatest preference for a flexible style and their likelihood to engage in risky or

rule-breaking behavior. The beginning of adolescence has been characterized as a time of experimentation with antisocial activities (Berndt, 1979).
Adolescents report higher levels of involvement in antisocial activities
(Steinberg & Silverberg, 1986). Problem behaviors in youth peak around
ages 15 and 16 across cultures and generations (Gottfredson & Hirischi,
1990; Kennedy, 1991; Lore & Schultz, 1993). Arrest rates among U.S. teens
ages 15 to 17 are higher than at any other time across the life span (Bee,
1995). However, the period of delinquency may be short-lived and serve as
a springboard for reconciliation with prevailing cultural and parental attitudes and beliefs (Kaplan, 1991; Smollar & Youniss, 1989; Steinberg &
Silverberg, 1986; Weissman, Cohen, Boxer, & Cohler, 1989).

REFERENCES

Ambert, A.M. (1997). *Parents, Children and Adolescents: Interactive Relationships
and Development in Context.* Binghamton, NY: Hawthorn Press.
Baltes, M.M., & Silverberg, S. (1994). The dynamics between dependency and
autonomy: Illustrations across the life span. In D.L. Featherman, R.M. Lerner, &
Perlmutter, M. (Eds.), *Life-Span Development and Behavior* (Vol. 12, pp. 41–90),
Hillsdale, NJ: Lawrence Erlbaum Associates.
Bandura, A., & Walters, R.H. (1963). *Social Learning and Personality.* New York:
Holt, Rinehart, and Winston.
Bassett, K.D. (2004). Nature, nurture, and temperament: Comparisons of tem-
perament styles displayed by U.S. students. Unpublished doctoral dissertation,
University of Florida, Gainesville.
Baumrind, D. (1971). Current patterns of parental authority. *Developmental Psy-
chology Monograph,* 4 (1, Pt. 2).
Bee, H. (1995). *The Growing Child.* New York: Harper Collins.
Bell, L., & Freeman, R. (1994). Why do Americans and Germans Work Differing
Hours? Paper No. 4808, Cambridge, MA: National Bureau of Economic
Research, pp. 2, 14–15
Bem, S.L. (1981). Gender schema theory: A cognitive account of sex typing.
Psychological Review, 88, 354–364.
Bem, S.L. (1983). Gender schema theory and its implications for child devel-
opment: Raising gender-aschematic children in a gender-schematic society.
Journal of Women in Culture and Society, Vol. 8, 4, pp. 598–616.
Berndt, T.J. (1979). Developmental changes in conformity to peers and parents.
Developmental Psychology, 15, 608–616.
Berndt, T.J. (1999). Friendships in adolescence. In M. Woodhead, D. Faulkner, &
K. Littleton (Eds.), *Making Sense of Social Development* (pp. 51–71). New York:
Routledge.
Benson, N., Oakland, T., & Shermis, N. (in press) Evidence for cross-national
invariance of children's temperament structure. *Journal of Psychoeducational
Assessment.*

Brown, B.B. (1989). The role of peer groups in adolescents adjustment to secondary school. In T.J. Berndt & G.W. Ladd (Eds.), *Peer Relationships in Child Development* (pp. 188–215). New York: Wiley.

Brown, B.B., Mounts, N., Lamborn, S.D., & Steinberg, L. (1993). Parenting practices and peer group affiliation in adolescence. *Child Development*, 64, 467–482.

Chodorow, N. (1999). *The Reproduction of Mothering: Psychoanalysis and the Sociology of Gender.* Los Angeles, CA: University of California Press.

Dindia, K., & Allen, M. (1992). Sex differences in self-disclosure: A metaanalysis. *Psychological Bulletin*, 112, 106–124.

Economist (1994a). Workaholics anonymous, Vol. 333, number 7886, Oct 22, 1994, p. 20.

Economist (1994b). The European Union, Vol. 333, number 7886, Oct 22, 1994, Survey, p. 4.

Eisenberg, N., & Lennon, R. (1983). Sex differences in empathy and related capacities. *Psychological Bulletin*, 94, 100–131.

Erikson, E. (1968). *Identity, Youth, and Crisis.* New York: Norton.

Fagot, B.I., & Hagan, R. (1991). Observations of parent reactions to sex-stereotyped behaviors: Age and sex effects. *Child Development*, 62, 617–628.

Feiring, C., & Lewis, M. (1989). The social networks of girls and boys from early through middle childhood. In D. Belle (Ed.), *Children's Social Networks and Social Supports* (pp. 119–150). New York: Wiley.

Fischer, A. (1998). Emotion. In K. Trew & J. Kremer (Eds.), *Gender and Psychology* (pp. 82–94). London, England: Arnold.

Freud, A. (1958). Adolescence. *Psychoanalytic Study of the Child*, 13, 255–278.

Furman, W. (1989). The development of children's social networks. In D. Belle (Ed.), *Children's Social Networks and Social Supports* (pp. 151–172). New York: Wiley.

Goldman, R., & Goldman, J. (1982). *A Comparative Study of Children aged 5 to 15 Years in Australia, North America, Britain and Sweden.* Boston, MA: Routledge & Keegan Paul.

Goldsmith, H.H., Buss, A.H., Plomin, R., Rothbart, M.K., Thomas, A., Chess, S., Hinde, R.A., & McCall, R.B. (1987). Roundtable: What is temperament? Four approaches. *Child Development*, 58, 505–529.

Gottfredson, M.R., & Hirischi, T (1990). *A General Theory of Crime.* Stanford, CA: Stanford University Press.

Grund, F.J. (1971). *The Americans in their Moral, Social and Political Relations.* New York: August M. Kelley (Original work published in 1837)

Hammer, A. (1996). MBTI research at CPP. *Bulletin of Psychological Type*, 19, 11.

Hammer, A.L., & Mitchell, W.D. (1996). The distribution of MBTI types in the US by gender and ethnic group. *Journal of Psychological Type*, 37, 2–15.

Higgins, E.T., & Parsons, J. (1983). Social cognition and the social life of the child: Stages as subcultures. In E.T. Higgins, D. Ruble, & W.W. Hartup (Eds.), *Social Cognition and Social Behavior: Developmental Perspectives* (pp. 15–62). New York: Cambridge University Press.

Hofstede, G.H. (1980). *Culture's Consequences: International Differences in Work-Related Values.* Beverly Hills, CA: Sage.

Horton, C., & Oakland, T. (1996) *Classroom Applications Booklet.* San Antonio, TX: The Psychological Corporation.

Joyce, D., & Oakland, T. (2005). Temperament differences among children with conduct disorder and oppositional defiant disorder, *California School Psychologist*, 10, 125–136.

Jung, C.G. (1953). *Two Essays on Analytical Psychology.* (R.F.C. Hull, Trans.). New York: Pantheon Books.(Original work published 1943.)

Jung, C.G. (1971). *Psychological Types.* (R.F.C. Hull, Revision of Trans. By H.G. Baynes). Princeton, NJ: Princeton University Press. (Original work published 1921.)

Kagan, J. (1989). Temperamental contributions to social behavior. *American Psychologist*, 44, 668–674.

Kagan, J. (1994a). *Galen's Prophecy: Temperament in Human Nature.* New York: Basic Books.

Kagan, J. (1994b). Inhibited and uninhibited temperaments. In W.B. Carey & S.C. McDevitt, (Eds.), *Prevention and Early Intervention: Individual Differences as Risk Factors for the Mental Health of Children* (pp. 35–41). New York: Brunner Mazel.

Kaplan, E.H. (1991). Adolescents, age fifteen to eighteen: A psychoanalytic developmental view. In S.I. Greenspan & G.H. Pollock (Eds.), *The Course of Life* (Vol. IV, pp. 201–233). New York: International Press.

Kaufman, A.S. (1979). *Intelligent Testing with the WISC-R.* New York: John Wiley & Sons.

Kaufman, A.S. (1994). *Intelligent Testing with the WISC-III.* New York: Wiley.

Kearney, M.C. (1998) Producing girls: Rethinking the study of female youth culture. In S.A. Innes (Ed.), *Delinquents and Debutantes: Twentieth-Century Girls' Encounters* (pp. 285–310). New York: University Press.

Keirsey, D. (1998). *Please Understand Me II: Temperament, Character, Intelligence.* Del Mar, CA: Prometheus Nemesis.

Kennedy, R.E. (1991). Delinquency. In R.M. Lerner, A.C. Petersen, & J. Brooks-Gunn (Eds.), *Encyclopedia of Adolescence* (pp. 199–206). New York: Garland.

Keogh, B.K. (2003). *Temperament in the Classroom*, Baltimore, MD: Brookes Publishing.

Kuebli, J., Butler, S., & Fivush, R. (1995). Mother-child talk about past emotions: Relations of maternal language and child gender over time. *Cognition and Emotion*, 9, 265–283.

León, C. Oakland, T., Wei, Y., & Berrios, M. (in press). Venezuelan children's temperament styles and comparison with their United States peers. *Interamerican Journal of Psychology.*

Lipset, M.S. (1996). *American Exceptionalism: A Double-Edged Sword.* New York: W.W. Norton & Company.

Lore, R.K., & Schultz, L.A. (1993), Control of Human Aggression. *American Psychologist*, 48, 16–25.

Lytton, H., & Romney, D.M. (1991). Parents' differential socialization of boys and girls: A meta-analysis. *Psychological Bulletin*, 109, 267–296

Maccoby, E.E., & Martin, J.A. (1983). Socialization in the Context of the Family: Parent Child Interaction. In E.M. Heatherington (Ed.), *Handbook of Child*

Psychology: Socialization, Personality, and Social Development (Vol. 4, pp. 1–102). New York: Wiley

Matas, L., Arend, R., & Sroufe, L.A. (1978). Continuity of adaptation in the second year: The relationship between quality of attachment and later competence. *Child Development*, 49, 547–556.

Mayall, B. (1999). Children in action at home and school. In M. Woodhead, D. Faulkner, & K. Littleton(Eds.), *Making Sense of Social Development* (pp. 199–213). New York: Routledge.

Moir, A., & Jessel, D. (1989). *Brain Sex: The Real Difference between Men and Women*. London: Mandarin.

Moran, P.B., & Eckenrode, J. (1991). Gender differences in the costs and benefits of peer relations during adolescence. *Journal of Adolescent Research*, 6, 396–409.

Myers, I.B., McCaulley, M.H., Quenk, N.L., & Hammer, A.L. (1998). *MBTI: Manual: A Guide to the Development and Use of the Myers-Briggs Type Indicator*. Palo Alto, CA: Consulting Psychologists Press.

Myers, I.B., & Myers, P.B. (1980). *Gifts Differing*. Palo Alto, CA: Consulting Psychologists Press.

Oakland, T., Faulkner, M. & Bassett, K. (2005). Temperament styles of children from Australia and the United States. *Australian Journal of Psychology*. 19, 35–51.

Oakland, T., Glutting, J.J., & Horton, C.B. (1996). *Student Styles Questionnaire*. San Antonio, TX: Psychological Corporation.

Oakland, T., Banner, D., & Livingston, R. (2000) Temperament-based learning styles of visually-impaired children. *Journal of Visual Impairment and Blindness*, January, 26–33.

Oakland, T., Joyce, D., Horton, C. & Glutting J. (2000). Temperament-based learning styles of male and female gifted and non-gifted children. *Gifted Child Quarterly*, 44, 183–189.

Oakland, T., Stafford, M., Horton, C., & Glutting, J. (2001). Temperament and vocational preferences: Age, gender and racial-ethnic comparisons using the Student Styles Questionnaire. *Journal of Career Assessment*, 9, (3), 297–314.

Oakland, T., Mogaji, A., & Dempsey, J. (2006). Temperament Styles of Nigerian and U.S. Children. *Journal of Psychology in Africa*, 16, 27–34.

Oakland, T. & Lu, L. (2006). Temperament styles of children from People's Republic of China and the United States. *School Psychology International*, 27, 192–208.

Oakland, T. & Mata, A. (2007). Temperament styles of children from the Costa Rica and the United States. *Journal of Psychological Type*, 67, 91–102.

Oakland, T., Mpofu, E., & Sulkowski, M. (2007). Temperament styles of Zimbabwe and U.S. children. *Canadian Journal of School Psychology*, 21, 139–153.

Oakland, T., Pretorius, J., & Lee, D.H. & (in press). Temperament Styles of Children from South Africa and the United States. *School Psychology Internationally*.

Oakland, T., Iliescu, D., Dinca, M., & Dempsey. A. Temperament styles of Romanian children. Submitted for publication.

Parker, S., & deVries, B. (1993). Patterns of friendship for women and men in same and cross-sex friendships. *Journal of Social and Personal Relations*, 10, 617–626.

Pogrebin, L.C. (1980). *Growing Up Free: Raising Your Child in the 80's*. New York: McGraw-Hill.

Potter, D.M. (1970). The quest for the national character. In M. McGiffert (Ed.), *The Character of Americans: A Book of Readings* (pp. 21–36). Homewood, IL: Dorsey.

Roback, A.A. (1927). *The Psychology of Character.* New York: Harcourt Brace.

Rothbart, M.K. (1989). Temperament and development. In G.A. Kohnstamm, J.E. Bates, & M.K. Rothbart (Eds.), *Temperament in Childhood* (pp. 59–73). Chichester, England: Wiley.

Ruble, T.L. (1983). Sex stereotypes: Issues of change in the 1970's. *Sex Roles, 9,* 397–402.

Selman, R.L. (1980). *The Growth of Interpersonal Understanding: Developmental and Clinical Analyses.* New York: Academic Press.

Smollar, J., & Youniss, J. (1989). Transformations in adolescents: Perceptions of parents. *International Journal of Behavioral Development, 12,* 71–84.

Stafford, M., & Oakland, T. (1996a). Racial-ethnic comparisons of temperament constructs for three age groups using the Student Styles Questionnaire. *Measurement and Evaluation in Counseling and Development, 29,* 108–110.

Stafford, M., & Oakland, T. (1996b). Validity of temperament constructs using the Student Styles Questionnaire: Comparisons for three racial-ethnic groups. *Journal of Psychoeducational Assessment, 14,* 109–120.

Steinberg, L., & Silverberg, S. (1986). The vicissitudes of autonomy in early adolescence. *Child Development, 57,* 841–851.

Strelau, J. (1998). *Temperament: A Psychological Perspective.* New York: Plenum Press.

Sullivan, H.S. (1953). *The Interpersonal Theory of Psychology.* New York: Norton.

Tegalsi, H. (1998a). Introduction to the mini-series: Implications of temperament for the practice of school psychology. *School Psychology Review, 27,* 475–478.

Teglasi, H. (1998b). Temperament constructs and measurement. *School Psychology Review, 27,* 564–585.

Thompson, S.K. (1975). Gender labels and early sex role development. *Child Development, 46,* 339–347.

Thomas, A., Chess, S., & Birch, H.G. (1968). *Temperament and Behavior Disorders in Children.* New York: New York University Press.

Triandis, H.C. (1995). *Individualism and Collectivism.* Boulder, CO: Westview Press.

Trompenaars, F., & Hampden-Turner, C. (1997). *Riding the Waves of Culture: Understanding Cultural Diversity in Business.* London, England: Nicholas Brealey.

Weber, M. (1958). *The Protestant Ethic and the Spirit of Capitalism* (T. Parsons, Trans.). New York: Charles Scribner's Sons. (Original work published in 1904.)

Weissman, S.H., Cohen, R.S., Boxer, A.M., & Cohler, B.J. (1989). Parenthood experience and the adolescent's transition to young adulthood: Self psychological perspectives. In S.C. Feinstein (Ed.), *Adolescent Psychiatry* (Vol. 16, pp. 155–174). Chicago, IL: Chicago University Press.

Whyte, J. (1998). Childhood. In K. Trew & J. Kremer (Eds.), *Gender and Psychology* (pp. 97–106). London, England: Arnold.

Whyte, W.H., Jr. (1956). *The Organization of Man.* New York: Simon and Schuster.

Williams, J.E., & Best, D.L. (1990). *Measuring Sex Stereotypes: A Multi-Nation Study.* Newbury Park, CA: Sage.

Wright, P.H. (1982). Men's friendship, women's friendships and the alleged inferiority of the latter. *Sex Roles*, 8, 1–20.

Yankelovich, D. (1994). How Changes in the economy are reshaping American values. In H.J. Aaron, T.E. Mann, & T. Taylor (Eds.), *Values and Public Policy* (pp. 16–53). Washington, DC: The Brookings Institution.

Youniss, J., & Smollar, J. (1985). *Adolescent Relations with Mothers, Fathers, and Friends*. Chicago, IL: University of Chicago Press.

7

Intelligent Intelligence Testing: The Influence of
Alan S. Kaufman

JACK A. NAGLIERI
George Mason University

INTRODUCTION

As I walked up to the third floor of Aderhold Hall at the University of Georgia (UGA) that fall day to attend a special meeting arranged by my PhD advisor, I had no idea that the field of intellectual assessment was about to make a dramatic course change. Dr. Alan S. Kaufman was about to tell a group of doctoral students about the intention he and Nadeen Kaufman had to build a new intelligence test. This challenge to the venerable Wechsler and Binet empires was equivalent to the challenge that formed the basis of the movie *The Mouse that Roared*. The plot of the 1959 Cold War era satire went like this: The Duchy of Grand Fenwick decides that the only way to get out of the country's economic woes is to declare war on the United States, lose, and then accept foreign aid. (Alan told me how he memorized the entire dialog of this movie when working as an usher in a local movie theater.) In the end, through a series of unbelievable comic circumstances, the little country wins! The mouse did roar. So too did Alan and Nadeen Kaufman when they published the *Kaufman Assessment Battery for Children* (K-ABC) and the many tests that followed.

Alan and Nadeen mounted a charge that provided alternative intelligence tests and, in addition, new tests of many types through their students. None of us could imagine the eventual effect that was beginning that day. In retrospect, it was a clear message that the field was evolving because of two psychologists from New York. The change would take time; after all, that first meeting was nearly 30 years ago. Like it or not, this was a revolution for evolution – and the change would be substantial.

The goal of this chapter is to help the reader understand how Alan Kaufman has been a catalyst for change that has profoundly influenced the field of assessment. He helped initiate a change in a field of intelligence,

73

which has been remarkably resistant to evolution, despite being described as one of the most important contributions psychology has made to society. His efforts helped start of a new era in intelligence testing and the work of his students has changed the face of assessment today. In order to segment the evolutionary nature of this revolution, I have organized this chapter into two main sections; first Alan Kaufman's influence on the field and second his influence on me.

MAKING INTELLIGENCE TESTS MORE INTELLIGENT

New Tests of Intelligence

Undoubtedly, Alan Kaufman's most important contribution to the field of assessment was to encourage an evolutionary step toward theory based tests of intelligence. The publication of the K-ABC in 1983 was both revolutionary and evolutionary on two dimensions. These dimensions were perhaps best illustrated by Alan's description of the WISC-R written on the chalk board during that first meeting in Aderhold Hall. He began writing that in his view, the WISC-R Verbal Scale was achievement (which formed the basis for the achievement portion of the K-ABC), the Performance Scale was holistic, gestalt, right brain (e.g., Simultaneous scale), and the third factor was serial, temporal, left brain (e.g., Sequential processing scale). With those strokes of chalk (by today's standards an old technology), he initiated a new technology and a revolt against the establishment.

The K-ABC, he codeveloped with Dr. Nadeen Kaufman, was and continues to be a monumental contribution to the field. The Kaufmans stressed theory at a time when IQ tests had no clear theoretical foundation. Just as Alan Kaufman's research and interpretive approaches helped bridge the gap between psychometrics and the practice of psychology, the K-ABC helped practitioners realize that an intelligence test should have some grounding in a theory and that intelligence could be conceptualized as cognitive processes. Whereas traditional IQ tests (e.g., Wechsler and Binet) emphasized the content of the items (verbal–nonverbal), the K-ABC switched the focus to the process (Sequential and Simultaneous) required to complete a task. This shift reflected a dramatic change in test development by emphasizing how children learn – an approach that is consistent with a variety of theories in cognitive psychology and neuropsychology.

Importantly, the K-ABC was also developed with the goal of greatly reducing the differences between the scores earned by European American and minority children. This goal was realized in several ways. Student interest was maintained by developing a variety of new tasks that were interesting to children. Students from low socioeconomic backgrounds performed better on this test because the content of the questions did not rely as much on school learning in favor of tasks that required new problem solving. In addition, novel, theory-based tasks were developed and a dramatic departure from the narrow and nontheoretical approach that characterized traditional IQ testing was provided. The result was to cut the typical European American-African American IQ difference in half and to greatly reduce the IQ differences between European American children and Hispanic American children, and between European American children and Native American children. That reduction in ethnic differences has been maintained on the KABC-II, underscoring the dramatic impact that Dr. Kaufman has made regarding the fair and nonbiased assessment of individuals from a variety of ethnic backgrounds.

Test Interpretation

Intelligent Testing with the WISC-R (Kaufman, 1979) was Alan's first book. This outstanding text encouraged practitioners to change the way they interpreted one of the gold standards of intelligence tests: the Wechsler scales. The Wechsler scales were, and continue to be, the most widely used tests of intelligence. What Alan Kaufman did was help practitioners use that test in a more scientifically defensible manner. He taught practitioners to use psychometrically defensible methods for test interpretation. For example, he helped practitioners use better methods of subtest analysis to understand the possible variables that influenced a subject's subtest variation. He did this using a mathematical system of comparing a child to themselves, sometimes referred to as an ipsative approach.

The ipsative methodology was originally proposed by Davis (1959) and popularized by Alan Kaufman in his WISC-R book (Kaufman, 1979). He encouraged the use of this method to determine when variability within a child is greater than what would be expected on the basis of unreliability of the subtest scores. Individual scores that were significantly below the child's average are labeled as a weakness and those significantly above the child's average described as a strength. Since then the ipsative method has been applied to a number of tests including the K-ABC and KABC-II (Kaufman & Kaufman, 1983, 2004), WISC-IV (Naglieri & Paolitto, 2005), the Wechsler Nonverbal and Scale of Ability (Wechsler & Naglieri, 2006), Binet-5 (Roid, 2003), and the Cognitive Assessment System (CAS) (Naglieri & Das, 1997a) to name a few. This method has also been recommended for determining relative strengths and weaknesses for the diagnosis of a specific learning disability (SLD), particularly when used to align the IDEA 2004 definition (e.g., a disorder in one or more of the basic psychological processes) with psychometric findings from tests of cognitive processing (Hale, Naglieri, Kaufman & Kavale, 2004). Naglieri (1999) further refined this method cautioning that the absolute value of a relative weakness could be significantly below the child's mean but still well within the average range. In order to ensure that a child has "a disorder" in processing, he recommended that a child's profile should show significant variability (using the ipsative method) and the lowest score should also fall below some normative cut-off designed to indicate what is typical or average. This type of finding was described as a "cognitive weakness" because it uses a dual criterion of a low score relative to the child's mean and a low score relative to the norm group. Naglieri (1999) further suggested a disorder in one or more of the basic psychological processes could be defined as a cognitive weakness accompanied by academic weakness (perhaps best identified using a standardized achievement test) comparable to the level of the processing scale cognitive weakness. Finding a cognitive weakness *and* an academic weakness provides evidence that contributes to the diagnosis of a SLD especially if other appropriate conditions are also met. The ipsative method advocated by Kaufman (1979) has evolved into a consistency/discrepancy model (see Naglieri, 1999), which is conceptually similar to the Hale–Fiorello concordance–discordance model described by Hale (2006) and the method used by Flanagan and Kaufman (2004) that can be used to help determine if a child has a SLD.

Alan Kaufman's application of the ipsative method to the subtest profiles of WISC-R scores has evolved into a method for comparing scores obtained on measures of cognitive processing which are, in turn, used to help make the diagnosis of SLD as well as attention deficit/hyperactivity disorders (ADHD) (see Naglieri, 2001, 2005). This technological and methodological contribution has provided practitioners a more scientific way to evaluate children with disabilities.

TEST INTERPRETATION AND LEARNING DISABILITIES

At the time when *Intelligent Testing with the WISC-R* was published, the use of concepts like statistical significance was mostly ignored by clinicians when interpreting test profiles and nonscientific approaches dominated. Freudian psychoanalytical interpretations were typical, as was overdiagnosis of brain damage from verbal-performance (V-P) IQ differences. Alan's research helped practitioners know what normal WISC-R subtest scatter was (see Kaufman, 1976a). Additionally, knowing what normal V-P IQ differences were (Kaufman, 1976b) gave clinicians yardsticks for evaluating whether the IQ discrepancies and range of subtest scores earned by their clients were common or rare within the normal population. V-P IQ differences of 15 or more points were commonly considered to denote learning disabilities or brain damage when, in fact, the research indicated that one normal child or adult out of four had differences of 15 points or greater. Similarly, children and adolescents were commonly diagnosed with learning disabilities because of variability (scatter) in the subtest profiles. His research indicated that the average person had a range of 7 ($\pm$ 2) points in their scaled scores on the WISC-R. That is, score ranges from 6 to 15 were normal and not cause for a diagnosis of any type of abnormality. These studies had a great effect on the diagnosis of brain damage, learning disabilities, and psychopathology by providing data on what was truly normal. At that time, clinicians and researchers lacked any conception of the fluctuations that characterize the test profiles of typical children and adults.

International Impact

Alan Kaufman's interpretive approach and cognitive tests have had dramatic impact on the testing and assessment practices throughout Canada, Europe, Africa, and Asia. Adaptations and translations of the K-ABC have been published throughout the world, and are extremely popular in a number of countries, including France, Germany, the Netherlands, Israel, Belgium, Switzerland, Korea, Japan, Egypt, Spain, Italy, and Canada. Other Kaufman tests have also been published in Europe (K-BIT, K-SNAP, KAIT, and K-CLASSIC). In addition, his books on the intelligence of children, adolescents, and adults – as well as his frequent invited talks throughout the world – have provided strong international guidance and leadership. His books (both the English and translated versions), tests, and lectures have had ground-breaking worldwide impact on the interpretation of the Wechsler and Kaufman tests and the diagnosis of learning disabilities in France, Sweden, Germany, Brazil, Japan, Spain, Korea, Netherlands, Israel, Canada, England, Egypt, Russia, and numerous other countries.

Test Developers

In the few years Alan Kaufman was on the faculty of the UGA, he provided his students with a wealth of knowledge and an opportunity to learn that went well beyond the classroom. His style was based on holding his students, and himself, to high standards and providing them with knowledge and opportunity. His wealth of knowledge was, and is, expansive, authoritative, and imaginative. His gift of opportunity encouraged us to do more than the PhD program required – and eventually, the opportunity to do as much as our imaginations allowed. The result has been amazing.

In addition to his role as a teacher and research supervisor for so many doctoral students at UGA, he gave us the opportunity to grow into national and international leaders in the field of assessment and school psychology. He informed and inspired us by his outstanding mentoring and the fine example he set as a scientist interested in the practical aspect of psychological assessment. Importantly, he provided opportunities for his students to learn the science and art of test development. As a group, his former students have themselves published many psychological tests and scientific papers and have gone on to produce a second generation of scholars under the Kaufman lineage. Alan's gift to his students became our gift to all those professionals who have used our instruments to influence the lives of so many children and adults who have taken the numerous tests we have produced. On behalf of all the children and adults whose lives have been improved because of the information those tests have provided and the knowledge that Alan Kaufman has generated, I extend my sincerest thanks.

PERSONAL INFLUENCE

It is impossible for me to write about the influence Alan S. Kaufman has had on the field without describing his impact on me. In order to better contextualize the impact, I will begin with my arrival at the UGA campus in the summer of 1977. It was somewhat of an unsettling culture shock and at the same time exhilarating. Culture shock – because I had had never been further south than the state of Delaware, knew little of southern culture, and had no idea what to expect once I traveled outside of the New York metropolitan area. Exhilarating – because I sensed this was the start of something really important. At that time I had no idea just how important my choice to go to UGA was. I did not know the young professor Alan S. Kaufman would become an icon in the field, but after only a few minutes in his office, it became clear that he was an extraordinary person and, more importantly, that there was some kind of connection between us. I also did not know that the knowledge and opportunity Alan provided me would be the catalyst for major changes my life and eventually allow me to touch the lives of many thousands of children and adults.

The knowledge that Alan provided his students at the UGA had depth and breadth of a magnitude that I had not seen before, nor seen since. Even though I had already taken classes in assessment and worked for two years as a school psychologist, I attended his courses on intelligence testing. He presented a way to interpret intelligence tests that was thoughtful, scientific, and definitely cutting edge. Alan's scientific method of examining test results, and the logical and psychometrically elegant way in which he examined each case, was as astonishing as the way he enveloped an incredible sense of humor within each sophisticated analysis.

As I acquired more knowledge of the field of assessment, my level of interest increased exponentially, but I could not have anticipated what would happen next. When Alan offered me, and several other students, the opportunity to work on the development of the K-ABC, I knew this was the start of something remarkable. We were given a framework and a research base and told to develop some experimental tests. That is, we were given the *opportunity* to contribute to the development of this test and given the freedom to explore how the basic concepts of the K-ABC could be operationalized. Importantly, we were told to be creative – something that in particular resonated with me. The essence of the framework for this new test was to start with a theoretical perspective and build tests that fit the theory. This was both logical and revolutionary, as IQ tests used at that time were based more on historical precedent than theory. For me, this experience was life-altering.

The opportunity and knowledge Alan Kaufman provided me changed the course of my life. Whereas my initial goal of attending UGA was to get my PhD and return to a school district in the New York area, a newly discovered love of research as a means of contributing to the field and society in general overwhelmed me. As a young school psychologist, I thought how nice it would be to make a small contribution to the field. Alan Kaufman gave me knowledge and opportunity to do that; but he actually gave me much more. He showed me how a professor could be a high-quality scholar, excellent teacher, and test developer at the same time. For me, my chance to demonstrate scholarship and teaching came with my first university position at Northern Arizona University. Alan's influence on me as a test developer emerged a few years later.

Alan's gifts of knowledge and opportunity taught me how to be a professional and gave me an understanding that I could also become a test author. Developing subtests for the K-ABC was an eye-opening activity for me; but seeing what I developed become part of the published test was exhilarating. Alan gave me the knowledge and opportunity, but going further was my responsibility. While teaching my assessment courses at The Ohio State University, it became clear to me that my experience building the K-ABC Matrix Analogies subtest provided me the basis for building my own test. I choose to build a test comprised of progressive matrix items. Partnering with Charles Merrill Publishing Company, which was located in Columbus, Ohio where I lived, I developed the Matrix Analogies Tests (Expanded and Short Forms) (Naglieri, 1985a, b). The 64-item Expanded Form was intended to be used as part of a comprehensive evaluation and the Short Form was designed for group screening (e.g., identification of children who may be gifted). I had no idea that this effort would eventually evolve into some of my most widely used tests – the Naglieri Nonverbal Ability Test Multilevel Form (NNAT) (Naglieri, 1997), Naglieri Nonverbal Ability Test Individual Form (Naglieri, 2003), and most recently the Naglieri Nonverbal Ability Test 2nd Edition Multilevel Form (NNAT2) (Naglieri, 2007) and the NNAT2-Online (Naglieri, 2008). All of this resulted from a request Alan made to me when the K-ABC was being developed. He told me that he was having trouble finding someone to write progressive matrix items that all could be solved with the same 6 options (which meant 6 movable pieces). I always liked a challenge and produced the items that became the Matrix Analogies subtest on the K-ABC. More importantly, however, this work not only led to the development of my own progressive matrix tests but also allowed me to begin studying the role such tests have in fair and equitable assessment of ability – something that Alan stressed.

Alan's view that the K-ABC should measure ability without the use of verbal and quantitative tests made sense to me and this approach to measuring intelligence without the requirement that a child know English and math has had particular relevance to the assessment of gifted minority children. The NNAT provides a way to measure general ability using tests that do not require verbal or quantitative skills. This chapter will include the examination of White and minority populations, bilingual children, gender differences, and relationships to achievement.

The first indications that the NNAT could fairly assess the ability of minority children was found when Naglieri and Ronning (2000a, b) studied mean score differences and correlations to achievement for matched samples of White (*n* = 2,306) and African-American (*n* = 2,306); White (*n* = 1,176) and Hispanic (*n* = 1,176); and White (*n* = 466) and Asian (*n* = 466) students in grades K through 12. The three pairs of groups were matched on the demographic characteristics of the U.S. population, including geographic region, socioeconomic status, ethnicity, and type of school setting (public or private). Only small differences were found between the NNAT scores for the white and African-American samples (Cohen's *d* ratio = .25 or about 4 standard score points). Minimal differences between white and Hispanic (*d* ratio = .17 or about 3 standard score points), as well as white and Asian (*d* ratio = .02 less than one standard score point) groups were also reported. Additionally, correlations between the NNAT and academic achievement were strong (e.g., *r* = .56 with Total Reading), consistent across the grades K through 12, and similar for the White, African-American, and Hispanic samples. The small mean score differences and the strong correlations suggested that the NNAT had utility for fair assessment of minority children. The utility of this test was more fully explored next.

Naglieri, Booth and Winsler (2004) studied differences between Hispanic children with (*n* = 148) and without (*n* = 148) limited English proficiency who were administered the NNAT and the Stanford Achievement Test – Ninth Edition. The two groups of Hispanic children were selected from 22,620 children included in the NNAT standardization sample and matched on geographic region, gender, socioeconomic status, urbanicity, and ethnicity. The results showed that there was only a small difference (*d* ratio = 0.1) between the NNAT standard scores for the Hispanic children with limited English proficiency and those without limited English proficiency. The NNAT scores also correlated similarly with achievement for the Hispanic children with and without limited English proficiency. The results suggested that the NNAT had utility for assessment of Hispanic children with and without limited English proficiency. Next, an examination of the utility of the NNAT for selection of gifted children was conducted.

The examination of mean score differences was evaluated by Naglieri and Ford (2003). They asked the practical question: if the NNAT yields small mean score differences between minority and majority groups, would it identify similar percentages of white, black and Hispanic children as gifted? They used a sample of 20,270 children from the NNAT standardization sample to determine if the percentages of children who earned NNAT standard scores from 120 to 140 were comparable by racial and ethnic groups.

Naglieri and Ford (2003) found that 5.6% of the White ($n = 14{,}141$), 5.1% of the Black ($n = 2{,}863$), and 4.4% of the Hispanic ($n = 1{,}991$) children earned an NNAT standard score of 125 (95th percentile rank) or higher and 2.5% of White, 2.6 % of Black, and 2.3% of Hispanic children earned NNAT standard scores of 130 or higher (98th percentile). Their findings suggested that the percentages of children who would be identified as gifted if the NNAT was used were similar across race and ethnic groups. This instrument, therefore, could help address the persistent problem of the underrepresentation of minorities in gifted education. This study was followed by a close examination of gender differences.

Gender differences on the NNAT were examined by Rojahn and Naglieri (2006) for the entire standardization sample. They found that the NNAT scores for children aged 6–9 years (14,468 males and 14,668 females) did not differ (100.2 for both genders). Males ($n = 14{,}273$) and females ($n = 14{,}443$) aged 10–13 years scored virtually the same on the NNAT (100.0 and 100.2, respectively). Finally, males ($n = 5{,}681$) and females ($n = 5{,}940$) aged 15–17 years also scored the same on the NNAT (99.1 for both genders). Scores for this sample by NNAT level yielded the same results, indicating that males and females earn nearly identical scores on this nonverbal measure of ability. Taken as a whole, these studies have shown that the NNAT provides a viable tool for equitable assessment of diverse populations – a goal that Alan emphasized when the K-ABC was being developed.

My work with the NNAT also evolved into the development of a nonverbal measure of ability that includes more subtests but retains the essential goal of measuring general ability nonverbally – the Wechsler Nonverbal Scale of Ability (Wechsler & Naglieri, 2006). The WNV is comprised of subtests that were either adapted from other Wechsler tests, are new, or are modeled after the NNAT (1997, 2003). There are six subtests: Matrices, Coding, Object Assembly, Recognition, Spatial Span, and Picture Arrangement, however, no more than four subtests are used at any one age. The WNV was standardized on a large representative sample of children aged 4 through 21 years who closely represented the U.S. population and a large sample of Canadian children aged 4 through 21 years who closely represented the characteristics of the Canadian population (for more details see Wechsler & Naglieri, 2006). One of the innovative features of this test is the administration format.

The WNV uses a new method for informing the examinee of the demands of the test called Pictorial Directions (patent pending), which are designed to provide a nonverbal and engaging method of communicating the task requirements to the examinee. Students are shown a series of pictures that illustrate what is required along with gestures by the examiner that draw attention to the correspondence between the pictured directions and the stimuli in front of the subject. In addition, Pictorial Directions are supplemented by simple verbal directions provided in English, French, Spanish, Chinese, German, and Dutch. The translated verbal directions are used only as needed and by a professional who speaks the language. If the use of the pictorial directions and supplemental verbal directions proves ineffective for explaining the demands of the subtest, examiners are instructed to provide additional help as needed. The amount and content of the assistance offered is based on professional judgment, reactions of the examinee, and the particular subtest. This approach to test directions is quite different from those employed by any other test; reflecting my efforts to find new and better ways to deliver instruction and Alan Kaufman's emphasis on innovation in test development. He noted this in the Foreword to the *Wechsler Nonverbal Administration and Scoring Manual* (Wechsler & Naglieri, 2006), writing ". . . the inclusion of instructions in six languages and the innovative pictorial directions, are brilliant and move the field of nonverbal assessment many paces forward" (p. iii).

The composition of the WNV reflects the recognition of the value of measuring general ability and the particular advantage of using nonverbal tests to do so. The WNV is like other Wechsler tests in that it uses subtests that vary in content and specific requirements but different from other Wechsler tests because it was designed to measure general ability using tests that do not have verbal or math content. The advantage of using nonverbal tasks to measure general ability is that the need for language skills is minimized, and requirements that the examinee have spoken or written language, as well as mathematical skills, is greatly reduced. While the nonverbal tests on the WNV are all alike in that they do not require language or arithmetic skills, they are diverse in their specific requirements. For example, some of the subtests have a strong visual–spatial requirement, others demand paper and pencil skills, and others require the recall of the sequence of information. This multidimensionality of task requirements distinguishes the WNV from tests that use one type of task requirement, such as the NNAT (Naglieri, 1997). Despite the variability of subtest content and task demands, the WNV, like other nonverbal tests, has essentially the same goal of measuring general ability nonverbally.

Due to the recent publication of the WNV, there are comparatively fewer published studies than on the NNAT, but there are important preliminary findings that will be briefly described here (see the test manual for more details). For example, the scores obtained from the WNV are strongly correlated with other Wechsler tests (see Wechsler & Naglieri, 2006), but more importantly it is an effective tool for measuring general ability for diverse populations. The WNV Manual provides a study of English language learners whose native language was not English, the primary language they spoke was not English, a language other than English was spoken at home, and their parents resided in the United States less than six years. The 55 students aged 8–21 years were administered the WNV and compared to a group matched on basic demographics. The results showed that the students learning English earned essentially the same score as the matched control of the English-speaking students group. These results indicate that the WNV measures general ability effectively and fairly for those with limited English language skills. Importantly, research findings for the deaf and hard of hearing also illustrate the value of this instrument.

Two studies of individuals who have varying degrees of hearing loss are presented in the WNV Manual. The first involved individuals who were selected based on their lack of ever having heard spoken language. They must not have been able to hear tones after the age of 18 months, nor read lips or use cued speech, and have severe to profound deafness (hearing loss measured with dB, Pure Tone Average greater than or equal to 55). The results showed that these deaf individuals earned very similar scores (mean = 102.5) as the matched control group (mean = 100.8). The second study involved examinees who were hard of hearing. This means that they had exposure to spoken language, either through hearing or lip reading, could have unilateral or bilateral hearing loss or deafness, their inability to hear could have begun at any age, and they could have cochlear implants but none of those included could have a disability or impairment other than being deaf or hard of hearing and no diagnosis of a neurological disorder. The scores these hard of hearing individuals earned (mean = 96.7) were also similar to the matched control group (mean = 100.5).

FROM TRADITIONAL TO NONTRADITIONAL
ASSESSMENT TOOLS

Alan's influence on my work was not only reflected by my research and publications in the area of nonverbal assessment of general ability, but also my efforts to further the evolution of the tests of ability that we have used since the early 1900s. One of the most important ideas that Alan taught us was that evolution of the field was needed. The work he and Nadeen

Kaufman did on the K-ABC was the best example of his conviction that the idea of an individual intelligence test could be reconceptualized. I used this perspective when I developed the *Cognitive Assessment System* (Naglieri & Das, 1997a) with my coauthor J. P. Das. Our test was a more complete extension of the basic principles for a test of ability than my nonverbal efforts because it has five basic components of a modern test of ability that Alan stressed. That is, a modern test of ability should (1) be based on a theory; (2) measure basic psychological processes; (3) be fair to a wide variety of individuals; (4) have relevance to intervention; and (5) have sensitivity to the problems that lead to learning difficulties. I will summarize the CAS research on these points next.

Theory-based Tests

Of all tests of its kind, the CAS is most clearly identified with a single theory of basic psychological processes. The CAS was explicitly designed to measure the four basic psychological processes described in the Planning, Attention, Simultaneous, Successive (PASS) theory of intelligence (Naglieri, 1999; Naglieri & Das, 2005), which was based on Luria's (1966, 1973) conceptualization of the three functional units of the brain. Using this approach meant that the essential ingredients of this theory were not constrained by notions of IQ represented by traditional tests such as the Wechsler and Binet. The familiar verbal, quantitative, and nonverbal partitions were abandoned in favor of an organization that represented cognitive processes. This provided a new way to conceptualize and measure the essential aspects of ability when reconceptualized as basic cognitive processes. These four PASS constructs are the result of a merger of cognitive and neuropsychological constructs like executive function (Planning), selective attention (Attention), visual–spatial ability (Simultaneous), and the serial nature of language and memory (Successive).

Measure of Basic Psychological Processes

The four PASS processes are described as follows:

Planning is a mental activity that provides cognitive control; use of processes, knowledge, and skills; intentionality; organization; and self-regulation. This includes self-monitoring and impulse control as well as generation, evaluation, and execution of a plan. Planning processing provides the means to solve problems and may involve control of attention, simultaneous, and successive processes, as well as acquisition of knowledge and skills. The essence of the construct of Planning, and tests to measure it, is that they provide a novel problem-solving situation for which children do not have a previously acquired strategy. This is also the hallmark of the concept of executive function (Hayes, Gifford & Ruckstuhl, 1996) and closely aligned with Goldberg's (2001) definition of Planning because it includes self-regulation, skillful and flexible use of strategies, allocation of attention and memory, inhibition, goal setting, self-monitoring, and self-correction.

Attention is a mental process that provides focused, selective cognitive activity over time and resistance to distraction. The process is involved when a person must demonstrate focused, selective, sustained, and effortful activity. Focused attention involves directed concentration toward a particular activity while selective attention is important for the inhibition of responses to distracting stimuli. Sustained attention refers to the variation of performance over time, which can be influenced by the different amount of effort required to solve the test. This construct is similar to the attention work of Schneider, Dumais, & Shiffrin (1984) and Posner and Boies (1971), particularly the selectivity aspect of attention which relates to intentional discrimination between stimuli.

Simultaneous processing is a mental activity by which a person integrates stimuli into interrelated groups or a whole. Simultaneous processing tests typically have strong spatial demands but the process is measured with tests that have nonverbal as well as verbal content. As long as the cognitive demand of the task requires the integration of information into groups, Simultaneous processing will be involved. The construct of Simultaneous processing is similar to the visual–spatial reasoning required in progressive matrices tests such as those originally developed by Penrose and Raven (1936) and now included in nonverbal scales of intelligence tests such as the Wechsler Nonverbal Scale of Ability (Wechsler & Naglieri, 2006) and the Stanford–Binet – Fifth Edition (Roid, 2003) as well as the simultaneous processing scale of the Kaufman Assessment Battery for Children – Second Edition (Kaufman & Kaufman, 2004).

Successive processing is a mental activity by which a person works with stimuli in a specific serial order that form a chain-like progression. Successive processing involves both the perception of stimuli in sequence and the formation of sounds and movements in order. For this reason, successive processing is involved with the recall of information in order as well as phonological analysis and the syntax of language. Successive processing has been conceptually and experimentally related to the concept of phonological analysis (Das, Naglieri, & Kirby, 1994). The concept of successive processing is similar to the concept of sequential processing included in the KABC-2 (Kaufman & Kaufman, 2004) and tests that require recall of serial information such as Digit Span Forward.

FAIR ASSESSMENT

One of the most important issues that Alan and Nadeen raised when they first published the K-ABC was that tests of intelligence needed to be fairer to minorities. As the characteristics of the U.S population continues to change, the need for fair assessment of diverse populations of children has become progressively more important. Federal law (e.g., IDEA 2004) stipulates that assessments must be selected and administered so as to be nondiscriminatory on a racial or cultural basis. It is, therefore, critical that any measures used within a problem-solving context be evaluated for bias. Some have suggested that tests of psychological processes are more appropriate for diverse populations than traditional IQ tests (Das, 2002; Fagan, 2000; Naglieri, 2002). Of the various processing options available, Suzuki and Valencia (1997) suggested that the CAS (Naglieri & Das, 1997a), based on the PASS theory, may be particularly useful for assessment of children from culturally and linguistically diverse populations. Alan's influence on me had a direct impact on the research I have conducted with groups of minority children.

Researchers have typically found a mean difference of about 12–15 points between Blacks and Whites on traditional measures of IQ. The results for PASS processing tests have been different. For example, the CAS scores of 298 Black children and 1,691 White children were compared by Naglieri, Rojahn, Matto, and Aquilino (2005). Controlling for key demographic variables, regression analyses showed a CAS Full Scale mean score difference of 4.8. They also found that correlations between the CAS scores and WJ-R Tests of Achievement were very similar for Blacks (.70) and Whites (.64). Similarly, Naglieri, Rojahn, and Matto (2007) compared the performance of Hispanic and White children on the CAS. They found that the two groups differed by 6.1 points using unmatched samples, 5.1 with samples matched on basic demographic variables, and 4.8 points when demographics differences were statistically controlled. They also found that the correlations between achievement and the CAS scores did not differ significantly for the Hispanic and White samples (Naglieri, Rojahn, & Matto, 2007). These studies suggest that assessment of PASS cognitive processes yields improved consequential validity (e.g., smaller differences between groups) without loss of criterion-related validity (correlations between processing and achievement) and therefore, such tests provide a fair way to assess diverse populations of children. Equally important, Alan Kaufman also stressed the utility of a test of processing for instructional decision-making.

DOES ASSESSMENT OF PROCESSING HAVE
RELEVANCE TO TREATMENT?

One of the most important influences that Alan Kaufman had on me was his desire to show that a test of cognitive processes could have relevance to instruction. My own work in this area has led me to study Planning Strategy Instruction, also known as the Planning Facilitation method, and to publish the book *Helping Children Learn: Intervention Handouts for Use in School and Home* (Naglieri & Pickering, 2003). I based the initial concept for Planning Strategy Instruction on the work of Cormier, Carlson, and Das (1990) and Kar, Dash, Das, and Carlson (1992). These authors found that students who performed poorly on measures of Planning from the CAS demonstrated significantly greater gains than those with higher Planning scores. This study was followed by two other research studies, which specifically examined the relationship between Planning scores and response to instruction. Naglieri and Gottling (1995, 1997) conducted two studies with children who had learning disabilities. Students were encouraged to recognize the need to plan and use strategies when completing mathematic problems during the intervention periods. The teachers provided probes that facilitated discussion and encouraged the students to consider various ways to be more successful. In both studies, we found that children who were poor in Planning improved considerably more in Math Computation than children who were good in Planning.

The relationship between Planning Strategy Instruction and the PASS profiles for children with learning disabilities and mild mental impairments was also studied next (Naglieri & Johnson, 2000). The findings from this study showed that children with a cognitive weakness in Planning improved considerably over baseline rates, while those with no cognitive weakness improved only marginally. Similarly, children with cognitive weaknesses in Simultaneous, Successive, and Attention showed substantially lower rates of improvement. The importance of this study was that the groups of children responded very differently to the same intervention and that Planning scores were the best predictor of the children's response to this math intervention (Naglieri & Johnson, 2000).

The effect of Planning Strategy Instruction on reading comprehension was the next study to be conducted (Haddad, Garcia, Naglieri, Grimditch,

McAndrews, & Eubanks, 2003). We assessed whether encouraging children to be strategic and use good plans would have differential benefits on reading comprehension based on PASS processing scores. Even though the groups did not differ by CAS Full Scale scores or pretest reading comprehension scores, children with a Planning weakness benefited substantially more from the instruction designed to encourage the use of strategies and plans. In contrast, children with no PASS weakness or a Successive weakness did not benefit as much, lending further support previous research that PASS profiles have relevance to response to this instruction.

The most recent examination of Planning Strategy Instruction was conducted with children who had learning disabilities and ADHD (Iseman, 2005). Students in the experimental group were provided Planning Strategy Instruction and a comparison group received additional math instruction. The results suggested that students who had learning disabilities and ADHD who were exposed to the Planning Strategy Instruction improved considerably more than the control group on math worksheets and standardized tests of math skills.

The results of these Planning Strategy Instruction studies suggest that changing the way aptitude is conceptualized (e.g., as the PASS rather than traditional IQ) increases the probability that an aptitude-by-treatment interaction (ATIs) is detected. Alan Kaufman was right when he suggested that cognitive processing tests held great promise in design of interventions. He recognized that past intervention research suffered from conceptualizations of aptitudes based on the concept of intelligence, which did not adequately differentiate those important abilities. In contrast, when intelligence is reconceptualized as cognitive processing (e.g., Planning ability), a relationship to instruction was found. My research, and the research of my colleagues, has suggested that the constructs included in the PASS theory and measured by the CAS do appear to have relevance to instruction. These studies also suggest that the PASS profiles can help predict which children will respond to a particular type of academic instruction and who will not. This offers an important opportunity for researchers and practitioners interested in the relationships between cognitive processing and instruction.

IS A COGNITIVE APPROACH SENSITIVE TO
LEARNING PROBLEMS?

Two major goals of assessment are (a) to discern variations in characteristics that help distinguish one group of children from another and (b) to determine if this information can help with intervention decisions. With these goals in mind, one way to examine the diagnostic utility of a cognitive approach is through the analysis of the frequency of the cognitive weaknesses found in children in regular and special educational settings. A second way to explore the diagnostic utility is by examining specific populations (e.g., ADHD and LD).

Naglieri (1999) defined three types of variation in one or more of the basic psychological processes using the methodology originally proposed by Davis (1959) and modified by Silverstein (1982, 1993). First, a relative weakness is a significant weakness which is low in relation to the child's mean processing score. In contrast, a disorder in one or more of the basic psychological processes can be operationalized as a cognitive weakness. A cognitive weakness is found when a child has a significant difference (using the ipsative method) and the lowest score also falls below some cut-off designed to indicate what is substantially below average. A cognitive weakness, therefore, is found when there is a low score relative to the child's mean and a low score relative to the norm group. Naglieri (1999) further suggested a third type of disorder where a cognitive weakness is accompanied by an achievement test weakness comparable to the level of the processing scale cognitive weakness. The children who have a cognitive weakness and an academic weakness should be considered candidates for special educational services if other appropriate conditions are also met (especially that the child's academic needs cannot be met in the regular educational environment) (Naglieri, 1999). This consistency/discrepancy model is conceptually similar to the concordance–discordance model described by Hale (2006).

Naglieri (2000) tested the consistency/discrepancy model and found that children with a weakness in one or more of the PASS scores earned lower scores on achievement. In fact, the more pronounced the cognitive weakness, the lower the achievement scores were. Additionally, children with a PASS cognitive weakness were more likely to have been previously identified and placed in special education. Finally, the presence of a cognitive weakness was significantly related to achievement, whereas the presence of a relative weakness was not. Naglieri's (2000) findings support the view that a cognitive processing disorder accompanied by academic failure could be used for the purpose of eligibility determination.

The profiles of the PASS processing scores obtained from populations of children with ADHD, mental retardation, and reading disabilities have been examined in several studies (Naglieri, 2005). The finding among the various studies has been that differences between groups have emerged in predictable and discriminating ways. That is, children with mental retardation earned low and similar PASS scores (Naglieri & Das, 1997b), while children with evidence of reading disabilities obtained average scores except for low Successive scores (Naglieri, 1999). In contrast, children diagnosed with ADHD hyperactive/impulsive (ADHD-H) type earned average scores except in Planning (Dehn, 2000; Paolitto, 1999; Naglieri, Goldstein, Iseman, & Schwebach, 2003; Naglieri, Salter & Edwards, 2004). These studies provided evidence that measuring cognitive processes can give important information about the cognitive characteristics of children who are experiencing learning problems. Differentiation of these groups is, of course, an important part of instructional planning.

SOMETHING OLD AND SOMETHING NEW

Alan Kaufman also taught by example. He believed that that we should look to ways of improving traditional approaches to assessment, as well as new constructs to assess while maintaining the highest psychometric standards. My first attempt to improve upon traditional approaches was illustrated by the Matrix Analogies Test (Naglieri, 1985a), which was a modernization of the well-known progressive matrix test. This test evolved into the Naglieri Nonverbal Ability Test (Naglieri, 1997) and most recently into the Naglieri Nonverbal Ability Test – Second Edition (Naglieri, 2007) and the Naglieri Nonverbal Ability Test – Online (Naglieri, 2008). The NNAT was also standardized and published in France (Naglieri, 1998). The computer-based version takes the traditional method to a modern platform. An adult nonverbal measure of ability, which was a traditional concept with new types of items called the General Ability Scale for Adults (GAMA), was also published in 1997 (Naglieri & Bardos, 1997). My interest in a very traditional approach involving human figure drawings led to two tests: one for assessing ability (Draw A Person: A Quantitative Scoring System; Naglieri, 1988) and the other for evaluating emotional problems (Draw A Person: Screening Procedure for Emotional Disturbance; Naglieri, McNeish, & Bardos, 1991). Next, were the Devereux Behavior Rating Scale School Form (Naglieri, LeBuffe, & Pfeiffer, 1993) and the Devereux Scales of Mental Disorders (Naglieri, LeBuffe & Pfeiffer, 1994). These two rating scales were designed to build upon the earlier versions and at the same time provide excellent reliability and validity evidence along with a national normative sample. We also introduced new methods for interpretation (e.g., building intervention plans on the basis of item level analysis and a psychometrically sound method for using the scales to examine treatment outcomes). Perhaps the best example of making a traditional approach modern is my work on the Wechsler Nonverbal Scale of Ability (Wechsler & Naglieri, 2006). Borrowing traditional tests, adding a new one, and including Pictorial Directions illustrates how the old and new were blended to provide a special tool for assessment of all children and adolescents, especially diverse populations.

As a group, these tests illustrated an emphasis on making the traditional modern, but the majority of the work I have done this century represents my, and Alan's, goal to encourage an evolution in the field of assessment. The evolution is well illustrated by my work with the CAS, which was conceptualized as a new way to think about ability and a new way to measure it. In a different arena, is the work that has been done to develop the Devereux Early Childhood Assessment (DECA; LeBuffe & Naglieri, 2002), the Devereux Early Childhood Assessment – Clinical Form (DECA-C; LeBuffe & Naglieri, 2003) and the forthcoming Devereux Elementary Student Strength Assessment (DESSA; LeBuffe, Shapiro, & Naglieri, in press). These instruments operationalized constructs that are related to resilience and represent a completely new dimension of personal attributes that have been shown to be related to emotional health and success in a variety of areas.

CONCLUDING COMMENTS

In this chapter, I have attempted to summarize the enormous contribution Alan S. Kaufman has had on the field and on me personally. The fact that his contributions cannot be adequately conveyed by one person is supported by the number of accomplished individuals who have contributed to this book. In my case, I have provided some of the more salient contributions to the field as an illustration. His contributions to me also illustrate the extent to which one person can impact hundreds of thousands of children and adults through the efforts of those he has taught. It is clear to me that my life's work was substantially influenced by, and I owe a great debt of gratitude to, Alan S. Kaufman for all he taught me in and out of the classroom, and for a lifelong friendship that is the most important gift anyone could give.

REFERENCES

Cormier, P., Carlson, J.S., & Das, J.P. (1990). Planning ability and cognitive performance: The compensatory effects of a dynamic assessment approach. *Learning and Individual Differences*, 2, 437–449.

Das, J.P. (2002). A better look at intelligence. *Current Direction in Psychology*, 11, 28–32.

Das, J.P., Naglieri, J.A., & Kirby, J.R. (1994). *Assessment of Cognitive Processes.* Needham Heights, MA: Allyn and Bacon.

Davis, F.B. (1959). Interpretation of differences among averages and individual test scores. *Journal of Educational Psychology,* 50, 162–170.

Dehn, M.J. (2000). Cognitive Assessment System performance of ADHD children. Paper presented at the Annual NASP Convention, New Orleans, LA.

Fagan, J.R. (2000). A theory of intelligence as processing: Implications for society. *Psychology, Public Policy, and Law,* 6, 168–179.

Flanagan, D.P., & Kaufman, A.S. (2004). *Essentials of WISC-IV Assessment.* New York, Wiley. (Spanish version published by Tea Ediciones of Spain, 2005).

Goldberg, E. (2001). *The Executive Brain: Frontal Lobes and the Civilized Mind.* New York: Oxford University Press.

Haddad F.A., Garcia Y.E., Naglieri, J.A., Grimditch, M., McAndrews, A., & Eubanks, J. (2003). Planning Facilitation and Reading Comprehension: Instructional Relevance of the PASS Theory. *Journal of Psychoeducational Assessment,* 21, 282–289.

Hale, J.B. (2006). Implementing IDEA 2004 with the three-tier model that includes response to intervention and cognitive assessment methods. *School Psychology Forum: Research into Practice,* 16–27.

Hale, J.B., Naglieri, J.A., Kaufman, A.S., & Kavale, K.A. (2004). Specific learning disability classification in the new Individuals with Disabilities Education Act: the danger of good ideas. *The School Psychologist,* 58, 6–13, 29.

Hayes, S.C., Gifford, E.B., & Ruckstuhl, L.E. (1996). Relational frame theory and executive function: A behavioral approach. In G.R. Lyon & N.A. Krasnegor (Eds.) *Attention, Memory and Executive Function* (pp. 279–306). Baltimore: Brookes.

Individuals with Disabilities Education Improvement Act of 2004, *Pub. L.* 108-446., 118 Stat. 2647 (2006).

Iseman, J.S. (2005). A cognitive instructional approach to improving math calculation of children with ADHD: Application of the PASS theory. Unpublished doctoral dissertation, George Mason University.

Kar, B.C., Dash, U.N., Das, J.P., & Carlson, J.S. (1992). Two experiments on the dynamic assessment of planning. *Learning and Individual Differences,* 5, 13–29.

Kaufman, A.S. (1976a). Do normal children have "flat" ability profiles? *Psychology in the Schools,* 13, 284–285.

Kaufman, A.S. (1976b). Verbal-performance IQ discrepancies on the WISC-R. *Journal of Consulting and Clinical Psychology,* 44, 739–744.

Kaufman, A.S. (1979). *Intelligent Testing with the WISC-R.* New York: Wiley Interscience.

Kaufman, A.S., & Kaufman, N.L. (1983) *Kaufman Assessment Battery for Children.* Circle Pines, MN: American Guidance Service.

Kaufman, A.S., & Kaufman, N.L. (2004) *Kaufman Assessment Battery for Children Second Edition.* Circle Pines, MN: American Guidance Service.

LeBuffe, P.A. & Naglieri, J.A. (2002). *Devereux Early Childhood Assessment.* Lewisville, NC: Kaplan Press.

LeBuffe, P.A. & Naglieri, J.A. (2003). *Devereux Early Childhood Assessment Clinical Form.* Lewisville, NC: Kaplan Press.

LeBuffe, P.A. Shapiro, V. & Naglieri, J.A. (2008). *Devereux Elementary Student Strength Assessment*. Lewisville, NC: Kaplan Press.

Luria, A.R. (1966). *Human Brain and Psychological Processes*. New York: Harper and Row.

Luria, A.R. (1973). *The Working Brain*. New York: Basic Books.

Naglieri, J.A. (1985a). *Matrix Analogies Test – Expanded Form*. San Antonio, TX: The Psychological Corporation.

Naglieri, J.A. (1985b). *Matrix Analogies Test – Short Form*. San Antonio, TX: The Psychological Corporation.

Naglieri, J.A. (1988). *Draw A Person: A Quantitative Scoring System*. San Antonio, TX: The Psychological Corporation.

Naglieri, J.A. (1997). *Naglieri Nonverbal Ability Test*. San Antonio, TX: The Psychological Corporation.

Naglieri, J.A. (1998). *NNAT: Test d'Aptitude Non Verbale de Naglieri*. Paris, France: ECPA.

Naglieri, J.A. (1999). *Essentials of CAS Assessment*. New York: Wiley.

Naglieri, J.A. (2000). Can profile analysis of ability test scores work? An illustration using the PASS theory and CAS with an unselected cohort. *School Psychology Quarterly*, 15, 419–433.

Naglieri, J.A. (2001). Cognitive Assessment System: A test built from the PASS theory. In A.S. Kaufman & N.L. Kaufman (Eds), *Learning Disabilities: Psychological Assessment and Evaluation* (pp. 141–177), Cambridge, England: Cambridge University Press.

Naglieri, J.A. (2002). Minority Children in Gifted Education: A Problem and a Solution. *Duke Gifted Letter*.

Naglieri, J.A. (2003). *Naglieri Nonverbal Ability Test – Individual Form*. San Antonio, TX: The Psychological Corporation.

Naglieri, J.A., (2005). *The Cognitive Assessment System*. In D.P. Flanagan and P.L. Harrison (Eds.) *Contemporary Intellectual Assessment* (2nd ed., pp. 441–460). New York: Guilford.

Naglieri, J.A. (2007). *Naglieri Nonverbal Ability Test Second Edition*. San Antonio, TX: The Psychological Corporation.

Naglieri, J.A. (2008). *Naglieri Nonverbal Ability Test – Online*. San Antonio, TX: The Psychological Corporation.

Naglieri, J.A., & Bardos, A.N. (1997). *General Ability Scale for Adults (GAMA)*. Minnetonka, NM: National Computer Systems.

Naglieri, J.A., & Das, J.P. (1997a). *Cognitive Assessment System*. Itasca, IL: Riverside Publishing Company.

Naglieri, J.A., & Das, J.P. (1997). Intelligence revised: The planning, attention, simultaneous, successive (PASS) cognitive processing theory. In R.F. Dillon (Ed.) *Handbook on Testing* (pp. 136–163). Westport, CT: Greenwood Press.

Naglieri, J.A. & Das, J.P. (2005). Planning, attention, simultaneous, successive (PASS) theory: a revision of the concept of intelligence. In D.P. Flanagan and P.L. Harrison (Eds.), *Contemporary Intellectual Assessment* (2nd ed., pp. 136–182). New York: Guilford.

Naglieri, J., & Ford, D.Y. (2003). Addressing Under-representation of Gifted Minority Children Using the Naglieri Nonverbal Ability Test (NNAT). *Gifted Child Quarterly,* 47, 155–16.

Naglieri, J.A., Goldstein, S., Iseman, J.S., & Schwebach, A. (2003). Performance of children with attention deficit hyperactivity disorder and anxiety/depression on the WISC-III and cognitive assessment system (CAS). *Journal of Psychoeducational Assessment,* 21, 32–42.

Naglieri, J.A. & Gottling, S.H. (1995). A cognitive education approach to math instruction for the learning disabled: An individual study. *Psychological Reports,* 76, 1343–1354.

Naglieri, J.A. & Gottling, S.H. (1997). The PASS theory and mathematics instruction: a summary of initial studies. *Journal of Cognitive Education,* 5, 209–216.

Naglieri, J.A., & Johnson, D. (2000). Effectiveness of a cognitive strategy intervention to improve math calculation based on the PASS theory. *Journal of Learning Disabilities,* 33, 591–597.

Naglieri, J.A., LeBuffe, P.A., & Pfeiffer, S.I. (1993). *Devereux Behavior Rating Scale-School Form.* San Antonio, TX: The Psychological Corporation.

Naglieri, J.A., LeBuffe, P.A., & Pfeiffer, S.I. (1994). *Devereux Scales of Mental Disorders.* San Antonio, TX: The Psychological Corporation.

Naglieri, J.A., McNeish, T.J., & Bardos, A.N. (1991). *Draw A Person: Screening Procedure for Emotional Disturbance.* Austin, TX: ProEd.

Naglieri, J.A. & Paolitto, A.W. (2005). Ipsative comparisons of WISC-IV Index scores. *Applied Neuropsychology,* 12, 208–211.

Naglieri, J.A. & Pickering, E.B. (2003). *Helping Children Learn: Intervention Handouts for Use at School and Home.* Baltimore, MD: Brookes Publishing.

Naglieri, J.A., Rojahn, J. & Matto, H. (2007). Hispanic and Non-Hispanic Children's Performance on PASS Cognitive Processes and Achievement. *Intelligence,* 35, 568–579.

Naglieri, J.A., Rojahn, J.R., Matto, H.C., & Aquilino, S.A. (2005). Black white differences in intelligence: A study of the PASS theory and Cognitive Assessment System. *Journal of Psychoeducational Assessment,* 23, 146–160.

Naglieri, J.A., & Ronning, M.E. (2000a). Comparison of White, African-American, Hispanic, and Asian Children on the Naglieri Nonverbal Ability Test. *Psychological Assessment,* 12, 328–334.

Naglieri, J.A., & Ronning, M.E. (2000b). The Relationships between General Ability Using the NNAT and SAT Reading Achievement. *Journal of Psychoeducational Assessment,* 18, 230–239.

Naglieri, J.A., Salter, C.J., & Edwards, G.H. (2004). Assessment of ADHD and Reading Disabilities Using the PASS Theory and Cognitive Assessment System. *Journal of Psychoeducational Assessment,* 22, 93–105.

Paolitto, A.W. (1999). Clinical validation of the Cognitive Assessment System with children with ADHD. *ADHD Report,* 7, 1–5.

Penrose, L.S., & Raven, J.C. (1936). A new series of perceptual tests: Preliminary communication. *British Journal of Medical Psychology,* 16, 97–104.

Posner, M.I., & Boies, S.J. (1971). Components of attention. *Psychological Review,* 78, 391–408.

Rojahn, J. & Naglieri, J.A. (2006). Developmental gender differences on the Naglieri Nonverbal Ability Test in a nationally normed sample of 5-17 year olds. *Intelligence,* 34, 253–260.

Roid, G. (2003). *Stanford–Binet Fifth Edition.* Itasca, IL: Riverside.

Schneider, W., Dumais, S.T., & Shiffrin, R.M. (1984). Automatic and controlled processing and attention. In R. Parasuraman & D.R. Davies (Eds.), *Varieties of Attention* (pp. 1–28). New York: Academic Press.

Silverstein, A.B. (1982). Pattern analysis as simultaneous statistical inference. *Journal of Consulting and Clinical Psychology,* 50, 234–240.

Silverstein. A.B. (1993). Type I, Type II, and other types of errors in pattern analysis. *Psychological Assessment,* 5, 72–74.

Suzuki, L.A., & Valencia, R.R. (1997). Race-Ethnicity and measured intelligence. *American Psychologist,* 52, 1103–1114.

Wechsler, D., & Naglieri, J.A. (2006). *Wechsler Nonverbal Scale of Ability.* San Antonio, TX: Harcourt Assessments.

PART 3

THE INTERSECTION OF THEORY AND MEASUREMENT

8

Kaufman on Theory, Measurement, Interpretation, and Fairness: A Legacy in Training, Practice, and Research

SAMUEL O. ORTIZ AND DAWN P. FLANAGAN
St. John's University

That the very words being read right now might actually find themselves in print was never a sure thing. It is no exaggeration when we say that it took us an inordinate amount of time to complete this chapter and that we needed every last "drop dead" deadline afforded us to accomplish it. Had this been the usual chapter on issues related to our research, we are quite certain we would have had it done much sooner. But this is not a usual chapter. This chapter is most extraordinary in that it is intended to serve as an acknowledgment and an expression of gratitude to a great man whose own professional work and personal character have influenced us in countless ways. Alan Kaufman is this man and we are proud to claim him as both a personal friend and a colleague.

The delays we experienced in writing this chapter had nothing to do with delineating the many ways in which Alan has influenced us. Quite to the contrary, his influence can be found in our own personal and professional histories to an extent that is truly amazing. Our real problem was in trying to limit what to say and in finding just the right tone and manner in which to convey our appreciation for what Alan has meant to us over the years. What follows in this chapter is only a fraction of the many ways in which Alan and his work have played a pivotal role in shaping not only our thinking and research but our careers and personal characters. Although late in its delivery to the publisher, it was necessary for us to take the time to write this tribute to make certain that we said it right. We believe we did.

Probably unbeknownst to him, Alan has been a central figure in both of our careers in school psychology; but, this did not happen by deliberate design or intention. Alan's influence on us seems to have occurred largely because we all share a great many common ideas and values about psychological testing, including intelligence theory, measurement, interpretation, and fairness. But there were also instances in which we were brought together less by commonalities than by serendipity. Whether through commonalities in thought or just plain karma, our paths crossed Alan's in ways we never could have hoped for or envisioned when we began our careers.

This chapter is a chronicling of some of the events that led to our current collaboration with, admiration of, and appreciation for Alan Kaufman. In an effort to provide some structure, this chapter is divided into three parts, corresponding to the periods of time when we were students (the training years), practitioners (the applied years), and academicians (the theoretical and empirical years). Each of these periods allows us to describe the nature and degree of Alan's influence on our career development. Because it is difficult for us to separate the personal from the professional encounters we have been so fortunate to have had with Alan (and often with Nadeen as well) our tribute to him includes both. For us, this chapter is a personal and professional way of saying *thank you* to a man whose values, work, attitudes, scholarship, mentoring, and most importantly, friendship, have meant more to us than he can imagine.

THE TRAINING YEARS

Given Alan's leadership in the field, it was not surprising that we, as students in the late 1980s and early 1990s, quickly encountered his name in our school psychology training. Although we were trained at about the same time, we had come from divergent backgrounds. In 1992, Dawn completed her PhD in school psychology at The Ohio State University under the tutelage of her mentor, Jack A. Naglieri, himself a former student of Alan. One year later, Sam completed his PhD in clinical psychology at the University of Southern California and after many twists and turns, enrolled at San Diego State University where he began his postdoctoral training in bilingual school psychology.

During our training, we were both introduced to the "Kaufman method" of test interpretation and profile analysis. Alan's book, *Intelligent Testing with the WISC-R* (1979), was required reading for both of us and proved to be a true revelation. In fact, this classic book (and the later edition, *Intelligent Testing with the WISC-III*, 1994) was the genesis of our subsequent interest in intelligence theory and testing, along with a few other factors that deserve mention.

For example, Sam had the good fortune of having John Horn serve as a co-mentor for his dissertation. Alan had also worked with John whose contributions to our understanding of human cognitive abilities are well known. Like the bane of many professors however, Sam readily admits that he had no idea who John really was or how much he had contributed to a field with which he would soon become exceedingly familiar. Since Sam's dissertation involved family systems theory and had nothing to do with intelligence (John was mentoring primarily for assistance in the then nascent statistical technique of structural equation modeling), his ignorance is somewhat forgivable.

Dawn's work with Jack Naglieri provided her with insights into several facets of testing and test development. Indeed, while Jack was a student of Alan's, he worked very closely on the development of the K-ABC. Dawn studied PASS theory, developed by Jack and his colleague, J.P. Das, which is an extension of the simultaneous–successive model that formed the foundation of the K-ABC. She also studied the many tasks and tests that later encompassed Jack's PASS-based intelligence test – the CAS. Jack's classes on intelligence testing were challenging and made Dawn realize that assessment would indeed become an important part of her career. As noted previously, students are often unaware of their mentor's accomplishments and stature. Thus, despite actually being trained by Jack directly, it was Alan himself who later made Dawn aware of the great talent Jack has for test development.

Our training in school psychology provided an introduction to psychological testing that was built around the typical exposure to the various popular tests and instruments. Neither of us, however, felt a tremendous amount of satisfaction with respect to how the tests were being interpreted and the reasons behind their structure. One particular observation that persisted in Dawn's mind and which fueled her sense of discomfort about testing was that few instruments seemed to have a basis in intelligence theory, let alone *modern* intelligence theory. The K-ABC and the CAS, however, by virtue of their structural foundation in Luria's work, were examples of tests that did follow theory. The importance of linking test construction with a theoretical framework was reinforced in the K-ABC administration manual. As part of this discussion, Alan and Nadeen suggested that in a way, the cognitive processing tests on the K-ABC could be construed as "*Gf*" and the available achievement tests were akin to "*Gc*," thereby implying that the K-ABC could also be interpreted from Cattell's original *Gf–Gc* theory. The connection between *Gf–Gc* theory and test design was made even more explicit later in the Kaufmans' design of the KAIT – a test which was subsequently reviewed by Dawn where she duly noted the reference to theory in the test's conceptualization and structure.

Another notable exception to the popular atheoretical tests was the WJ-R. Richard Woodcock developed a psychoeducational battery in 1977 that he readily acknowledged as largely atheoretical. He published a revision of that test in 1989 (WJ-R), which was explicitly based on a current theoretical cognitive framework – modern *Gf-Gc* theory – as espoused and developed by Raymond Cattell and John Horn. Despite the availability of empirically validated theories of intelligence, it seemed that most intelligence batteries continued to be published with little theoretical underpinnings beyond Spearman's *g*. And so, the Wechsler Scales, with the inertia of tradition on their side, continued to rein supreme. The K-ABC, however, filled an important niche in the field and therefore was used with some regularity.

As part of our training, we both recall well our introduction to the K-ABC. Despite the fact that it was housed in a purple case that very much resembled a bowling ball bag, the K-ABC quickly became a favorite. Alan and Nadeen's expressed intention of making their test more fair and suitable for culturally and linguistically diverse individuals, as compared to the Wechsler Scales, was apparent in our training and in our work with diverse children. It was clear, both in Alan's writings and in the very tests he developed, that attention needed to be paid to the measurement of abilities in individuals who were not proficient in English or fully acculturated to the U.S. mainstream.

The training years, in short, provided us exposure to many of the issues that we found troubling, particularly the relative lack of theory in test design and development and the presumed fairness in the measurement of abilities in diverse populations. The principles and ideas we gleaned from Alan's writings and his tests were the sign posts along the roads which helped guide and enlighten us as we embarked on our later careers as practitioners and academicians.

THE APPLIED YEARS

As practitioners, we were able to compare the day to day use of the K-ABC with day-to-day use of other batteries, such as the WISC-III and WJ-R. As any school psychologist knows, results from testing the same individual often vary from battery to battery, sometimes considerably. It was during this time that we noticed particular aspects or characteristics of certain tasks and subtests that seemed to give rise to the differences. Problems in equitable evaluation of abilities for individuals with different backgrounds and languages were readily evident. For example, a vocabulary test that required the examinee to provide the exact name for an object was invariably more difficult for English learners than one in which the examinee simply had to point to a picture that represented a word or concept spoken by the examiner. Likewise, the concept of antonyms was not something that was mediated at an early age for Hispanics, for example, as it was for young children in mainstream U.S. culture. These experiences gave us some insight into the various limitations of all batteries in evaluating the broad range of children's abilities and the degree to which other factors, notably cultural and linguistic differences, might be affecting both the measurement and interpretation of test data.

Being culturally and linguistically different himself and trained in multicultural service delivery, fairness in testing quickly became a central concern in Sam's work as a school psychologist. He found the ability to mediate task concepts prior to administration of actual items on the K-ABC to be invaluable in his work. The K-ABC also provided instructions for administration in Spanish. These characteristics remain part of the KABC-II and are unique among the cadre of standardized tests of intelligence and cognitive ability available today. Because of the various innovations in its design and structure, the K-ABC was one of the primary tools in Sam's arsenal of nondiscriminatory instruments.

The innovations inherent in the K-ABC were no accident, as Alan had openly expressed his concern about fairness and his desire to create instruments that were more responsive to the cultural differences of individuals. These concerns were described in an eloquent and witty tribute to his own mentor, David Wechsler, in the preface to *Intelligent Testing with the WISC-III*. Alan relates that many executives at the publishing company were hesitant to tell Wechsler directly that "there are a number of black psychologists who don't much care for the WISC, and there have been some serious complaints with a lot of specific items" (p. x). Wechsler apparently became fed up with the whole ordeal and invited Alan to his apartment where they, alone, would hammer out the revision of the WISC. During some of his initial discussions with Wechsler about the various items on the tests, Alan describes how he tried to keep his feelings relatively secret until he was apparently chided by Wechsler for holding back. Alan then writes:

> From that point on, I never held back anything. He would usually respond calmly, but occasionally I'd strike a raw nerve, and his grandfatherly smile would evaporate. His temples would start to pulse, and his entire face and scalp would turn crimson. I'd unconsciously move my chair back in self-protection, the way I did when I tested hard-core

prisoners on the old WAIS and had to ask the question, "Why should we keep away from bad company?" I struck that exposed nerve when I urged him to eliminate the Comprehension item about walking away from a fight if someone much smaller starts to fight with you. The argument that you can't walk away from any fight in a black ghetto just added fuel to his rage. When I suggested, at a later meeting, that he just *had* to get rid of the item "Why should women and children be saved first in a shipwreck?" or incur the wrath of the new wave of militant feminists, his response was instant. With red face and pulsing head, he stood up, leaned on his desk with extended arms, and said as if he were firing a semiautomatic, "Chivalry may be dying. Chivalry may be dead. *But it will not die on the WISC.*" (p. x; emphasis in original).

This classic story has become a staple in our presentations and we have retold it countless times to audiences as a way of illustrating the degree to which a single individual's cultural values and beliefs influence the content and potential fairness of a test. We even had the good fortune of hearing Alan tell it in person at the 1998 NASP Convention in Las Vegas where he participated on an esteemed panel on testing with Colin Eliott, Richard Woodcock, Gale Roid, Aurelio Prifitera, and Jack Naglieri. As we all know, chivalry apparently did die on the WISC but the "fight" item remains intact on the WISC-IV to the present day. The point, however, is that it was abundantly clear that Alan was a pioneer in the area of fairness and that he was keenly aware of such problems more than a decade before the K-ABC was published and that its design was in direct response to long-held concerns he had harbored about fairness.

Consistent with the intent of the K-ABC, our experiences with its use in evaluating culturally and linguistically diverse students provided a large part of the basis upon which our understanding of issues relative to non-discriminatory assessment evolved. Use of the K-ABC alone did not necessarily result in a fair evaluation of the abilities of diverse individuals, but it did provide more opportunities to engage in practices that were eminently more equitable than that which was available from the use of other instruments at that time. The ability to compare tasks and individual performances from different batteries not only informed us about fairness but also heightened our concern with measurement and interpretation. It is easy to see that the K-ABC was pivotal in setting the stage for the two main areas of our current research interest – theoretically based measurement and interpretation, as well as nondiscriminatory assessment.

Alan's work continued to influence our practice and eventually so did Alan himself. Consider, for example that during his work as a practitioner,

Sam had the pleasure of meeting Alan and Nadeen in a manner that came about in an extraordinary fashion. While a professor at the University of Georgia, Alan had trained a Japanese psychologist Toshinori Ishikuma who subsequently found himself in Solana Beach, California (adjacent to the city of Encinitas where Sam worked). Toshinori had gone there to complete a school psychology internship under the supervision of Sharon Loveman, a graduate from the SDSU School Psychology Program. Upon finishing his internship, Toshinori returned to Japan and later became the point person in the eventual translation and adaptation of the K-ABC into Japanese. The Japanese K-ABC was published by a company called Marusen Mates, Inc., which was a rather risky venture at the time, considering that there were no actual school psychologists in Japan because the profession did not yet exist there. However, by 1995, the Japanese Ministry of Education had created school psychology as an experimental profession to gauge the need for it, especially in addressing the growing recognition of mild disabilities (e.g., learning disability, attention deficit/hyperactivity disorder [ADHD]). Marusen Mates, eager to promote the K-ABC to the new profession, sponsored a type of school psychology training junket where Japanese professionals (most of them professors, teachers, and psychologists in other fields) would each receive a new Japanese version of the K-ABC and a two week trip to the United States for training in its use, including lectures directly from the authors, Alan and Nadeen. The training was to include tours of U.S. schools and special education programs along with other lectures providing information about the clinical utility of the K-ABC.

Of course, Toshinori was asked by Marusen Mates to provide the names of people in San Diego who might be able to arrange for some of these experiences and lectures. It is likely that San Diego was chosen for several reasons, including the fact that Alan and Nadeen had a home just outside the city. Naturally, Toshinori's internship supervisor's name (Sharon Loveman) was on that list and the representative from Marusen Mates arrived one day to visit with her and to begin making plans for school visits and special education program demonstrations. Unfortunately, the representative arrived on a Sunday, relatively unannounced, and was hoping to meet Sharon the following day. However, Sharon was already scheduled to be in meetings all day and could not arrange time to meet with him.

For some reason, perhaps as simple as proximity, Sharon called Sam to see if he might be able to accommodate the representative's needs that day. Sam recalls this incident with significant clarity as Sharon phoned in a panic at about 6:00 AM, a time of the day in which he is most susceptible to suggestion. So, of course, he agreed to meet with the representative. Sam was assured by Sharon that the representative only wanted to see what some special education programs looked like and that this was a "one time thing."

So that morning, Sam, who knew no Japanese whatsoever, met with the representative from Japan who knew no English whatsoever, at Capri Elementary School in Encinitas. After several problems in establishing comprehensible communication, Sam finally managed to determine the representative's desires. Sam was able to arrange for several observations and the representative appeared very happy with what he had seen. Upon his mid-day departure, the representative offered a small gift to Sam in gratitude (a typical Japanese cultural gesture).

About a month later, Sam received a phone call from a woman who explained that she was to be the translator/interpreter for a group visiting from Japan (educators who had signed up for the training sponsored by Marusen Mates) and she wanted to know the schedule for their school visit and observations of the special education programs (the responsibility of which had apparently been assigned to Sam as a consequence of his meeting with the representative) as well as the topic of his lecture for the afternoon (for some unknown reason they had presumed that Sam must be an expert on the K-ABC and its application in diagnosing learning disability). What was thought to have been a brief "one time thing" to help a colleague suddenly ballooned into a lot more than that, and through what can only be described ironically as a cultural misunderstanding, Sam was placed officially on the schedule for the Japanese visitor's training on the K-ABC.

And so it was that Sam found himself in the middle of an unusual set of circumstances that bore Alan's handprint. And who in their right mind would turn their back on such an incredible cultural and professional opportunity? In keeping with Japanese tradition and customs, Sam was invited to a dinner party hosted by the Japanese contingent at the end of their visit to celebrate, honor, and thank those involved in the training. The event was held at a downtown hotel in San Diego and it was here that Sam met Alan and Nadeen for the very first time.

Sam recalls meeting Alan and Nadeen at the dinner party with great fondness. At that time, 1995, Sam had only just begun his career in school psychology and as a practitioner had given just a few presentations at professional conferences but had done little other academic work of note. And yet there he stood, shaking hands with Alan and Nadeen and having his picture taken alongside of them. It was surreal. The Kaufmans were, well, they were the Kaufmans, the authors of several major psychological tests, text books, and journal articles, with reputations at the height of the field. Having gone to college in Los Angeles where movie stars were a dime a dozen, Sam was never all that fazed by silver screen reputation. But they were not merely Hollywood mortals, they were the Kaufmans! In the field of school psychology, Alan and Nadeen were celebrities among celebrities and it is with no shame that Sam admits to feelings of hero worship and awe at that dinner.

Given the massive differences in stature, Sam never imagined that either Alan or Nadeen would remember him from Adam. After all, they must meet dozens of people every day. What's another school psychologist from some small district in yet another state or country to them? Many years later, after Sam had developed his own modest reputation, he vividly remembers meeting Alan and Nadeen again at a professional conference. This time, Nadeen took Sam aside and said that she and Alan had always felt they sort of discovered him and that they knew him "when" (i.e., in 1995 when no one knew who he was). It was the kind of compliment that one never forgets for at the same time that it recognized the development of Sam's own professional development and accomplishments, it also acknowledged and expressed a personal connection that meant even more. Thus, it is with very special pride that Sam acknowledges Alan and Nadeen, not just as professional influences, but personally as two of only a small cohort who know from where he had come and how far, and as caring individuals who had followed his career from the very beginning, not unlike proud parents.

THE THEORETICAL AND EMPIRICAL YEARS

The knowledge of problems in theory, measurement, fairness, and invalidity in assessment gained largely through Alan's writings were reinforced by our experiences during our time as practitioners. The persistent limitations of existing batteries were issues that we could not ignore for long. Indeed, our experiences as practicing school psychologists were relatively short lived as both of us moved rather quickly into academia. The move was a natural extension for us in that it accorded us an opportunity to address and deal with many issues empirically and ultimately offer solutions to psychometric problems that plagued practitioners and that remain problematic in the field today.

As academicians, we began to echo Alan's words and assert the critical nature of theory in establishing the validity of cognitive and intelligence batteries. We believed that if tests were limited in the number of cognitive constructs they measured and if problems existed with regard to how those constructs were measured, then perhaps the use of tests from more than one cognitive or intelligence battery might help address current limitations. For our ideas to materialize and gain merit, they had to be firmly grounded in theory. From this line of reasoning emerged the foundations of what eventually became known as Cross-Battery Assessment (XBA).

Consistent with Alan's vision, one of the major pillars supporting XBA was an empirically validated theory – the Cattell–Horn–Carroll (CHC) theory of cognitive abilities. CHC theory was based on an integration of the Cattell–Horn *Gf–Gc* theory and John Carroll's Three-Stratum theory. This integration was made possible by a series of analyses that were conducted by Kevin McGrew. In a book that we authored with Kevin, *The Wechsler Intelligence Scales and Gf–Gc Theory: A Contemporary Approach to Interpretation*, we presented the integrated model, which shortly thereafter became known as "CHC theory." Having CHC theory as the foundation of the XBA method was our way of responding to Alan's pleas for theory-based assessment to guide practice.

Another major influence of Alan's thinking on our work also appeared in our Wechsler book, namely the notion of *supplemental* testing. Alan has always discussed the need to supplement the Wechsler Scales to round out the assessment and follow up on hypotheses about an individual's functioning. He recognized that intelligence batteries did not always evaluate important abilities well, and possibly not at all. At a time when the Wechsler Scales were administered largely without question or concern for their measurement accuracy or construct validity, Alan urged practitioners not to be content with results from a single Wechsler administration and to evaluate individuals more thoroughly using supplemental tests. The name of our approach, *cross-battery*, reflects Alan's long-held belief that a single battery often does not provide sufficient data to draw diagnostic conclusions about an individuals profile of cognitive strengths and weaknesses.

Another notable aspect of XBA and our research that stems directly from Alan's influences involves issues of fairness. As we have noted, Alan was always sensitive to the problems inherent in the use of standardized tests with culturally and linguistically diverse individuals. It may be true that others have understood and even researched this topic intensively, but we have seen few more dedicated to the ideal than Alan.

In our experience as practitioners, it had become clear that existing tests were at the very least problematic when used with individuals from diverse cultural and linguistic backgrounds. In addition, it seemed improbable that there would ever be enough culturally and linguistically diverse school psychologists available to manage the increasing number of referrals for evaluation of diverse students. And although there were some tests available in languages other than English, there were hardly enough to cover the great variety of mother tongues occurring with increasing frequency in the schools.

Alan's work helped us to see that culture was embedded in tests and we recognized that language was often a barrier that needed to be overcome, hence the common use of the PIQ, nonverbal indexes, and nonverbal tests with English language learners. To help practitioners select tests that were less influenced by exposure to U.S. mainstream culture and less reliant upon English language proficiency, we classified tests according to their degree of cultural loading and degree of linguistic demand and thus was born the Culture-Language Test Classifications (C-LTC) and the Culture-Language Interpretive Matrix (C-LIM), both extensions of the XBA.

The C-LTC were based on notions that had been ingrained in us for some time and which had come from our readings and understanding of Alan's concerns with fairness in testing. By categorizing tests on the basis of cultural loading and linguistic demand, as either "low," "moderate," or "high," we were able to assist practitioners in addressing issues of fairness in testing directly. That is, we designed the C-LIM to help practitioners differentiate culture and language *difference* from *disability* based on expected patterns of performance on cognitive tests.

Because our classification of tests according to cultural loading and language demand follows Alan's teachings on fairness in testing, it is not surprising to see parallels in our work. For example, the KABC-II Nonverbal Index is made up of tests that we classified as "low" in both cultural loading and linguistic demand. Although this index is the narrowest measure of general ability on the KABC-II, it is also the fairest estimate. The Mental Processing Index is a broader measure than the Nonverbal Index but less equitable in the sense that it includes tests classified as "moderate" in cultural loading and linguistic demand. The most comprehensive measure of general intelligence on the KABC-II is the Fluid-Crystallized Index, but because it includes tests that are classified as "high" in cultural loading and linguistic demand, it is very likely to underestimate generally ability for children from diverse backgrounds. Thus, the design of the KABC-II is consistent with the principles by which the C-LTC and C-LIM were developed.

The concerns that Alan has always espoused regarding theory, measurement, interpretation, and fairness all found their way into our Wechsler book and therefore we believed it most appropriate to ask Alan to write its forward. Alan ended the foreward to our book by stating that we might even understand his method of profile interpretation better than he does. This summary statement is profound in that it is self-effacing, a characteristic not common to many in our field. Alan's ability to find the positives in others work, respect disparate opinions, be self-critical, and help others achieve success is a testament to his professional and personal character.

Since Alan wrote the foreward to our book, we have come to know him well. Our continued professional discourse and contact with Alan over the years about science and research have fostered a greater sense of appreciation for and understanding of our work – to the extent that it led to a series of collaborative efforts that continue to the present day. That this collaboration proceeded rather rapidly is also a reflection of the type of man and professional Alan is – one who is open to new ideas and not afraid to question the status quo.

Dawn's first meeting with Alan was poignant and demonstrated the uncanny coincidental crossings that seem to characterize our relationship with him. In 1997, Dawn was receiving the Lightmer–Witmer Award from APA Division 16 in recognition of her early career contributions to school psychology. At the same time and at the same event, Alan was receiving the Senior Scientist Award in recognition of his career contributions to school psychology. As award recipients, Alan and Dawn were naturally seated at the same table and meeting each other was therefore assured. But Alan went beyond making simple acquaintances that day. In another impressive demonstration of his ability to respect new ideas, he asked Dawn if she would be willing to write a book on the topic of XBA for his Essentials Series. Dawn, of course, jumped at the opportunity and to this day she remembers that moment as one of the most exciting of her career. *Essentials of Cross-Battery Assessment* was published in 2001.

Of significant note is that when the time came for us to revise *Essentials of Cross-Battery Assessment*, we requested that the publisher allow us to include a CD-ROM with software that would greatly facilitate and automate the XBA process. The publisher initially balked at our idea because the "Essentials" series was meant to be consistent across topics and the formats of the books were carefully crafted to give the same look and feel for readers irrespective of volume. Adding a CD-ROM would not only introduce an element not found in any of the other books in the series but it would also add to the price of the book, which the publisher also wanted to keep constant. In the end, it was Alan's support of our idea that persuaded the publisher to accept our proposal and allow the CD-ROM to become a part of the *Essentials of Cross-Battery Assessment*, Second

Edition, which was published in 2007. If not for Alan's steadfast support of our ideas and confidence in our scholarship, neither of these books may have ever seen the light of day.

Other recent examples of our collaboration with Alan can be seen in *Essentials of WISC-IV*, which Dawn coauthored with Alan. In this book, Dawn worked closely with Alan on developing a theory-based interpretive framework for the WISC-IV. Although the ideas presented in this book represent an integration of the interpretive methods of both Alan and Dawn, it could not have been achieved without the theoretical, psycho-metric, clinical, and empirical basis for Weschsler test interpretation that Alan has spent most of his career building. Due to the success of *Essentials of WISC-IV Assessment*, the next edition is due to the publisher in just three months. Help!

Some of the most enjoyable and enriching professional experiences Dawn has had were with Alan and Nadeen brainstorming in their living room about what to do instead of "another book." Well, they all came up with the idea of a multimedia course that would cover a variety of topics germane to the field of school psychology. The idea was eventually embraced by Pearson Assessments and, in collaboration with our dear friend and colleague, Liz Lichtenberger, we have been working on this project for well over a year. Although we refer to this professional de-velopment program as "Agora" – a name none of us would have ever chosen – its official title is *Agora: The Marketplace of Ideas. Best Practices: Applying Response to Intervention (RTI) and Comprehensive Assessment for the Identification of Specific Learning Disabilities*. While Dawn, Alan, Nadeen, and Liz have found this project to be exciting, they have also found it to be quite challenging, demanding, and overwhelming. Indeed, they have expressed emotions ranging from loving the project to hating it. Dawn can just hear Alan saying now, "I never said I loved the project!" Regardless of the highs and lows associated with developing Agora, one thing was clear to Dawn – there is no greater gift one can receive during the course of a professional career than to be able to work closely with an icon. Being able to watch Alan work, generate ideas, reason through problems, maintain focused attention longer than anyone else, and inter-ject humor when weariness set in was truly amazing. But what Dawn gained most from her days of working closely with Alan was a sense of respect that can only be accorded to a person whose depth of character matches his level of genius.

CONCLUSION

Given that we came from very different backgrounds and experiences, the number of times in which Alan's path has crossed ours is truly remarkable. Many of the commonalities we described here were coincidental, yet pivotal, and demonstrate the nature of our history with Alan, the professional, and Alan, the man. The Wechsler Scales, Cattell–Horn *Gf–Gc* theory, CHC theory, Japanese K-ABC, Essentials books, San Diego, Jack Naglieri, John Horn, SLD, and RTI brought us into contact again and again. And, the nature of our contact with Alan has allowed us to venture farther and reach higher than we ever thought was possible. To a very large extent, our success is Alan's success.

It is impossible to truly thank you, Alan, for what you have done for us, both intentionally and unintentionally, but we sincerely want you to be aware of what you have meant to us over these many years. We attribute many of our accomplishments to you and we hope that you take pride in knowing just how much our achievements are a reflection of you. We hope that the stories and anecdotes we have related here demonstrate in some small way our appreciation for what you have done. We count ourselves among the lucky few who can say that *Alan Kaufman* is our mentor and our colleague, but, most importantly, he is our friend. Thank you.

REFERENCES

Flanagan, D.P., McGrew, K.S. & Ortiz, S.O. (2000). *The Wechsler Intelligence Scales and Gf-Gc Theory: A Contemporary Interpretive Approach*. Boston, MA: Allyn & Bacon.

Flanagan, D.P. & Ortiz, S.O. (2001). *Essentials of Cross-Battery Assessment*. New York: Wiley.

Flanagan, D.P. & Ortiz, S.O. & Alfonso, V.C. (2007). *Essentials of Cross-Battery Assessment* (2nd ed.). New York: Wiley.

Kaufman, A.S. (1994). *Intelligent Testing with the WISC-III*. New York: Wiley.

McGrew, K.D. & Flanagan, D.P. (1998). *The Intelligence Test Desk Reference (ITDR): Gf-Gc Cross-Battery Assessment*. Boston, MA: Allyn & Bacon.

9

Theory of Successful Intelligence as a Basis for New Forms of Ability Testing at the High School, College, and Graduate School Levels

ROBERT J. STERNBERG
Tufts University

AN APPRECIATION

I first met Alan S. Kaufman in 1968 when I was 18 years old. I had gone to work in New York City as a research assistant in the Test Division at the Psychological Corporation. Kaufman was a high-level staff member. He was older than I was, but not by all that much! We had only brief and casual contact. I had no idea at the time that this man would become a one-man publishing industry. Perhaps that is an overstatement. Much of his work has been done with his wife, Nadeen, as well as other collaborators, including his son James, who many years later was to become one of my graduate students, and shortly afterward, another one-man publishing industry. It runs in the family.

If one were to ask who are the people who most have influenced and impacted ability testing, almost certainly Alfred Binet would be #1. David Wechsler would probably be #2. In my mind, Alan Kaufman would be #3. And in terms of productivity, he surpassed Binet and Wechsler relatively early in his career. Kaufman's career started with his writing books for psychologists to help them administer conventional standardized tests. He has continued to author and coauthor such books, even to the present day (e.g., Flanagan & Kaufman, 2004; Kaufman & Lichtenberger, 1999, 2005; Lichtenberger & Kaufman, 2003). But far more important than these books have been his tests, which have reshaped the industry (see Kaufman, Lichtenberger, Fletcher-Janzen, & Kaufman, 2005; Lichtenberger, Broadbooks, & Kaufman, 2005). These tests include the Kaufman Assessment Battery for Children (KABC), the Kaufman Adolescent and Adult Intelligence Test (KAIT), the Kaufman Brief Intelligence Test (KBIT), the Kaufman Functional Academic Skills Test (K-FAST), the Kaufman

Short Neuropsychological Assessment Procedure (K-SNAP), and various other tests.

These tests have reshaped the way psychologists think about intelligence testing. The original edition of the KABC was the first large-scale intelligence based upon a psychological theory of Luria (1973). His later tests have been based on this theory and other theories, such as that of Cattell (1971). Next to the Wechsler series and Stanford–Binet series, Kaufman's tests have probably been the most widely used, at least in the United States. They are also used abroad, often in translation.

The testing industry has been, to me, often a disappointing one. Tests often tend to differ from each other somewhat in surface structure, but little, if at all, in deep structure. Kaufman has changed that pattern. He has not made a career imitating, in the manner of the early IBM clones. Rather, he has blazed his own path, much as I see his son James doing today in his studies of creativity. It is an honor to be a part of this volume.

Had Kaufman done nothing more than write wonderful tests and books, he would be remembered in the annals of the history of psychology. But he (and his son James) will be remembered beyond that. You want to find out what makes a baseball pitcher really bad? Read *The Worst Baseball Pitchers of All Time: Bad Luck, Bad Arms, Bad Teams, and Just Plain Bad* (Kaufman & Kaufman, 1993). Amazingly, the book is brought to you from the same scholars who study intelligence and, in the case of the son, creativity as well. The pitcher is the member of a baseball team who is most remembered. In the same way, the contributions of Alan Kaufman and his collaborators, including those in his own family, will never be forgotten.

Although this book is an appreciation of the father, I must say something about the son – James – as he was my advisee, and as we continue to work together. One can leave a legacy in one's work and in one's family. James enables Alan Kaufman and his wife Nadeen to leave a legacy in both. I have no doubt that James, like his father, will become one of the most eminent psychologists of his day.

ADMISSIONS TESTING

My own contribution to testing has been orders of magnitude more modest than those of Alan Kaufman. In this chapter, I will say just a little bit about these very modest contributions. I will focus particularly on admissions testing.

For many years, admissions testing has been dominated by a conventional psychometric model of intelligence, dating back to Binet and Simon

(1916) and Spearman (1904). In this chapter, I will describe three relatively large-scale admissions-testing projects, based on a new model of intelligence, in which we at the Center for the Psychology of Abilities, Competencies, and Expertise (PACE Center) at Yale have been involved. The three projects are the Choate Rosemary Hall Project (Sternberg et al., 2003), which was designed to predict success at a competitive independent secondary school; the Rainbow Project (Sternberg & the Rainbow Project Collaborators, 2005; Sternberg, The Rainbow Project Collaborators, and the University of Michigan Business School Project Collaborators, 2004), which was designed to provide assessments to augment the SAT (an acronym that originally stood for Scholastic Aptitude Test but that now stands for nothing in particular); and the University of Michigan Business School Project (henceforth referred to as "the Michigan Project"; Hedlund, Wilt, Nebel, & Sternberg, 2006), which was designed to provide assessments to augment the Graduate Management Admissions Test (GMAT). The theoretical basis for all three projects is the theory of successful intelligence.

Theory of Successful Intelligence

Definition of Successful Intelligence

1. *Intelligence* is defined in terms of the ability to achieve success in life in terms of one's personal standards, within one's sociocultural context. The field of intelligence has at times tended to put "the cart before the horse," defining the construct conceptually on the basis of how it is operationalized rather than vice versa. This practice has resulted in tests that stress the academic aspect of intelligence, or intelligence relevant only to the classroom, which is not surprising given the origins of modern intelligence testing in the work of Binet and Simon (1916) in designing an instrument that would distinguish children who would succeed from those who would fail in school. But the construct of intelligence needs to serve a broader purpose, accounting for the bases of success in all of one's life. The use of societal criteria of success (e.g., school grades, personal income) can obscure the fact that these operationalizations often do not capture people's personal notions of success. Some people choose to concentrate on extracurricular activities such as athletics or music and pay less attention to grades in school; others may choose occupations that are personally meaningful to them but that never will yield

the income they could gain doing work that is less personally meaningful. Although scientific analysis of some kinds requires nomothetic operationalizations, the definition of success for an individual is idiographic. In the theory of successful intelligence, however, the conceptualization of intelligence is always within a sociocultural context. Although the processes of intelligence may be common across such contexts, what constitutes success is not. Being a successful member of the clergy of a particular religion may be highly rewarded in one society and viewed as a worthless pursuit in another culture.

2. *One's ability to achieve success depends on one's capitalizing on one's strengths and correcting or compensating for one's weaknesses.* Theories of intelligence typically specify some relatively fixed set of skills, whether one general factor and a number of specific factors (Spearman, 1904), seven multiple factors (Thurstone, 1938), eight multiple intelligences (Gardner, 1983, 1999), or 150 separate intellectual abilities (Guilford, 1982). Such a nomothetic specification is useful in establishing a common set of skills to be tested. But people achieve success, even within a given occupation, in many different ways. For example, successful teachers and researchers achieve success through many different blendings of skills rather than through any single formula that works for all of them.

3. *Balancing of skills is achieved in order to adapt to, shape, and select environments.* Definitions of intelligence traditionally have emphasized the role of adaptation to the environment (*Intelligence and its measurement,* 1921; Sternberg & Detterman, 1986). But intelligence involves not only modifying oneself to suit the environment (adaptation), but also modifying the environment to suit oneself (shaping), and sometimes, finding a new environment that is a better match to one's skills, values, or desires (selection). Not all people have equal opportunities to adapt to, shape, and select environments. In general, people of higher socioeconomic standing tend to have more opportunities and people of lower socioeconomic standing have fewer. The economy or political situation of the society also can be factors. Other variables that may affect such opportunities are education and especially literacy, political party, race, religion, and so forth. For example, someone with a college education typically has many more possible career options than does someone who has dropped out of high school in order to support a family. Thus, how and how well an individual adapts to, shapes, and selects environments must always be viewed in terms of the opportunities the individual has.

4. *Success is attained through a balance of three aspects of intelligence: analytical, practical, and creative skills.* Analytical skills are the skills primarily measured by traditional tests. But success in life requires one not only to analyze one's own ideas as well as the ideas of others, but also to generate ideas and to persuade other people of their value. This necessity occurs in the world of work, as when a subordinate tries to convince a superior of the value of their plan; in the world of personal relationships, as when a child attempts to convince a parent to do what he or she wants or when a spouse tries to convince the other spouse to do things his or her preferred way; and in the world of the school, as when a student writes an essay arguing for a point of view.

Defining the Three Aspects of Successful Intelligence
According to the proposed theory of human intelligence and its development (Sternberg, 1980, 1984, 1985, 1990, 1997, 1999), a common set of processes underlies all aspects of intelligence. These processes are hypothesized to be universal. For example, although the solutions to problems that are considered intelligent in one culture may be different from the solutions considered to be intelligent in another culture, the need to define problems and translate strategies to solve these problems exists in any culture. However, although the same processes are used for all three aspects of intelligence universally, these processes are applied to different kinds of tasks and situations depending on whether a given problem requires analytical thinking, practical thinking, creative thinking, or a combination of these kinds of thinking.

> *Analytical intelligence.* Analytical intelligence is involved when skills are used to analyze, evaluate, judge, or compare and contrast. It typically is involved when processing components are applied to relatively familiar kinds of problems where the judgments to be made are of a fairly abstract nature.

> *Creative intelligence.* Creative intelligence is involved when skills are used to create, invent, discover, imagine, suppose, or hypothesize. Tests of creative intelligence go beyond tests of analytical intelligence in measuring performance on tasks that require individuals to deal with relatively novel situations. Sternberg and his colleagues have shown that when one enters the range of unconventionality of the conventional tests of intelligence, one starts to tap sources of individual differences measured little or not at all by the tests (Sternberg, 1985). Thus it is important to include problems that are relatively novel in nature. These problems can be either convergent or divergent in nature.

Practical intelligence. Practical intelligence is involved when skills are utilized, implemented, applied, or put into practice in real-world contexts. It involves individuals applying their abilities to the kinds of problems they confront in daily life, such as on the job or in the home. Practical intelligence involves applying the components of intelligence to experience so as to (a) adapt to, (b) shape, and (c) select environments. Adaptation is involved when one changes oneself to suit the environment. Shaping is involved when one changes the environment to suit oneself. And selection is involved when one decides to seek out another environment that is a better match to one's needs, abilities, and desires. People differ in their balance of adaptation, shaping, and selection, and in the competence with which they balance among these three possible courses of action.

Practical intelligence often has been equated with the notion of "common sense." It involves knowing how to navigate effectively through the problems of everyday life. Individuals who are successful at solving these everyday problems also are said to rely, to some extent, on their "intuition." In other words, they develop effective solutions to problems without necessarily being able to explain or justify their decisions. This "intuition" or "common sense" has been attributed in the practical intelligence literature to *tacit knowledge* (see Polanyi, 1976). The concept of tacit knowledge reflects the idea that much of the knowledge relevant to real-world performance is acquired through everyday experiences without conscious intent. Tacit knowledge guides action without being easily articulated.

We have defined this construct as the knowledge needed in order to work effectively in an environment that one is not explicitly taught and that often is not even verbalized (Sternberg et al., 2000; Sternberg & Hedlund, 2002; Sternberg & Wagner, 1993; Sternberg, Wagner, & Okagaki, 1993; Sternberg, Wagner, Williams, & Horvath, 1995; Wagner, 1987; Wagner & Sternberg, 1986). Sternberg and his colleagues represent tacit knowledge in the form of production systems, or sequences of "if–then" statements that describe procedures one follows in various kinds of everyday situations.

The projects described here applied the theory of successful intelligence in the creation of tests that capture, in the case of the Rainbow Project, analytical, practical, and creative skills; and in the case of the Choate Rosemary Hall and Michigan Projects, primarily practical skills. More details regarding the theory of successful intelligence and its validation can be found in Sternberg (1985, 1997, 1999) and Sternberg, Lautrey, & Lubart (2003).

Introduction to the Current Projects

Our main goal in both projects was to enhance secondary and university admissions testing using the theory of successful intelligence. In the first project, we tested students at Choate Rosemary Hall for their skills and attitudes regarding school work. We predicted that those who did better on our measures also would do better in their work at Choate Rosemary Hall, independent of Secondary School Admission Test (SSAT) and other measures of analytical abilities. In the second project, a test battery was administered to more than 1000 students at a variety of institutions across the country, and was used to predict success in school as measured by grade point average (GPA). The hypotheses were twofold: First, we expected that the battery of tests based on the theory of successful intelligence would predict a substantial proportion of variance in GPA above and beyond that captured by the SAT. Second, we expected that this battery of tests would reduce racial and ethnic differences in scores that are typically found in current standardized college entrance examinations such as the SAT. In the second project, a test battery was administered to over 700 business-school students at the University of Michigan. Our goal was to improve predictive validity for both course and independent-project grades in the business school, and to reduce both ethnic and sex differences relative to those that would be obtained with the GMAT alone.

Choate Rosemary Hall Project

Predicting Academic Success of Students in a Competitive Independent School

Many independent schools use tests such as the SSAT and prior GPA to predict success of applicants for admission to their individual academic programs. The efficacy of these and other measures is good, but is it possible to design a new generation of assessments that will improve prediction of success? We have sought to design such measures, with considerable success, at least in the context of the single competitive independent school for which the measures were designed and in which they were evaluated.

Study 1

In this study, we examined the ability of our measures to predict performance of students in a special program that admitted students from families of relatively low socioeconomic status. Students were in a special summer program to orient them to the independent-school environment. In performing our study, we made two key decisions upfront. The first was to use a "salad-bar" approach to devising measures. In other words, we used measures that varied considerably in the kinds of personal attributes they measured and in the ways they measured these attributes. Our goal here was to ensure that we did all we could to pick up on the unexplained variation in performance in independent school – that is, the variation not accounted for by traditional predictors. The second decision was to measure both *hard-side variables* and *soft-side variables*. The former include measures of academic intelligence and practical intelligence. The latter include measures of self-reported character, values, and motivation. Initially, we also sought reports from parents and teachers. However, the reports from parents showed ceiling effects: All parents seemed to believe that their children were extremely talented and special. As a result, there was little variation in ratings obtained from parents. There was more variation in ratings from teachers, but we did not receive back enough teacher rating forms in order to obtain reliable data.

The study sought to assess several attributes, namely (1) type of tasks preferred (too hard, hard, not too hard, easy); (2) self-awareness of (a) modifiability of intellectual abilities and (b) modifiability of character; (3) self-confidence in (a) intellectual abilities, (b) learning potential, and (c) social abilities; (4) Commitment to learning and achievement through (a) goal choice, (b) self-efficacy, and (c) attribution of academic success; (5) Locus of control; (6) Sources of support (self, peers, friends, teachers); and (6) Resilience.

Here is an example of a self-report item measuring type of task preferred:

You think that if you put enough work into it, you will do well in any academic subject. _____

Ratings were from 1 (strongly agree) to 7 (mostly disagree).

A hard-side instrument, the School-Life Questionnaire, was constructed on the basis of interviews with alumni, interviews with current students, and conversations with teachers at the independent school. It was designed to measure management of oneself, of others, and of tasks in five domains: motivating, interpreting situations, behaving, following directions, and organizing.

Here is an example of an item from the School-Life Questionnaire:

In day schools you rarely see your teachers outside of class. Some of them might be engaged in sports or other extracurricular activities, but mostly you only see them in school-related circumstances. At boarding school the situation is quite different, because many teachers live on campus and you get to see them outside the classroom a lot.

Given this situation, rate the quality of the following behavior choices:

1. Always greet teachers and smile, but avoid seeing them outside of class.
2. Take advantage of this situation to talk to teachers about your school-related problems.
3. Wait and see if teachers approach you, and if so, what kinds of things they talk to you about.
4. Talk to your teachers but avoid discussing your problems as this might give them a negative impression of you.
5. Try to be sensitive and make a distinction between situations when teachers are available and are not available to you.
6. Always try to be noticed – the more that teachers talk to you, the better your grades will be.
7. Always ask whether it is a good time or not to discuss your problems with teachers.

The scale for answering these items ranged from 1 (strongly agree) to 7 (strongly disagree).

Grades for schooling before Choate Rosemary Hall showed substantial right skewness, meaning that there were many high grades. Grades for achievement at Choate Rosemary Hall showed only a modest amount of right skewness, meaning that grades were, for the most part, normally distributed.

We also looked at the incremental validities of three variables entered in a fixed order: pre-enrollment GPA, followed by SSAT (Quantitative – the best predictor of the SSAT series), followed by the Yale indicators we used. A very substantial increase in predictive validity was obtained as a result of using the Yale measures. In particular, predictive validity as expressed by percentage of variance accounted for in the criterion (independent-school GPA) increased from 31 to 53 percent, an increase in excess of over 70 percent in predictive efficacy. Including all SSAT measures made no significant difference in prediction.

Analysis of the predictive efficacy of individual measures showed that three variables were particularly important in prediction of independent-school GPA: (1) Very high motivation to achieve (internal locus of control); (2) Sensible self-confidence (neither too much nor too little); (3) "Expert" knowledge of the independent-school environment.

Students were evaluated by their teachers each day of the summer-school program. Each day, teachers or administrative staff completed a

14-item survey evaluating student progress on a number of dimensions. Examples of such dimensions were (1) Does s/he accept the workload? (2) Is s/he asking for help from faculty and/or administrators? (3) Does s/he display curiosity about the independent school? and (4) Does s/he adjust smoothly to the new environment? Students also completed the School Life Inventory on a daily basis so we could track changes in students' tacit knowledge about the school environment.

The results were unanticipated. Generally, ratings first rose, and then fell. In other words, adjustment initially increased, and then decreased. There could be many reasons for such a curvilinear pattern, of course. We suspect that students initially found themselves quite able to handle the workload and stress of the independent-school environment. But as the workload and stress increased over time, their adjustment decreased.

Not everyone showed the pattern of an initial increase followed by a decline. We did an analysis of those who declined after the initial increase versus those who did not. Our goal was to determine whether we could predict which students would show a decline in adjustment following an initial incline. We found that decliners did indeed differ from other students. In particular, decliners showed (a) more self-confidence, (b) less motivation, (c) an external locus of control (i.e., a tendency to blame others rather than themselves for failures), (d) less adaptation to the independent-school environment, and (e) relatively little change over time in adjustment as measured by the School-Life Inventory.

After the summer program ended and the term began, we compared the students' performance on the School Life Inventory to the performance of newly recruited students for the special program. Students how had completed the summer program and three months of school scored significantly higher than did students who were newly recruited. On average, therefore, students were gaining an understanding of the tacit knowledge of school life.

Our first study thus led to the conclusions that both hard-side and soft-side inventories provide substantial increase in prediction of academic success at the Independent School, and that student inventories, in general, can be useful supplemental measures of potential achievement. Particularly relevant variables proved to be tacit knowledge about the independent-school environment, internal locus of control (i.e., blaming oneself rather than others for one's failures), and sensible self-confidence. We also found curvilinear functions of adjustment, and that it was possibly to predict reasonably well which students would show the most decline.

Study 2

Study 1 was sufficiently successful that it was decided to try out the new measures on *all* students in the entering class who wished to volunteer. There were 173 volunteers among newcomers to the school.

The Yale measures were very successful with the new sample. SSAT scores (all of them) alone predicted only 3 percent of the variation in first-year GPA, whereas our measures added to SSAT predicted 25 percent of the variation, an increase of 83 percent. The variables that best predicted success were very high motivation to achieve (internal locus of control), sensible self-confidence (neither too high nor too low), and tacit knowledge about the independent-school environment.

From this group, those who were admitted through the special program were studied for their performance on the School Life Inventory at three times during their initial few weeks in the new environment. It was found that scores increased each time. In other words, as in Study 1, students in the program, on average, were mastering the independent-school environment over time.

Conclusion

Independent schools are constantly looking for new ways of improving their selection process. When students fail in the independent-school environment, it is unfortunate both for them and for the school. It is unfortunate for them because they may have to face the humiliation of leaving or of having poor grades; it is unfortunate for the school because someone else might have been admitted instead who would have better adapted to the independent-school environment. Our research suggests that it is possible to improve prediction of academic success, at least in one school. We believe it may be worthwhile to try out a similar approach in other schools. It might be possible to construct a battery that would work across many schools, or it might be better to customize batteries to individual schools. Whichever is the case, prediction of school success apparently can be enhanced by thinking more broadly about the skills that are measured at the time of application.

The Rainbow Project

The Rainbow Project is fully described in Sternberg and the Rainbow Project Collaborators (2003), upon which this description is based. The Rainbow measures supplement the SAT-I. The SAT-I is a three-hour examination currently measuring verbal comprehension and mathematical thinking skills, with a writing component to be added in the near future. A wide variety of studies have shown the utility of the SAT as a predictor of college success, especially as measured by GPA (e.g., Bridgeman, McCamley-Jenkins, & Ervin, 2000; Ramist, Lewis, & McCamley, 1990).

A recent meta-analysis of the predictive validity of the SAT, encompassing roughly 3000 studies and over 1 million students, suggested that the SAT is a valid predictor of early-college academic performance (as measured by first-year GPA), with validity coefficients generally in the range of .44 to .62 (Hezlett et al., 2001). The validity coefficients for later-college performance were somewhat lower but still substantial – generally ranging from the mid .30s to the mid .40s. Ramist, Lewis, and McCamley (1990) found that the validity of the SAT-I at 39 colleges was better than that of high-school GPA for predicting individual course grades, but that high-school GPA was a better predictor of overall first-year GPA. The correlations (corrected for shrinkage, restriction of range, and criterion unreliability) were .60 for SAT-I, .62 for SAT-II, and .63 for high school GPA. The multiple correlation of SAT-I and SAT-II with freshman GPA was .63. The multiple correlation of high school GPA and SAT-I with freshman grades was .71. Correlations for females were generally higher than for males. Correlations of the SAT-II differed somewhat for different ethnic groups.

Kobrin, Camara, and Milewski (2002) examined the validity of the SAT for college-admissions decisions in California and elsewhere in the United States. They found that, in California, SAT-I and SAT-II both showed moderate correlations with family income (in the range of .25 to .55 for SAT-I). Correlations with parental education ranged from .28 to .58. These findings indicate that SAT scores may be a function, in part, of social class. Predictive effectiveness of the SAT was similar for different ethnic groups; however, there were important mean differences for the different ethnic groups on the SAT (see also Bridgeman, Burton, & Cline, 2001). The group differences are reflected by the number of standard deviations away from the White students' mean each group scored. On average, African-American students scored about one full standard deviation below the White students on both the verbal and mathematics tests. Latino students scored about 3/4 of a standard deviation lower than the White students, and Native Americans scored about 1/2 of a standard deviation lower than White students on the two tests. Asian students scored higher than White students by about a third of a standard deviation on the math test but about a third lower on the verbal test.

Taken together, these data suggest reasonable predictive validity for the SAT in predicting college performance. Indeed, traditional intelligence or aptitude tests have been shown to predict performance across a wide variety of settings (Brody, 1997; Schmidt & Hunter, 1998). But as is always the case for a single test or type of test, there is room for improvement. The theory of successful intelligence (Sternberg, 1997, 1999) provides one basis for improving prediction and possibly for establishing greater equity. It suggests that broadening the range of skills tested to go beyond analytical skills, to include practical and creative skills as well, might significantly enhance the prediction of college performance beyond current levels. Thus, the theory does not suggest *replacing*, but rather, *augmenting* the SAT in the college-admissions process. A collaborative team of investigators sought to study how successful such an augmentation could be.

We have had some past experience in such work. In one study (Sternberg, Grigorenko, Ferrari, & Clinkenbeard, 1999), we used the so-called Sternberg Triarchic Abilities Test (STAT – Sternberg, 1993) to investigate the internal validity of the theory. Three hundred twenty-six high school students, primarily from diverse parts of the United States, took the test, which comprised 12 subtests in all. There were four subtests each measuring analytical, creative, and practical abilities. For each type of ability, there were three multiple choice tests and one essay test. The multiple choice tests, in turn, involved, respectively, verbal, quantitative, and figural content.

1. Analytical-Verbal: Figuring out meanings of neologisms (artificial words) from natural contexts. Students see a novel word embedded in a paragraph, and have to infer its meaning from the context.
2. Analytical-Quantitative: Number series. Students have to say what number should come next in a series of numbers.
3. Analytical-Figural: Matrices. Students see a figural matrix with the lower right entry missing. They have to say which of the options fits into the missing space.
4. Practical-Verbal: Everyday reasoning. Students are presented with a set of everyday problems in the life of an adolescent and have to select the option that best solves each problem.
5. Practical-Quantitative: Everyday math. Students are presented with scenarios requiring the use of math in everyday life (e.g., buying tickets for a ballgame), and have to solve math problems based on the scenarios.
6. Practical-Figural: Route planning. Students are presented with a map of an area (e.g., an entertainment park) and have to answer

questions about navigating effectively through the area depicted by the map.

7. Creative-Verbal: Novel analogies. Students are presented with verbal analogies preceded by counterfactual premises (e.g., money falls off trees). They have to solve the analogies as though the counterfactual premises were true.

8. Creative-Quantitative: Novel number operations. Students are presented with rules for novel number operations, for example, "flix," which involves numerical manipulations that differ as a function of whether the first of two operands is greater than, equal to, or less than the second. Participants have to use the novel number operations to solve presented math problems.

9. Creative-Figural: In each item, participants are first presented with a figural series that involves one or more transformations; they then have to apply the rule of the series to a new figure with a different appearance, and complete the new series.

Methodological Considerations

Data were collected at 15 schools across the United States, including 8 four-year colleges, 5 community colleges, and 2 high schools.[1] Most of the data were collected from mid-April, 2001 through June, 2001, although some institutions extended their data collection somewhat further into the summer.

The participants received either course credit or money. They were 1,013 students predominantly in their first year of college or their final year of high school. In this report, we discuss analyses only for college students because they were the only ones for whom we had available college performance. The final number of participants included in these analyses was 793.

Baseline measures of standardized test scores and high-school GPA were collected to evaluate the predictive validity of current tools used for college admission criteria, and to provide a contrast for our current measures. Students' scores on standardized college entrance exams were obtained from the College Board.

---

[1] Participating institutions in the Rainbow Project included Brigham Young University; Florida State University; James Madison University; California State University, San Bernardino; University of California, Santa Barbara; Southern Connecticut State University; Stevens Institute of Technology; Yale University; Mesa Community College; Coastline Community College; Irvine Valley Community College; Orange Coast Community College; Saddleback Community College; Mepham High School; and Northview High School. Participating institution in the University of Michigan Business School Project was the University of Michigan.

Measuring analytical skills. The measure of analytical skills was provided by the analytical items of the STAT (Sternberg, 1993) as described above.

Measuring creative skills. Creative skills were measured by STAT multiple-choice items, as described above, and by performance-based items. Creative skills also were measured using open-ended measures. One measure required writing two short stories with a selection from among unusual titles, such as "The Octopus's Sneakers," one required orally telling two stories based upon choices of picture collages, and the third required captioning cartoons from among various options. Open-ended performance-based answers were rated by trained raters for novelty, quality, and task-appropriateness. Multiple judges were used for each task and satisfactory reliability was achieved (details in Sternberg and the Rainbow Project Collaborators, 2003).

Measuring practical skills. Multiple-choice measures of practical skills were obtained from the STAT. Practical skills also were assessed using three situational-judgment inventories: the Everyday Situational Judgment Inventory (Movies), the Common Sense Questionnaire, and the College Life Questionnaire, each of which tap different types of tacit knowledge. The general format of tacit-knowledge inventories has been described in detail elsewhere (Sternberg et al., 2000), so only the content of the inventories used in this study will be described here. The movies presented everyday situations that confront college students, such as asking for a letter of recommendation from a professor who shows, through nonverbal cues, that he does not recognize you very well. One then has to rate various options for how well they would work in response to each situation. The Common Sense Questionnaire provided everyday business problems, such as being assigned to work with a coworker whom one cannot stand, and the College Life Questionnaire provided everyday college situations for which a solution was required.

Unlike the creativity performance tasks, in the practical performance tasks the participants were not given a choice of situations to rate. For each task, participants were told that there was no "right" answer, and that the options described in each situation represented variations on how different people approach different situations.

All materials were administered either in paper-and-pencil format (for the college students, $N = 325$) or on the computer via the World Wide Web (for the college students, $N = 468$). Participants were either tested individually or in small groups. During the oral stories section, participants who were tested in the group situation either wore headphones or were directed into a separate room to not disturb the other participants during the story dictation.

There were two discrete sessions, conducted one directly after the other, for each participant. The first session included the informed-consent procedure, demographics information, the movies, the STAT batteries, and the cartoons, followed by a brief debriefing period. The second session included obtaining consent again, followed by the rest of the demographics and "additional measures" described earlier, the Common Sense or College Life Test (depending on the condition), the Written or Oral Stories (depending on the condition), and ending with the final debriefing. The order was the same for all participants. No strict time limits were set for completing the tests, although the instructors were given rough guidelines of about 70 minutes per session. The time taken to complete the battery of tests ranged from two to four hours.

As a result of the lengthy nature of the complete battery of assessments, participants were administered parts of the battery using an intentional incomplete overlapping design, as described in McArdle and Hamagami (1992; also McArdle, 1994). The participants were randomly assigned to the test sections they were to complete. Details of the use of the procedure are in Sternberg and the Rainbow Collaborators (2003).

What We Found

Basic statistics. When examining college students alone, one can see that this sample also shows a slightly higher mean level of SAT than that found in colleges across the country. Our sample means on the SATs were, for two-year college students, 491 verbal and 509 math, and for four-year college students, 555 verbal and 575 math. These means, although slightly higher than typical, are within the range of average college students.

There is always a potential concern about restriction of range in scores using the SAT when considering students from a select sample of universities, especially when the means run a bit high. However, our sample was taken from a wide range in selectivity of institutions, from community colleges to highly select four-year institutions. Additionally, the standard deviation of the SAT scores (for the college sample, $SD_{SAT\ Verbal} = 118.6$, and $SD_{SAT\ Math} = 117.6$) was comparable to the standard deviation of the SAT tests in the broader population. If anything, an analysis of variance test suggests that the variance for the sample for these items is statistically larger than for the typical population of SAT examinees ($p < .05$). For these reasons, the concern of restriction of range of SAT scores across the whole sample is reduced.

Factor structure of the Rainbow measures. An exploratory factor analysis with Varimax rotation was conducted to explore the factor structure underlying the Rainbow measures. Three factors were extracted with eigenvalues greater than 1 and these accounted for 59.2 percent of the variation between the measures. One factor represented practical performance tests. A second, weaker factor represented the creative performance tests. A third factor represented the multiple-choice tests (including analytical, creative, and practical). Thus, method variance proved to be very important in this as in past studies (Sternberg, Grigorenko, Ferrari, & Clinkenbeard, 1999). The results show the importance of measuring skills using multiple formats, precisely because method is so important in determining factorial structure.

Predicting College GPA.[2] In order to test the incremental validity provided by Rainbow measures above and beyond the SAT in predicting GPA, a series of hierarchical regressions was conducted that included the items analyzed above in the analytical, creative, and practical assessments.

In one set of hierarchical regressions, the SAT-V, SAT-M, and High School GPA were included in the first step of the regression because these are the standard measures used today to predict college performance. Only

---

[2] One problem when using College GPA from students across different colleges is that a high GPA from a less selective institution is equated to a high GPA from a highly selective institution. One could make the argument that the skills needed to achieve a high GPA at a selective college are greater than the skills needed to achieve a high GPA at a less selective college. There are a number of ways one could account for this problem of equated GPAs. (1) One could assign a weight to GPA based on the selectivity of the students' institution, such that more selective institutions are given a weight that increases the GPA relative to less selective institutions. However, this procedure assumes that the variables used to predict GPA are measured independently of the weight, namely the selectivity of the school. Because SAT is used to determine the selectivity of the school to which a student matriculates, and therefore results in a violation of independence of independent and dependent variables, we could not run this procedure because it would artificially inflate the relationship between SAT and weighted GPA. Adjusting for the SAT/Selectivity relationship by partialling out selectivity from the SAT would artificially deflate the relationship between SAT and weighted GPA. (2) A second procedure would be to standardize all scores, including the dependent variable and all independent variables, within levels of selectivity of the institution, or even within each school, and then run these scores together in all analyses. This standardization procedure effectively equates students at highly selective institutions with students from less selective institutions, and produces results that would be essentially a rough summary of the analyses done within each level of selectivity or within each school. One problem with this procedure is that it loses the elegance of involving schools in a large range of selectivity (e.g., University of California at Santa Barbara versus Mesa Community College), if all students become equated by standardization. Nevertheless, when this procedure is run, the pattern of results is essentially the same as an analysis that does not use a standardization adjustment to the data; in fact, the only substantive change is that, across the board, all coefficients become attenuated (including correlations, beta coefficients, R^2 squared, etc.). Consequently, we have chosen to report the results based on scores that are unadjusted for institutional selectivity.

High School GPA contributed uniquely to R^2. In Step 2 we added the analytic subtest of the STAT, because this test is closest conceptually to the SAT tests. The analytical subtest of the STAT slightly increased R^2, with a statistically significant beta-weight. In Step 3, the measures of practical ability were added, resulting in a small increase in R^2. Notably, the latent variable representing the common variance among the practical performance measures and High School GPA were the only variables to significantly account for variance in College GPA in Step 3. The inclusion of the creative measures in the final step of this regression indicates that, by supplementing the SAT and High School GPA with measures of analytical, practical, and creative abilities, a total of 22.6 percent of the variance in GPA can be accounted for. Inclusion of the Rainbow measures in steps 2, 3, and 4 represents an increase of about 8.5 percent (from .141 to .226) in the variance accounted for over and above the typical predictors of College GPA. Including the Rainbow measures without high school GPA, using only SAT scores as a base, represents an increase in percentage variance accounted for of about 8.6 percent (from .084 to .170). Looked at in another way, this means that the Rainbow measures almost doubled prediction versus the SAT alone.

In another set of hierarchical regressions, SAT and High School GPA were entered in the last steps. These regressions showed that SAT did not add significant incremental validity above and beyond the Rainbow measures in the penultimate step, although High School GPA did in the final step. Approximately 16.3 percent of the variance in College GPA could be accounted for by using Rainbow measures alone. With the addition of High School GPA in the last step, at least one task from each of the Rainbow components also contributed to the incremental prediction of college GPA above and beyond High School GPA and the SAT, significantly by the STAT-analytic ($p < .05$) and the oral stories ($p < .001$), and marginally by the latent practical-ability measure underlying performance on the three tacit-knowledge tasks ($p < .08$).

These multiple regression analyses pose some concern because of the large number of measures used representing each of analytic, creative, and practical skills. This risks a great deal of construct overlap. To account for this problem, a final multiple regression analysis was conducted that included only High School GPA, SAT, and one measure from each of analytic, creative, and practical skills. For analytic skills, we used the only measure available from the new measures, the $STAT_{Analytical}$. For creative skills, we used the only statistically significant predictor, the oral stories measure. For practical skills, we used the methodology that did not overlap with other methodologies in the study, namely the practical performance measures as represented by the practical performance latent variable. The results from this analysis support the claim that measuring analytic, creative, and practical skills using different methodologies can substantially improve upon predicting College GPA beyond High School GPA and the SAT. All three representatives of the Rainbow measures and high school GPA maintained a statistically significant beta coefficient. The beta weights were .307 for high school GPA, -.034 for SAT-M, .001 for SAT-V, .117 for Rainbow Analytical, .110 for Rainbow Practical, and .239 for Rainbow Creative.

Group differences. Although one important goal of the present study was to predict success in college, another important goal involved developing measures that reduce racial and ethnic group differences in mean levels. There are a number of ways one can test for group differences in these measures, each which involves a test of the size of the effect of race. We chose two: omega square (ω^2), and Cohen's *D*.

We first considered the omega squared coefficients. This procedure involves conducting a series of one-way analyses of variance (ANOVA) considering differences in mean performance levels among the six ethnic and racial groups reported, including White, Asian, Pacific Islander, Latino, Black, and Native American, for the following measures: the baseline measures (SAT-V and SAT-M), the STAT ability scales, the creativity performance tasks, and the practical-ability performance tasks. The omega-squared coefficient indicates the proportion of variance in the variables that is accounted for by the self-reported ethnicity of the participant. The omega squared values were .13 for SAT-V, .16 for SAT-M, and .15 for combined SAT. For the Rainbow measures, omega square ranged from .00 to .07 with a median of .02. Thus, the Rainbow measures showed reduced values relative to the SAT.

The test of effect sizes using the Cohen's *D* statistic allows one to consider more specifically a standardized representation of specific group differences. For the test of ethnic group differences, each entry represents how far away from the mean for whites each group performs in terms of standard deviations. For the test of gender differences, the entries represent how far away women perform from men in terms of standard deviations.

The median Cohen's *D* relative to whites, for SAT, was −.70 for blacks, −1.05 for Latinos, .07 for Asians, and −.82 for Native Americans. For Rainbow Analytical, the respective median *D* values relative to whites were −.26 for blacks, −.35 for Latinos, .24 for Asians, and −.46 for Native Americans. For Rainbow Practical, the values were −.71 for blacks, −.31 for Latinos, .06

for Asians, and −.60 for Native Americans. Finally, for Rainbow Creative, the corresponding values were −.30 for blacks, −.44 for Latinos, −.22 for Asians, and .26 for Native Americans.

These results indicate two general findings. First, in terms of overall differences represented by omega squared, the triarchic tests appear to reduce race and ethnicity differences relative to traditional assessments of abilities like the SAT. Second, in terms of specific differences represented by Cohen's D, it appears that the Latino students benefit the most from the reduction of group differences. The black students, too, seem to show a reduction in difference from the white mean for most of the triarchic tests, although a substantial difference appears to be maintained with the practical performance measures. Important reductions in differences can also be seen for the Native American students relative to white. Indeed, their median was higher for the creative tests. However, the very small sample size suggests that any conclusions about Native American performance should be made tentatively.

Although the group differences are not perfectly reduced, these findings suggest that measures can be designed that reduce ethnic and racial group differences on standardized tests, particularly for historically disadvantaged groups like black and Latino students. These findings have important implications for reducing adverse impact in college admissions.

Implications

The SAT is based on a conventional psychometric notion of cognitive skills. Using this notion, it has had substantial success in predicting college performance. But perhaps the time has come to move beyond conventional theories of cognitive skills. Based on multiple regression analyses, the triarchic measures alone nearly double the predictive power of College GPA when compared to the SAT alone (comparing R^2 of .163 to .084, respectively). Additionally, the triarchic measures predict an additional 8.5 percent of College GPA beyond the initial 14.1 percent contributed by the SAT and High School GPA. These findings, combined with encouraging results regarding the reduction of between-ethnicity differences, make a compelling case for furthering the study of the measurement of analytic, creative, and practical skills for predicting success in college.

One important goal for the current study, and future studies, is the creation of standardized test measures that reduce the different outcomes between different groups as much as possible to maintain test validity. Our measures suggest results toward this end. Although the group differences in the tests were not reduced to zero, the tests did substantially attenuate group differences relative to other measures such as the SAT. This finding could be an important step toward ultimately ensuring fair and equal treatment for members of diverse groups in the academic domain. Although this first study presents a promising start for the investigation of an equitable yet powerful predictor of success in college, the study is not without its share of methodological problems. Better tests and scoring methods, larger samples, and more representative samples all are needed in future work. Future development of these tests will help sort out some of the problems borne out of the present findings.

In sum, the theory of successful intelligence appears to provide a strong theoretical basis for augmented assessment of the skills needed for college success. There is evidence to indicate that it has good incremental predictive power, and serves to increase equity. As teaching improves and college teachers emphasize more the creative and practical skills needed for success in school and life, the predictive power of the test may increase. Cosmetic changes in testing over the last century have made relatively little difference to the construct validity of assessment procedures. The theory of successful intelligence could provide a new opportunity to increase construct validity at the same time that it reduces differences in test performance between groups.

The University of Michigan Business School Project

As noted above, researchers and practitioners have increasingly recognized that reliance solely on conventional standardized testing in undergraduate and graduate admissions has several limitations (Bracey, 2001; Darling-Hammond, 1991). These limitations are clearly demonstrated by the GMAT, the most widely used assessment in business school admissions (Dobson, Krapljan-Barr, & Vielba, 1999; Hancock, 1999; Wright & Palmer, 1994). First, the GMAT, like most standardized tests, tends to explain less than 20 percent of the variance in graduate GPA (Ahmadi, Raiszadeh, & Helms, 1997; Graham, 1991; Hancock, 1999; Nilsson, 1995; Paolillo, 1982; Wright & Palmer, 1994; Youngblood & Martin, 1982). From one point of view, 20 percent is impressive. Relatively rarely in psychological measurement can we consistently predict 20 percent of the variance in a dependent variable. From another point of view, it leaves 80 percent of the variance unexplained and suggests that no matter how good the GMAT is, its prediction might benefit from supplementation by other kinds of assessments. Second, the GMAT has been found to exhibit similar patterns of gender and racial disparities as other standardized tests (Dobson et al.,

1999; Hancock, 1999). These differences tend to favor males over females and whites over blacks. A supplement might be found, at least in theory, that reduced these differences but that nevertheless increased prediction.

The purpose of the research described here was to explore alternative ways to assess a business school applicant's potential for success that address, although certainly do not fully circumvent, some of the limitations identified above. This presentation of the research is based on Hedlund, Wilt, Nebel, and Sternberg (2003). The goal is not to replace the GMAT or comparable assessments, but rather, to supplement them using the theory of successful intelligence (Sternberg, 1997) and thus to improve the process of business-school admissions.

The admission process in Masters of Business Administration (MBA) programs involves assessing each candidate's demonstrated and potential abilities to be a successful student, manager, and business leader. The two most common indicators used to evaluate candidates are undergraduate GPA and scores on the GMAT. The GMAT consists of multiple-choice questions that measure verbal and quantitative skills and essay questions that measure analytical skills. According to Jaffe and Hilbert (1994), "The purpose of the GMAT is to measure your ability to think systematically and to employ the verbal and mathematical skills that you have acquired throughout your years of schooling" (p. 3). Research has found these two factors to be somewhat predictive of graduate school performance (Ahmadi et al., 1997; Graham, 1991; Hancock, 1999; Nilsson, 1995; Paolillo, 1982; Wright & Palmer, 1994; Youngblood & Martin, 1982). However, as indicated above, a large amount of variance is not accounted for by these two skills.

In addition to GMAT scores and undergraduate GPA, admissions officers may review resumes, letters of recommendation, and essays, or conduct interviews to evaluate a candidate's work experience, interpersonal skills, and leadership potential. However, these additional items typically are weighed heavily for candidates who have borderline GMAT scores. With some MBA programs receiving thousands of applications each year, it is challenging, if not impossible, to evaluate all candidates on all criteria. Therefore, some initial screening process is often desirable. GMAT scores often play a central role in determining whether a candidate makes it past this initial screening and thus is given any further consideration. The problem occurs when the screening criterion or criteria potentially (a) leads to the rejection of applicants who possess other qualities relevant to success or (b) disfavors members of certain groups. In order to address some of the limitations in the use of the GMAT (or, potentially, any other single test or verbal and mathematical skills) in MBA admissions, other forms of assessment should be explored. The goal of such exploration is to determine whether skills exist that, in combination with the verbal and mathematical skills measured by the GMAT, would be important for business-school and, ultimately, business success.

The purpose of our research was to develop a measure of practical ability that would predict an individual's success as a business student and business leader. We chose to explore two methods of assessing practical skills that incorporate features from the various approaches described above.

Measurements of Tacit Knowledge and its Acquisition

The first method incorporates features of the in-basket and case-based interview techniques, and asks individuals to sort through detailed case-study problems (CSPs) and to develop solutions to those problems. The advantages of the CSPs are that (a) they assess an individual's potential abilities rather than acquired knowledge and (b) they have more ecological validity in the sense that what respondents are asked to do (e.g., identify the problem, generate solutions) is more representative of real-world problem-solving. The limitations of CSPs are that (a) the questions requires more time to complete, reducing the number that can be administered in a given time, and (b) scoring the questions is somewhat more subjective and time-consuming because raters must evaluate the quality of each response.

Given the potential drawbacks of the CSPs, we chose also to explore a second method based on prior research on tacit knowledge and situational-judgment testing. The second method involves using SJPs to assess an individual's practical ability. The advantages of SJPs are that (a) a greater number of questions can be included in the assessment, thus enhancing reliability, and (b) the response format allows answers to be more readily quantified. The limitation of SJPs is that responses may depend largely on an individual's ability to draw on knowledge gained from prior training or experience. Thus, it may unduly favor MBA candidates who have specific managerial experience or training.

General Methodology

We developed measures based on the two methods described above and conducted two studies to validate these new measures with samples of MBA students. The studies entailed administering the new items to incoming MBA students and tracking their success in the program and immediately following graduation. We present the method and results of these two studies below. However, we first describe the development of the new items and scoring keys.

Item Development

The development of the items involved several steps. First, we constructed a set of six case scenarios representing problems that business leaders might encounter on the job. Each scenario describes a fictitious business problem and consists of an overview of the situation, the respondent's role, and a brief history of the company and/or department. This overview is accompanied by various documents such as organizational charts, departmental memos, e-mail correspondence, financial tables, or product descriptions. Individuals are instructed to read through all the materials and to answer a set of questions, based on the metacomponents (higher order metacognitive processes) in Sternberg's (1985, 1997) theory:

- *Problem identification and rationale.* What do you see as the main problem in this situation? Why do you consider it to be the main problem? What additional problems need to be addressed?
- *Solution generation and rationale.* What would you do to address the main problem you have identified? What alternative courses of action did you consider? Why did you choose your particular course of action?
- *Use of information and prior experience.* What information did you focus on in developing a response to the situation? How did you use the information to arrive at a response to the situation? Did you draw on any personal experiences in developing a response to the situation? If so, please explain. What additional information/resources would you need to address this problem?
- *Outcome monitoring and obstacle recognition.* What outcome do you hope will result from the course of action you have chosen? What obstacles, if any, do you anticipate to obtaining this outcome?

In developing these scenarios, we sought to cover a broad range of management/leadership issues (planning, decision making, communicating, managing and developing subordinates, managing conflict, adapting to demands, and handling stress) as well as diverse business settings (finance, manufacturing, technology, nonprofit) and functions (marketing, accounting, information systems, general management). The situations represented in these scenarios included (a) Personnel Shortage,

(b) Strategic Decision-Making, (c) Problem Subordinate, (d) Consulting Challenge, (e) Interdepartmental Negotiations, and (f) Project Management. In developing the scenarios, we further sought to include enough information to provide a rich context for assessing practical problem-solving abilities, but to avoid details that would present an advantage to someone with prior business experience.

Next, we asked 27 business-school alumni and students to complete the scenarios and rate them in regard to adequacy. Lastly, we derived a set of SJPs from the longer case scenarios. Based on reviewer responses, we identified a set of subproblems in each scenario. For each subproblem, we developed brief descriptions that attempted to capture, in a paragraph, the key issues pertaining to that problem. For example, in Scenario 1, we isolated problems pertaining to understaffing, employee turnover, and job satisfaction. Although in the overall scenario these problems were all symptoms of a larger problem (i.e., a mismatch between employee values and management policies), they all can be viewed as significant problems in themselves. We then identified a set of possible solutions for each problem, drawing again on the reviewers' responses. For example, suggestions for dealing with the problem of understaffing included hiring temporary employees, offering overtime to current employees, asking individual departments to evaluate their personnel needs, and hiring full-time employees with the understanding that they may be laid off if demand decreases. This process resulted in a total of 18 SJPs (three problems representing each of the six scenarios).

Answers to the structured, open-ended questions of the CSPs and the closed-ended alternatives of the SJPs serve as the basis for assessing an individual's practical abilities. To develop the scoring keys for both question formats, we relied on expert opinions of the quality of various responses that individuals might provide.

Implementation of the Study
Our study represented the first administration of the new items. We sought to evaluate the new measures in terms of four main criteria: (1) the ability of the CSPs and SJPs to predict indicators of academic and employment success; (2) the ability of these measures to explain performance beyond GMAT scores and undergraduate GPA; (3) the potential of these measures to compensate for disparities in test scores on the GMAT; and (4) the perceived value and relevance of these measures for MBA admissions and managerial development.

Measures. For the purpose of administering the new items and evaluating them related to the above criteria, we created an assessment, called the Successful Intelligence Assessment (SIA). Three versions of the SIA were developed, each consisting of two CSPs plus six SJPs drawn from two alternate case scenarios. We used alternate forms of each version in which the order of the case scenario and SJPs varied so to control for potential confounds (e.g., fatigue and time constraints). We paired scenarios for inclusion in each version based on their time requirements, difficulty, functional areas addressed, and abilities measured.

Each student received one score for the SJPs and another for the CSPs. Scores on the SJPs represented the similarity of the student's ratings to those of the experts across all response options. For our purposes we chose a similarity index (Pearson correlation), which looks at how closely the profile of ratings provided by the student relates to the profile provided by the experts. The Pearson *r* was preferred as it allowed for more straightforward interpretation of the results and enables comparisons to be made across SJPs. Scores on the CSPs reflect the overall quality of an individual's answer to the set of open-ended questions at the end of the scenario. Ratings are based on a scoring key derived from expert judgments and can range from 1 (poor answer) to 5 (excellent answer).

The SIA included several other measures to help evaluate the SJPs and CSPs. These measures assessed motivation, self-efficacy, and reactions to the questionnaire.

In addition to SIA data, we tracked students' performance in the MBA program, participation in extracurricular activity, and placement success. We used several indicators of performance in the MBA program, including the average GPA at the end of the 1st year and the end of the program, as well as a score on an team-consulting project called the Multidisciplinary Action Project (MAP). The consulting project was evaluated on a scale of 1 = Low Pass, 2 = Pass, 3 = Good, or 4 = Excellent.

We also looked at indicators of participation in extracurricular activities. These indicators included participation in student clubs, involvement in volunteer organizations, and leadership positions held while in the MBA program. Finally, we monitored success outside of school by collecting data on the number of interviews and offers received for internships and jobs, as well as starting salary.

We did two studies in two consecutive years. Because of space limitations, only the first study is described in any detail here. The SIA was administered to 422 incoming MBA students at the University of Michigan Business School during orientation in the Fall of 1999. The sample consisted of 313 (74 percent) males and 109 (26 percent) females. The racial composition was 28 (7 percent) African American, 124 (29 percent) Asian, 213 (50 percent) Caucasian, 22 (5 percent) Hispanic, and 26 (6 percent) classified as "Other." Nine (2 percent) did not provide information regarding race. The majority (81 percent) of the students were between 26 and 35 years of age and none were older than 45 years of age.

What We Found
Scores on the SJPs represent Pearson correlation coefficients. The average score on the SJPs was .66, indicating that the students' ratings, on average, correlated fairly high with the experts' ratings. Spearman-Brown coefficients were computed on the two sets of SJPs completed by each student to assess reliability of the SJP scores. Reliabilities ranged from .61 to .73 across the three assessment versions. Scores on the CSPs represent the average quality rating an individual received from two raters on the two scenarios she or he completed. Quality ratings ranged from 1 (poor) to 5 (excellent). The mean rating on the CSPs was 3.05, indicating that students, on average, received a satisfactory rating. The average inter-rater reliability across all scenarios was .68. It also is worth noting that although the grades on the consulting project ranged from 1 to 4, 65 percent of the students received a rating of 3 or "good," suggesting a possible restriction of variance in this measure. Finally, many of the extracurricular and placement variables were log transformed prior to the analyses to correct for skewness in the data.

Predictive validity. We performed correlational analyses to determine the predictive validity of SJP and CSP scores relative to the various performance indicators. We also compared these validities to those associated with existing predictors (prior experience, GMAT scores, undergraduate GPA).

Scores on both the SJPs and CSPs were predictive of academic performance. Students with higher scores on the SJPs had significantly higher first year and final GPAs ($r = .18$ and .19 respectively), and also received higher grades on the team consulting project ($r = .17$). Similarly, students with higher scores on the CSPs had significantly higher first year and final GPAs ($r = .21$ and .29 respectively) and higher consulting project grades ($r = .17$).

Both GMAT scores and undergraduate GPA also were significant predictors of academic performance. However, GMAT scores did not correlate significantly with the consulting project grade ($r = .06$, ns). Prior work experience was not a significant predictor of academic performance.

SJP and CSP scores were somewhat predictive of involvement in extracurricular activity. Students who scored higher on the SJPs participated in more student clubs ($r = .15$) and held more leadership positions ($r = .11$). CSP scores also exhibited a significant positive correlation with leadership ($r = .18$). GMAT scores exhibited some relationship with extracurricular activity, but in the opposite direction. Specifically, students with higher GMAT scores participated in fewer student clubs ($r = -.13$) and volunteered less ($r = -.12$).

Finally, there were few significant predictors of internship or job placement success as measured by the number of interviews, number of offers, and base salary. Students with higher CSP scores received more full-time job offers ($r = .11$) and students with higher GMAT scores received higher base salaries ($r = .13$). The latter finding may be attributable to the fact that many employees look at the GMAT scores of job applicants, which ultimately may influence the salary they are willing to offer.

Incremental validity. Next, we sought to determine the validity of the SJPs and CSPs relative to two most commonly used criteria in MBA admissions, undergraduate GPA and GMAT scores. First we observed that scores on the SJPs and CSPs were unrelated to GMAT scores, suggesting that the new measures tap distinct abilities from the GMAT. Similarly, scores on the SJPs were unrelated to undergraduate GPA. Scores on the CSPs, however, did correlate modestly but significantly with undergraduate GPA ($r = .12$). The latter finding is likely attributable to the large reading and writing requirement of the CSPs compared to the SJPs.

We followed up the correlational analyses with a set of hierarchical regression analyses in order to determine the extent to which SJP and CSP scores explained individual differences in MBA performance beyond undergraduate GPA and GMAT scores. In the following hierarchical regressions, we entered GMAT scores and undergraduate GPA in the first step, followed in the second step by either SJP or CSP scores. We examined three dependent variables: first year GPA, final GPA, and consulting project grade.

Both SJP and CSP scores accounted for significant variance in MBA grades beyond GMAT scores and undergraduate GPA. In predicting first year GPA, SJP and CSP scores each accounted for an additional 3 percent of variance beyond GMAT and undergraduate GPA. In predicting final GPA, SJP and CSP scores accounted for 4 and 6 percent incremental validity respectively. SJP and CSP scores also accounted for significant incremental variance in consulting project grades, whereas GMAT was not a significant predictor.

We also compared CSP and SJP scores directly and found that CSP scores were better predictors of final GPA than were SJP scores ($\beta = .21$

and .14, respectively). In addition, CSP scores accounted for an additional 4 percent variance in final GPA after accounting for SJP scores. In comparison, SJP scores only accounted for 2 percent variance beyond CPS scores. There were virtually no differences between SJP and CSP scores in regard to predicting first year GPA or the consulting project grades.

Group differences. A concern with standardized ability or aptitude tests is that they often result in disparities between members of gender, racial or ethnic groups. There is evidence, for example, that females and African Americans score significantly lower on the GMAT than do other gender and racial groups (Dobson et al., 1999; Hancock, 1999). Therefore, we assessed the extent to which group differences emerged in scores on the SJPs and CSPs, and compared them to differences in GMAT scores.

We found significant gender differences for GMAT scores, SJP scores, and CSP scores. Males scored .34 standard deviations higher than did females on the GMAT ($Ms = 681$ and 666 respectively, $t = -3.05$, $p < .01$). Females, however, scored .24 standard deviation higher than did males on the SJPs ($Ms = .68$ and .65 respectively, $t = 2.29$, $p < .05$) and .39 standard deviation higher on the CSPs ($Ms = 3.26$ and 2.98 respectively, $t = 3.53$, $p < .01$).

With regard to socially defined race, individuals were classified based on self-report data as African American, Asian, Caucasian, Hispanic, or Other.

African Americans scored 1.24 standard deviations lower than did Caucasians on the GMAT. In contrast, African Americans scored only .14 of a standard deviation lower on the SJPs and .42 of a standard deviation lower on the CSPs than did Caucasians.

Other disparities emerged on the new measures that were not found on the GMAT. Overall, the differences on the SJPs were modest, with the most notable disparity between Caucasians and Asians ($d = -.38$), favoring the Caucasians. Differences on the CSPs were more pronounced, with the largest disparities between Caucasians and Asians ($d = -.63$), favoring Caucasians, followed by Caucasians and Hipanics ($d = -.57$), also favoring Caucasians.

One possible explanation for the pattern of disparities on the SJPs and CSPs is that not all students were native English speakers. In fact, 34 percent of the students in the sample classified themselves as non-U.S. citizens. These students may have had more difficulty with the problems, given the extensive reading and writing requirements and the fact that the problems were presented in U.S. business contexts. After controlling for citizenship status, differences in scores among self-designated racial groups on the SJPs were reduced to nonsignificance. Differences in CSP scores remained, but were somewhat mitigated. Most notably, the disparity in scores between Asians and Caucasians was reduced from −.63 to −.24. Interestingly, differences in scores among self-designated racial groups on the GMAT were only exacerbated after controlling for citizenship status. The disparity between African Americans and Caucasians increased to 1.43 standard deviations, which represents a disparity three times greater than that for the CSPs. Overall, these findings indicate that the SJPs and CSPs mitigate some of the disparities inherent in the GMAT, although it is clear that the CSPs present some of their own disparities that need to be addressed in future test development.

Summary

The results of the study indicate that the SJPs and CSPs are predictive of success both inside and outside the classroom. Additionally, both the SJPs and CSPs appear to measure abilities that are distinct from those measured by the GMAT or undergraduate GPA, and contribute beyond GMAT scores and undergraduate GPA to the prediction of success in the MBA program.

In developing these new measures, we also sought to offset some of the disparities in scores associated with traditional aptitude tests like the GMAT. Although we found significant differences in SJP and CSP scores as a function of gender and race, the pattern and magnitude of these differences varied from those observed for the GMAT. In particular, gender differences on the GMAT favored males, but on the SJPs and CSPs, the differences favored females. In terms of differences in scores as a function of self-designated race, African Americans scored significantly lower than all other groups on the GMAT, but significant differences on the SJPs and CSPs were largely attributable to differences between Caucasians and Asians. The latter disparity was explained, in part, by differences in test performance between U.S. and non-U.S. citizens, the latter having typically grown up speaking a language other than English and in a culture different from that of the United States.

In comparing the two formats, we found that the predictive and incremental validities were slightly higher for the CSP than the SJP format. The SJPs, however, exhibited less disparity in scores across gender and self-designated racial groups.

The Second Study

A second study was conducted in order to replicate the findings of the study with a new sample of MBA students. The second study followed the methodology of the first study and found similar results with minor exceptions (see Hedlund et al., 2003). Both the SJPs and CSPs were predictive of academic performance and accounted for variance beyond GMAT scores and undergraduate GPA. However, the effect sizes were slightly smaller in the second study compared with the first, perhaps because the test was not mandatory and was given under less than idea conditions of testing.

With regard to group differences, the findings of the second study were fairly consistent with those of the first.

General Discussion

Our research was prompted by concerns regarding the heavy reliance on conventional standardized testing in (private) secondary-school admissions and in university admissions. The concerns with standardized tests are that (a) they measure skills that are more relevant to academic than practical problems (although the skills are relevant to both), (b) they account for a relatively small, although by no means trivial, proportion of the variance in criterion performance, and (c) they produce disparities in scores among gender and socially defined racial groups.

Our projects represent an attempt to redefine but also revitalize secondary-school and university admissions assessments. We believe that theory-based tests can supplement conventional tests in a way that provides information additional to that obtained from more traditional forms of assessments. The result we have seen, at least in our work so far, is increased predictive validity and reduction in differences between ethnic groups and sexes. Obviously, our samples are small and they are less than fully representative. The tests are new and in need of improvement. We have not had 100 years to create standardized tests that match conventional ones in terms of reliability or, when used alone, predictive validity. But too often new tests have been little more than variants of old tests. The result has been minimal gains in predictive validity and patterns of group differences that never change. We believe that psychological theories, such as ours, or the theory of multiple intelligences (Gardner, 1983), or the theory of emotional intelligence (Mayer, Salovey, & Caruso, 2000), may provide a new basis for better understanding the full range of student qualifications, and thereby improving admissions testing. In doing so, they will do a service to students who wish to optimize their chances for admissions; parents who want a "fair shake" for their children; schools that wish to obtain the best students possible; and a society that cannot afford to waste talent.

ACKNOWLEDGMENT

The research reported in this chapter was supported by the Icahn Foundation (Choate Rosemary Hall Project), the College Board (Rainbow Project), and the University of Michigan Business School (University of Michigan Business School Project).

REFERENCES

Ahmadi, M., Raiszadeh, F., &Helms, M.(1997). An examination of the admission criteria for the MBA programs: A case study. *Education*, 117, 540–546.

Binet, A., & Simon, T. (1916). *The development of intelligence in children.* Baltimore: Williams & Wilkins (Originally published in 1905).

Bracey, G.W. (2001). Test scores in the long run. *Phi Delta Kappan*, 637–638.

Bridgeman, B., Burton, N., & Cline, F. (2001). *Substituting SAT II: Subject Tests for SAT I: Reasoning Test: Impact on Admitted Class Composition and Quality.* (College Board Report No. 2001-3). New York: College Entrance Examination Board.

Bridgeman, B., McCamley-Jenkins, L., & Ervin, N. (2000). *Predictions of freshman grade-point average from the revised and recentered SAT I: Reasoning test* (College Board Report No. 2000-1). New York: College Entrance Examination Board.

Brody, N. (1997) Intelligence, schooling, and society. *American Psychologist*, 52, 1046–1050.

Cattell, R.B. (1971). *Abilities: Their structure, growth and action.* Boston, MA: Houghton Mifflin.

Darling-Hammond, L. (1991). The implications of testing policy for quality and equality. *Phi Delta Kappan*, 73, 220–225.

Dobson, P., Krapljan-Barr, P., & Vielba, C. (1999). An evaluation of the validity and fairness of the Graduate Management Admissions Tests (GMAT) used for MBA selection in a UK business school. *International Journal of Selection & Assessment*, 7, 196–202.

Flanagan, D.P., & Kaufman, A.S. (2004). *Essentials of WISC-IV Assessment.* New York: Wiley.

Gardner, H. (1983). *Frames of Mind: The theory of multiple intelligences.* New York: Basicbooks.

Gardner, H. (1999). *Intelligence Reframed: Multiple Intelligences for the 21st Century.* New York: Basicbooks.

Graham, L.D. (1991). Predicting academic success of students in a Masters of Business Administration Program. *Educational and Psychological Measurement*, 51, 721–727.

Guilford, J.P. (1982). Cognitive psychology's ambiguities: Some suggested remedies. *Psychological Review*, 89, 48–59.

Hancock, T. (1999). The gender difference: Validity of standardized American tests in predicting MBA performance. *Journal of Education for Business*, 75, 91–94.

Hedlund, J., Forsythe, G.B., Horvath, J., Williams, W.M., Snook, S., & Sternberg, R.J. (2003). Identifying and assessing tacit knowledge: Understanding the practical intelligence of military leaders. *The Leadership Quarterly*, 210, 1–24.

Hedlund, J., Wilt, J. M., Nebel, K. R., Ashford, S. J., & Sternberg, R. J. (2006). Assessing practical intelligence in business school admissions: A supplement to the graduate management admissions test. *Learning and Individual Differences*, 16, 101–127.

Hezlett, S., Kuncel, N., Vey, A., Ones, D., Campbell, J., & Camara, W.J. (2001). *The effectiveness of the SAT in predicting success early and late in college: A comprehensive meta-analysis.* Paper presented at the annual meeting of the National Council of Measurement in Education, Seattle, WA.

Intelligence and its measurement: A symposium. (1921). *Journal of Educational Psychology*, 12, 123–147, 195–216, 271–275.

Jaffe, E.D., & Hilbert ,S. (1994). *How to Prepare for the Graduate Management Admission Test* (10th Ed.). Hauppauge, NY: Barron's Educational Series.

Kaufman, A.S., & Kaufman, J.C. (1993). *The Worst Baseball Pitchers of All Time: Bad Luck, Bad Arms, Bad Teams, and Just Plain Bad.* Jefferson, North Carolina: McFarland.

Kaufman, A.S., & Lichtenberger, E.O. (1999). *Essentials of WAIS-III Assessment.* New York: Wiley.

Kaufman, A.S., & Lichtenberger, E.O. (2005). *Assessing Adolescent and Adult Intelligence* (3rd ed.). New York: Wiley.

Kaufman, A.S., Lichtenberger, E.O., Fletcher-Janzen, E., & Kaufman, N.L. (2005). *Essentials of KABC – II assessment.* New York: Wiley.

Kobrin, J.L., Camara, W.J., Milewski, G.B. (2002). *The Utility of the SAT I and SAT II for Admissions Decisions in California and the Nation* (College Board Report No. 2002-6). New York: College Entrance Examination Board.

Lichtenberger, E.O., Broadbooks, D.Y., & Kaufman, A.S. (2000). *Essentials of Cognitive Assessment with KAIT and other Kaufman Measures.* New York: Wiley.

Lichtenberger, E.O., & Kaufman, A.S. (2003). *Essentials of WPPSI-III Assessment.* New York: Wiley.

Luria, A.R. (1973). *Working Brain: An Introduction to Neuropsychology.* New York: Basic.

Mayer, J.D., Salovey, P. Caruso, D. (2000). Emotional intelligence. In R.J. Sternberg (Ed.), *Handbook of Intelligence,* (pp. 396–421). New York: Cambridge University Press.

McArdle, J.J. (1994). Structural factor analysis experiments with incomplete data. *Multivariate Behavioral Research*, 29(4), 409–454.

McArdle, J.J., & Hamagami, F. (1992). Modeling incomplete longitudinal and cross-sectional data using latent growth structural models. *Experimental Aging Research*, 18(3), 145–166.

Nilsson, J.E. (1995). The GRE and the GMAT: A comparison of their correlations to GGPA. *Educational and Psychological Measurement*, 55, 637–641.

Paolillo, J. (1982). The predictive validity of selected admissions variables relative to grade point average earned in a Masters of Business Administration program. *Educational and Psychological Measurement*, 42, 1163–1167.

Polanyi, M. (1976). Tacit knowledge. In M. Marx & F. Goodson (Eds.), *Theories in Contemporary Psychology* (pp. 330–344). New York: Macmillan.

Ramist, L., Lewis, C., & McCamley, L. (1990). Implications of using freshman GPA as the criterion for the predictive validity of the SAT. In Willingham, W.W., Lewis, C., et al. *Predicting College Grades: An Analysis of Institutional Trends Over Two Decades* (pp. 253–288). xviii.

Schmidt, F.L, & Hunter, J.E. (1998). The validity and utility of selection methods in personnel psychology: Practical and theoretical implications of 85 years of research findings. *Psychological Bulletin*, 124, 262–274.

Spearman, C. (1904). 'General intelligence,' objectively determined and measured. *American Journal of Psychology*. 15(2), 201–293.

Sternberg, R.J. (1980). Sketch of a componential subtheory of human intelligence. *Behavioral and Brain Sciences*, 3, 573–584.

Sternberg, R.J. (1984). Toward a triarchic theory of human intelligence. *Behavioral and Brain Sciences*, 7, 269–287.

Sternberg, R.J. (1985). *Beyond IQ: A Triarchic Theory of Human Intelligence*. New York: Cambridge University Press.

Sternberg, R.J. (1990). Behind closed doors: Unlocking the mysteries of human intelligence. In J. Brockman (Ed.), *Speculations: The Reality Club* (pp. 186–207). Englewood Cliffs, NJ: Prentice Hall.

Sternberg, R.J. (1993). *Sternberg Triarchic Abilities Test*. Unpublished test.

Sternberg, R.J. (1997). *Successful Intelligence*. New York: Plume.

Sternberg, R.J. (1999) The theory of successful intelligence. *Review of General Psychology*, 3, 292–316.

Sternberg, R.J., & Detterman, D.K. (1986). *What is Intelligence?* Norwood, N.J.: Ablex Publishing Corporation.

Sternberg, R.J., Forsythe, G.B., Hedlund, J., Horvath, J., Snook, S., Williams, W.M., Wagner, R.K., & Grigorenko, E.L. (2000). *Practical Intelligence in Everyday Life*. New York: Cambridge University Press.

Sternberg, R.J., Grigorenko, E.L., Ferrari, M., & Clinkenbeard, P. (1999). A triarchic analysis of an aptitude-treatment interaction. *European Journal of Psychological Assessment*, 15(1), 1–11.

Sternberg, R.J., & Hedlund, J. (2002). Practical intelligence, g, and work psychology. *Human Performance* 15(1/2), 143–160.

Sternberg, R.J., Lautrey, J., & Lubart, T.I. (2003). Where are we in the field of intelligence, how did we get here, and where are we going? In R.J. Sternberg, J. Lautrey, & T.I. Lubart (Eds.), *Models of Intelligence: International Perspectives*, (pp. 3–26). Washington, DC: American Psychological Association.

Sternberg, R.J., & the Rainbow Project Collaborators (2005). Augmenting the SAT through assessments of analytical, practical, and creative skills. In W. Camara & E. Kimmel (Eds.). *Choosing Students. Higher Education Admission Tools for the 21st Century* (pp. 159–176). Mahwah, NJ: Lawrence Erlbaum Associates.

Sternberg, R.J., The Rainbow Project Collaborators, & University of Michigan Business School Project Collaborators (2004). Theory based university admissions testing for a new millennium. *Educational Psychologist*, 39(3), 185–198.

Sternberg, R.J., & Wagner, R.K. (1993). The geocentric view of intelligence and job performance is wrong. *Current Directions in Psychological Science*, 2, 1–5.

Sternberg, R.J., Wagner, R.K., & Okagaki, L. (1993). Practical intelligence: The nature and role of tacit knowledge in work and at school. In H. Reese & J. Puckett (Eds.), *Advances in Lifespan Development* (pp. 205–227). Hillsdale, NJ: Erlbaum.

Sternberg, R.J., Wagner, R.K., Williams, W.M., & Horvath, J.A. (1995). Testing common sense. *American Psychologist*, 32, 912–927.

Thurstone, L.L. (1938). *Primary Mental Abilities*. Chicago, IL: University of Chicago Press.

Wagner, R.K. (1987). Tacit knowledge in everyday intelligent behavior. *Journal of Personality and Social Psychology*, 52, 1236–1247.

Wagner, R.K., & Sternberg, R.J. (1986). Tacit knowledge and intelligence in the everyday world. In R.J. Sternberg & R.K. Wagner (Eds.), *Practical Intelligence: Nature and Origins of Competence in the Everyday World* (pp. 51–83). New York: Cambridge University Press.

Wright, R.E., & Palmer, J.C. (1994). GMAT scores and undergraduate GPAs as predictors of performance in graduate business programs. *Journal of Education for Business*, 69, 344–349.

Youngblood, S.A., & Martin, B.J. (1982). Ability testing and graduate admissions: Decision process modeling and validation. *Educational and Psychological Measurement*, 42, 1153–1161.

10

Kaufman's Work in the Penumbra between Measurement Science and Clinical Assessment

RANDY W. KAMPHAUS

Georgia State University

CECIL R. REYNOLDS

Texas A & M University

Like all chapters in this book, we wish to document another one of Dr. Alan S. Kaufman's contributions, one that we think is of greatest impact on the disciplines of psychology, school psychology, educational psychology, and related fields. We think that his most innovative work, and the contribution likely to have the most long-term impact, was his joining of the two disciplines of measurement science and clinical assessment practice. He did so by essentially creating a new methodology of intelligence test interpretation, a method that has spread to clinical assessment practice in general, and it may be characterized in today's terminology as an early form of "evidence-based" test interpretive practice, one that emphasizes a psychometric approach to evaluating individual performance on a battery of tests as expressed as test scores.

Professor Kaufman's innovative insight is typical of breakthroughs that are made in the space between traditional boundaries, in this case, between two disciplines that were not closely aligned prior to the publication of his seminal 1979 work, *Intelligent Testing with the WISC-R*. His work takes its place alongside other breakthroughs such as the merger of mathematical modeling and chemistry to form the field of quantitative chemistry, combining the fields of physics and mathematics to create magnetic resonance imaging equipment, and merging information technology and health care to create the field of health informatics.

Professor Kaufman referred to his new method of clinical test interpretation as "Intelligent Testing," a term that he took from the prestigious psychometrician Alexander Wesman, who was Director of the Test

Division at the Psychological Corporation during the time of Seashore, Wechsler, and other luminaries. We do not think that this term adequately describes the source of his innovation, and the merger of his measurement science's background, knowledge, and expertise with clinical assessment practice. Thus, we will use this chapter to explicate the key insights and works that joined measurement science and clinical practice in such a way that they are no longer separable, as they were for most of the twentieth century. Prior to his work, clinical test interpretation practice was largely governed by practices that were handed down in an apprenticeship tradition, based on the "clinical experience" of the supervising psychologist, and relatively uninformed by scientific evidence. In other words, clinical test interpretation practice was typical of physician practices of the day in that it constituted a case of "action in the absence of evidence" (Kamphaus, 1999), and is perhaps exemplified in a quote (the veracity of which is unknown) often attributed in clinical folklore to Ralph Reitan. When asked how one could learn to interpret the Halstead–Reitan test batteries at as high a level as Reitan, he is purported to have replied, "Follow me around for 30 years." Even though Reitan was a consummate actuarialist in his approach to test interpretation, there still existed no codified, psychometrically sound, evidence-based approach to test interpretation, at least outside of the heads of many early pioneers.

Kaufman's breakthroughs in clinical assessment interpretive practice were presented in his 1979 textbook, the first of its kind to ground clinical assessment practice in principles of normative base rates, variance partitioning, and principles of factor analysis, among other measurement concepts. Prior to this publication, basic measurement principles were elucidated primarily in tests and measurement sources, and rarely well developed in clinical test interpretation texts. Specifically, Kaufman's book stood in contrast to the prior three decades of work in clinical test interpretation that was governed by the work of Rapaport, Gil, and Schafer's (1945–6) post–World War II text. Their classic work, *Diagnostic Psychological Testing*, documented the clinical profiles of the Wechsler–Bellevue scales for adult patients with various psychopathological conditions, such as "simple schizophrenia." In contrast to earlier interpretive traditions, where emphasis was placed on ranking individuals according to their overall intelligence quotient (IQ) or intelligence test composite score, Rapaport et al. (1945–6) emphasized the importance of understanding an individual's abilities and functioning by considering the entire profile of scores and their relationships to one another (Kamphaus, Winsor, Rowe, & Kim, 2005). Of course, the publication of the Wechsler scales in the 1930s made this interpretive process possible, because it yielded multiple IQs and subtest scores, whereas the Binet scales offered only a single general intelligence score (Kamphaus, 2001). Thus, this interpretive practice was made possible by the presence of the new Wechsler "technology," an intelligence test that offered multiple scores.

In their own words, Rapaport et al. (1944–5) described their interpretive practice based on patterning of scores by defining "scatter" as follows:

> Scatter is the pattern or configuration formed by the distribution of the weighted subtest scores on an intelligence test . . .the definition of scatter as a configuration or pattern of all the subtests scores implies that the final meaning of the relationship of any two scores, or of any single score to the central tendency of all the scores, is derived from the total pattern. (p. 75)

Their work was well-reasoned, detailed, thorough, and innovative and, for these reasons, it became the dominant model for interpretive practice in clinical psychology for several decades. Rapaport et al. (1945–6) were also objective in their analysis of their own work. They noted a lack of clear differentiation between profiles for various clinical samples observing, "The standardization of the [Wechsler–Bellevue] left a great deal to be desired so that the average scattergrams of normal college students, Kansas highway patrolmen . . . and applicants to the Meninger School of Psychiatry . . . all deviated from a straight line in just about the same ways" (p. 161). Results such as these do not constitute a ringing endorsement of the effectiveness of using profiles of intelligence test scores to make differential diagnostic decisions. Contemporaneously, Wechsler (1944) himself espoused the use of profiles of scores for diagnostic decision making. He described, for example, a "Psychopathic Profile" of a 15-year-old male as follows:

> Psychopathic patterning: Performance higher than verbal, low similarities, low Arithmetic, sum of Picture Arrangement plus Object Assembly greater than sum of scores on Blocks and Picture Completion. (p. 164)

This practice of interpreting score patterns was and is alluring to practitioners, and it remains commonplace at the time of this writing (Kamphaus, 2001) despite evidence contrary to its utility (e.g., see Reynolds & Kamphaus, Chapter 1). For nearly 50 years post–World War II, psychologists were taught by their mentors to search for such diagnostic profiles and, when encountered, use said profiles to make important conclusions about individuals, such as making a diagnosis. Dr. Kaufman's text started the sea change away from the search for intelligence test based diagnostic profiles, a process that is ongoing.

NORM REFERENCING AND BASE RATES

Dr. Kaufman provided a measurement science alternative to intelligence test-based diagnostic profiling by proposing in his 1979 text that it was of little value to compare the profiles for one clinical sample to another. He pointed out a key problem for interpreting a profile of test scores: a profile must not only be deviant from other profiles for other diagnostic groups, they must also be deviant with respect to population base rates, that is, the norm or typically developing populations. Deviance cannot be judged in the absence of an understanding of normalcy. Many breakthroughs appear simple due to their clarity, and this premise fits that description. Dr. Kaufman simply asked practitioners to use norms to detect intellectual pathology, not the profiles and practices passed down from supervisor to intern unchecked by referencing to norms or other scientific evidence. In so doing, he also created a method that was definable and perhaps even more importantly, clearly teachable in an academic setting as a replicable practice that did not require following anyone around for some period of years to understand.

He first made a clear data-based argument for the premise that many of the Verbal versus Performance IQ discrepancies that were deemed indicative of psychopathology by Wechsler users were, in fact, prevalent in the standardization sample of the various Wechsler Scales, and therefore typical of children in general. In his own words Kaufman (1979) stated his case eloquently:

Large V-P differences have frequently been associated with possible brain damage, with differences exceeding 25 points considered suggestive of neurological dysfunction (Holroyd & Wright 1965). Black (1974b) found an index of neurological impairment to be significantly related to the absolute magnitude of the WISC V-P discrepancy and also discovered larger V-P differences in children with documented brain damage than in children with suspected neurological impairment or in normal youngsters (Black 1974a, 1976). He concluded that differences exceeding 15 points may be predictive of neurological dysfunction. Assertions such as those made by Holroyd and Wright or by Black must be tempered by contradictory findings [Bortner, Hertzig, et al. (1972), for example, found the WISC V-P discrepancies of brain-damaged children to be comparable to the V-P differences of normal youngsters], by the fact sizable V-P differences can be traced to a variety of causative factors other than neurological impairment (Simensen and Sutherland 1974), and by data on normal children (see Table 2.1) showing that V-P differences as large as 17 points cannot be considered "abnormal" by any reasonable statistical standard.

(Kaufman 1976c; Seashore 1951) (pp. 24–25)

Professor Kaufman used normative data and base rates of occurrence to overturn an interpretive conclusion of long standing usage, i.e., differences of 12 of 15 points between the verbal and performance IQs, were "psycho-pathological" and, thus, may warrant a diagnosis. His measurement science-based approach may have saved thousands of children from unwarranted diagnoses, and parents from unnecessary worry about their offspring. It was difficult for many to give up on this treasured set of myths as is often the case. One of the authors (C.R.R.), in a presentation discussing Kaufman's work in the late 1970s, encountered a director of special education who argued vehemently that if these profiles were commonplace in the Wechsler standardization samples, then it was the samples that were faulty and not the interpretation, the solution to their dissonance being that the WISC-R standardization sample must be full of children with a learning disability because "everyone knows that a 15 point Verbal-Performance IQ discrepancy defines a learning disability."

Kaufman (1979) went on to explicate the difference between statistical significance and rarity of score differences, a subtlety that was not widely understood by intelligence test users of the Rapaport et al. tradition and which unfortunately remains difficult for some to understand even today. In fact, statistical guidelines for interpretation were not part of this clinical interpretation tradition (Kamphaus, 2001). Professor Kaufman explained the differences between these two concepts in the following way.

Statistical criteria, based on the standard error of measurement of the difference between IQs on the Verbal and Performance Scales, have been provided by Wechsler (1974, p. 35) to help the examiner identify significant V-P discrepancies. The values required for significance, as stated earlier (p. 24), are 9 points ($p < 0.15$), 12 points ($p < 0.05$), and 15 points ($p < 0.01$). When examiners use these values they determine whether any particular discrepancy is "real," as opposed to purely a function of chance error; the level of significance chosen merely translates to the amount of confidence that can be placed in the conclusion that a child's Verbal and Performance IQs are really different (e.g., $p < 0.05$ means 95% confidence). The issue of significance, however, says nothing about the frequency with which discrepancies of various magnitudes occur within the normal population. Yet the degree to which an individual's discrepancy is common or rare, compared to others of his or her approximate ability level and background, has important interpretive significance. Analysis of standardization data (Kaufman 1976c) revealed that the average WISC-R discrepancy (regardless of direction) was 9.7 IQ points [standard deviation (SD) = 7.6] for all children aged 6–16 years. (pp. 50–51)

Kaufman (1979) went further and demonstrated that much of the observed scatter of subtest scores was not clinically meaningful, because it was typical – but unexpectedly so – of children as indicated by results from the WISC-R normative sample.

If the scaled scores on the 10 regular WISC-R subtests are rank ordered from high to low for all of the normal children in the stand-ardization sample, what will the *average difference* be between each child's highest and lowest scaled score? That is the question I posed to clinicians and then determined the answer by analyzing the WISC-R standardization data. Their answers soon became predictable: 3 or 4 points, with some bold individuals suggesting a possible range of 5 or 6 points. And yet the answer is 7 *points* (more than 2 SDs!) – based on systematic analysis of the 2200 children in the WISC-R standardization sample (Kaufman 1976b). The 7-point range so surprised me that I had the computer programmer thoroughly recheck the program and rerun the data, and I personally computed the scaled-score range by hand for an entire age group before I was able to accept the results as valid. But 7 points it was, with a standard deviation of 2 points. Two-thirds of all normal children had scaled-score ranges of 7 ± 2. From that perspective, ranges as large as 9 points were within one standard deviation of the mean and hence legitimately termed "normal." Thus the average child had a scaled-score range of 6–13 or 7–14, and even ranges of 3–12 or 9–18 fit easily into the category of normal (i.e., expected) variability. How often have children with scaled-score profiles such as these been diagnosed as learning disabled or neuro-logically impaired at least in part because of their subtest scatter? (p. 196)

Thanks to Kaufman's compelling data-based argument, the practice of interpreting scatter of typical score differences was effectively challenged, a challenge that has changed intelligence test interpretive practice forever, and likely saved children from unwarranted diagnostic labels and accusa-tions of psychopathology.

VARIANCE PARTITIONING

Dr. Kaufman introduced principles of measurement variance to clinical and school psychologists that were long understood by measurement scientists. Long before Kaufman's landmark work, Jacob Cohen (1959) published an incisive factor analytic study of the 1949 WISC that reiterated important understandings of variance components of subtests.

Kaufman built on this work and introduced it to clinicians in an understandable and usable way. In one case, he introduced the notion that reliability estimates for subtests could be partitioned into error, reliable-specific, and reliable-shared variance. Heretofore, the concept of reliable-specific variance or "subset specificity" was unknown to the practitioner psychologist. Subtest specificity (Cohen, 1959) refers to the amount of reliable variance attributable to the latent trait presumed to be measured by a single subtest. The clarity of Kaufman's prose is evident in the following explication of the concept of subtest specificity:

> First, an estimate of the common or shared variance for each subtest has to be obtained. The common variance is then subtracted from the subtest's reliability coefficient (which equals the total reliable variance for the subtest), yielding the reliable unique variance or subtest specificity. When the specificity is compared to the error variance for the subtest (equal to 1 minus the reliability), one can determine whether it is sensible to interpret that task's uniqueness. (pp. 111–112)

These concepts required clinicians to rethink their understanding of the reliability of a subtest in support of test interpretation. For the first time, it became clear to clinicians that a seemingly high reliability coefficient of .90 may, in fact, be insufficient to support an interpretive conclusion based on a single subtest score. This "reliable" subtest, for example, may be comprised of mostly shared variance, warranting interpretation of the subtest largely untenable, due to the fact that there is little subtest specific variance to support an interpretation about a uniquely measured latent trait. Of course, with the introduction of principles of structural equation modeling and its requirement for two or three indicators (e.g. subtests) to assess a latent trait, the wisdom of Kaufman's cautions regarding subtest interpretation are increasingly clear as research on intelligence test interpretation progresses.

FACTOR ANALYSIS

During the decades leading up to Kaufman's landmark work, psychologists interpreted the part (i.e. composite scores other than the Full Scale IQ) scores, e.g., Verbal and Performance IQs of the Wechsler scales at face value, without considering evidence of internal validity. Citing Cohen's (1959) and his own (Kaufman, 1975) factor analytic findings, Professor Kaufman made a strong case that these Verbal and Performance IQs were flawed measures of the latent traits of verbal and spatial abilities. He offered considerable factor analytic evidence to show that both the WISC and WISC-R measured three constructs, not two, thus rendering the obtained IQ scores less than ideal for interpretive purposes. Again, Kaufman was requiring that practitioners understand principles of measurement science that, in this instance, call for factor analytic support for obtained scores.

Dr. Kaufman's and Cohen's analyses provided compelling evidence that the Digit Span, Coding, and Arithmetic subtests were poor measures of the Verbal and Performance IQs and, in fact, shared variance adequate to create a third factor, for which a composite score was not offered. Clinicians intuited these results as they often saw these three subtest scores deviated from their composites.

Today, factor analytic studies are routinely conducted during the test development phase and used to guide the construction of part scores. At the time of publication of Kaufman's book, Wechsler used content analysis and his expert judgment to assign subtests to scales. While generally accurate, Wechsler's judgment was flawed enough to shed doubt on the interpretability of the part scores. Professor Kaufman's work not only raised the standard for internal validity (factor analytic) evidence to support score interpretation, he effectively created the standard.

Kaufman (1979) also created what has become referenced as the psychometric method of ipsative analysis of subtest profiles on aptitude tests. He carefully laid out a sound psychometric method for analyzing the performance of individuals on a battery of tests that would allow the determination not just of differences in cognitive profiles relative to a reference group such as the standardization sample, but relative to the examinee's own overall level of performance. Based in an evaluation of the standard errors associated with difference scores, which have long been known to have relatively poor reliability, Kaufman's approach provided clinicians with a practical method for partialling error variance from the profiles to reveal real differences in patterns within the aptitude spectrum of the individual. While historically clinicians had made many such interpretations, prior to Kaufman's (1979) work, they did so without a sound psychometric or statistical basis. For more than 25 years, this method captured the field and was the dominant method of intelligence test interpretation and remains widely used today. While the validity of the interpretations many clinicians have made of

Wechsler profiles based on the application of this method have not been well supported, the method itself finally allowed careful research to be conducted on the practices of clinicians and systematized much of what was a field of idiopathic interpretive methods. It is from this foundation that the field has been able to move forward.

CONCLUSIONS

Like many eminent scientists, thinkers, and talents, Dr. Alan S. Kaufman's work was precocious. His 1979 book, the impact of which is still unfolding, was completed as an assistant professor at the University of Georgia. He also inspired several generations of test authors. His former students have accounted for the conceptualization, development, and authorship of more than 40 commercially available psychological and educational tests, some of which are among the most frequently administered individual psychological tests in the United States. Not only his science but his mentorship thus has changed the face of clinical assessment for tens of millions of individuals over the years, and he remains a vital contributor to the applied measurement field. We look forward to learning from his continuing contributions.

REFERENCES

Cohen, J. (1959). The factorial structure of the WISC at ages 7-6, 10-6, and 13-6. *Journal of Consulting Psychology*, 23, 285–299.

Kamphaus, R.W. (1999). Intelligence test interpretation: Acting in the absence of evidence. In A. Prifitera & D. Saklofske (Eds.). *WISC-III Clinical Use and Interpretation: Scientist – Practitioner Perspectives* (pp. 39–57). San Diego, CA: Academic Press.

Kamphaus, R.W. (2001). *Clinical Assessment of Children's Intelligence* (2nd Ed.). Needham Heights, MA: Allyn & Bacon.

Kamphaus, R.W., Rowe, E.W., Winsor, A.P., & Kim, S. (2005). A history of intelligence test interpretation. In D. Flanagan & P. Harrison (3rd Ed) (Eds.). *Contemporary Intellectual Assessment* (pp. 23–38). New York: Guilford.

Kaufman, A.S. (1975). Factor Analysis of the WISC-R at eleven age levels between 6 ½ and 16 ½ years. *Journal of Consulting and Clinical Psychology*, 43, 135–147.

Kaufman, A.S. (1979). *Intelligent Testing with the WISC-R*. New York: Wiley.

Rapaport, D., Gil, M., & Schafer, R. (1945–1946). *Diagnostic Psychological Testing* (2 Vols.). Chicago, IL: Year Book Medical.

Reynolds, C.R., & Kamphaus, R.W. (2003). *Reynolds Intellectual Assessment Scales and Reynolds Intellectual Screening Test: Professional Manual*. Odessa, FL: Psychological Assessment Resources.

Seashore, R.H. (1951) Work & motor performance. In Stevens, S. S. (Ed.), *Handbook of experimental psychology*. New York: Wiley.

11

Success Is a Latent Variable: How Alan Kaufman Shaped Intelligence Test Theory, Interpretation, and Psychometrics with Factor Analysis

JASON C. COLE

Institute of Consulting Measurement Group

Kaufman (1990) has noted that there seems nothing more irresistible to a psychometrician than factor analysis of an IQ test. I certainly fall into that category, and therefore jumped at the opportunity to provide a chapter on Alan's influence on and with factor analysis for this book. The Kaufman Intelligent Testing system is one of the most widely used tools in cognitive assessment, which essentially mandates assessors validate the use of factors for each person they assess. I therefore do not find it an overstatement to say that Alan Kaufman's imprint on cognitive assessment with and on factor analysis is not only veritably omnipresent, but perhaps unparalleled.

Before I get too carried away discussing how Kaufman has used and refined factor analysis to the benefit of the study of cognitive assessment, I feel it appropriate to begin with a limitation. Above all, Kaufman places the most emphasis on understanding the person behind the test scores rather than the interrelationships among the measures used. "Many psychological reports stress what the scales or subtests measure instead of what aspects of the person are particularly well developed or in need of improvement; many reports are so number-oriented that the reader loses sight of the person's uniquenesses" (Kaufman & Lichtenberger, 2006, p. 22). Hence, part of the intelligent testing system of interpreting results from an IQ test is to assure that the person is always the center of attention, not the psychometrics. Psychometrics are only a litmus – once they are sufficient, the understanding of people becomes the crux of the matter.

With the disclaimer set aside, let us talk about the most exciting topic in this book: factor analysis. I have attempted to avoid much technical jargon throughout the chapter, and any such jargon is explained. Because factor analysis can be explained with different terms, it is prudent to quickly review these and their differences. Factor analysis is a nice general term that refers to evaluating the relationship between measured variables and latent variables. Equally as generic, or maybe even more so, latent structure (or latent model) refers to a specific set of relationships among manifest and latent variables (such as PIQ having influence on block design and symbol search, whereas VIQ has influence on vocabulary and number recall). Factor analysis and latent structure (latent model) can be used interchangeable. Exploratory factor analysis (EFA) refers to a technique wherein the research basically says "show me how the manifest variables cluster together so I can infer what latent variables may lead to that grouping." Conversely, confirmatory factor analysis (CFA) is a technique wherein the researcher models a specific set of relationships (X latent variable influences Y1, Y2, and Y3 manifest variables, all of which have some unreliability) and then asks the statistical software "how well does my model fit that data?"

Whether from latent modeling, factor analysis, or some other name, Alan Kaufman has helped shape the current landscape of cognitive assessment through his use of "it." Alan is an integrator when it comes to theory and factor analysis: he has merged various theories together through creative use of factor analysis to help better understand the veracity of theories for certain tests. When it comes to interpretation, perhaps no one has influenced the field more than Alan with his omnipresent intelligent testing system, which has been honed through the use of factor analysis. Finally, Alan's influence on factor analysis itself has helped keep psychometricians honest during the analyses and presentation of results. All of these concepts are detailed throughout this chapter, which I hope will better acquaint the reader with Dr. Kaufman's profound impact on cognitive assessment through the use of factor analysis.

ADVANCES TO THEORY FROM FACTOR ANALYSIS

Kaufman is an integrator. Whether he was integrating clinically driven tests with theory-driven tests or integrating multiple theoretical interpretations into a single test, Kaufman's suave understanding and exploration of factor structures has allowed for many applied advances in the theories surrounding intelligent testing. Kaufman has provided much research integrating the structures of different tests (Daleo et al., 1999; Kaufman, 1993; Kaufman, Ishikuma, & Kaufman, 1994a,b; Kaufman & McLean, 1987; Kaufman & O'Neal, 1988). According to Alan (personal communication, December 27, 2006), the most important of these was the tithing of the clinically driven Wechsler scales to the theoretically driven Kaufman scales.

Kaufman is also an innovator integrator in his (and Nadeen Kaufman's) blending of multiple theoretical perspectives into a single intelligence test. The KABC-II provides a formalized representation of this integration, but the origins of such integration go back to the Kaufmans' first test, the K-ABC. Alan's tithing of the Kaufman and Wechsler scales as well as his use of multiple theories in a single test are discussed next.

From the strongest critics (Lezak, 1988) through favorable reviews (Groth-Marnat, 1997) to Kaufman's books (Kaufman, 1994;Kaufman & Lichtenberger, 2006), the Wechsler scales have been noted to be essentially atheoretical. The concepts of Verbal and Performance IQ are clinically derived concepts rather than theoretically derived concepts (Kaufman, 1994; Kaufman & Lichtenberger, 2006). Whereas "the validity evidence from thousands of research investigations indicates the practical and clinical utility..." of the Wechsler scales and their clinical derivation (Kaufman & Lichtenberger, 2006, p. 49), there was previously little empirical evidence linking the Wechsler scales to theoretical constructs.

In the mid-1980s, Alan sought to change the lack of a link between the Wechsler scales and cognitive theory through the use of joint EFA. Joint EFA is conducted by examining the scores on two tests (e.g., IQ subtest scores) in order to see if the scores on the tests reflect similar underlying latent constructs (factors). Therefore, an atheoretical measure such as the Wechsler Intelligence Scale for Children – Revised (WISC-R; Wechsler, 1974) could be jointly factor analyzed with theoretical measures such as the K-ABC. In doing so, one could determine which of the clinically driven Wechsler factors loads on the various theoretical factors from the K-ABC. Although the K-ABC scales were developed from a cerebral specialization and Luria-Das sequential and simultaneous processing, the entire K-ABC has its roots in the general Horn and Cattell (1966) fluid-crystallized (FC) theory of intelligence. Previous research found that the three scales of the K-ABC can be conceptualized in the FC theory as follows: Achievement Scale is akin to crystallized IQ (Kaufman & Kaufman, 1983), Sequential Processing is a measure of short-term acquisition and retrieval (short-term memory) (Kaufman & Kaufman, 1983), and the Simultaneous Processing is a fluid IQ, perhaps most akin to Gv (Horn, 1991; Woodcock, 1990).

The joint factor analysis of the WISC-R and K-ABC revealed that Wechsler's clinically inspired Perceptual Organization factor measures the same construct as FC theory's fluid (or Gv) scale, a finding which holds for normal children (Kaufman & McLean, 1987; Naglieri & Jensen, 1987) and for children with learning problems (Kaufman & McLean, 1986;

Keith & Novak, 1987). Moreover, Verbal IQ and K-ABC Achievement were found to load similarly (except for two deviant subtests for children with learning disabilities, an expected result).

These joint factor analysis findings not only provided further validation of the Wechsler scales, but they also fermented a rich allotment of enhanced interpretation based on theoretical models (Kaufman, 1994). For example, by tithing the K-ABC and WISC-R, deficits on the WISC-R could be tied back to cerebral specialization theories, deficits in FC components, and more. All of these could then generate hypotheses for further specific tests in order to hone in on the exact nature of a cognitive deficit, including providing for a richer array of educational remedies. Moreover, these results have been carried forward by Kaufman, showing that the KAIT and WAIS-III are similarly aligned (Kaufman et al., 1994a), and that there is sufficient overlap between FC theory and Luria's cerebral specialization as shown via joint factor analysis of the K-ABC and KAIT for the overlapping 11- and 12-year-old children (Kaufman, 1993).

Another example of Kaufman's innovative integration with factor analysis is readily found in the KABC-II. To my knowledge (and via confirmation of Kaufman's belief, A. S. Kaufman, personal communication, December 27, 2006), the KABC-II is the first test to readily integrate summary scores for two different, though complimentary, scoring systems: Luria's sequential-simultaneous processing and the CHC cognitive theory. To be fair, Alan reminded me (personal communication, December 27, 2006) that the use of multiple theoretical perspectives was born in the original K-ABC with the integration for theories from Luria (1966, 1970, 1973) and his sequential-simultaneous processing, the cerebral specialization from Sperry (1968), and overall placed within the FC theory (Horn & Cattell, 1966). The KAIT was also a blend of FC and simultaneous-sequential theories (Lichtenberger, Broadbooks, & Kaufman, 2000).

With the KABC-II, children's intellectual performance can be examined and interpreted from one of two major current theories. Although the onus is on the examiner to select which theory shall be used a priori (Kaufman & Kaufman, 2004), the ability to create a different set of summary scores within the framework most appropriate for the child, most familiar to the assessor, or both provides an unprecedented flexibility. Research already noted demonstrated the shared variance of FC (for which CHC is mostly just an expansion) and Luria-based factors. Thus, it was not a marked stretch to affirm both factors in the KABC-II. However, because of the novelty of allowing for two different scoring systems in the KABC-II, both systems had to be examined with factor analysis to affirm their validity. Kaufman and Kaufman (2004) demonstrated in the K-ABC-II manual that each of the theoretical models yielded appropriately fitted factor models using CFA. Independent review of the standardization data from Reynolds, Keith et al. (Reynolds, Keith, Fine, Fisher, & Low, in press) also provided support that the KABC-II is well fit within the CHC model (though some small discrepancies were found). Additionally, Cole, Kaufman, and Dang (in press) conducted an exhaustive set of CFAs on ethnic and gender differences on the KABC-II for children aged 7 to 18 years. Our results indicated that both the standard and expanded versions of the CHC and Sequential-Simultaneous scores of the KABC-II were appropriately fit, including for females and males, and for African Americans, Caucasians, and Hispanics. Moreover, our results provided strong support for the structural invariance for gender and for ethnicity with either theory on either length form. In other words, the latent structure was the same for each of these demographic groups regardless of the theoretical perspective employed.[1]

ADVANCES TO INTERPRETATION FROM FACTOR ANALYSIS

The synergy between psychometrics (and factor analysis) with theory is what leads to cogent and sagacious interpretation. Kaufman has a rich history of providing us with his mastery of blending empirical results with theory in order to give us a sound system for interpretation. Indeed, this book you are reading is named after Kaufman's system of interpretation: Intelligent Testing. In addition to Kaufman's omnipresent intelligent system, he has used factor analysis in other key interpretive functions. None of these is more famous than his assignment to the named factor in the WISC-R, Freedom from Distractibility. I will attempt to provide some clarity there. Finally, Alan has noted (personal communication, December 27, 2006) that his most important advancement in interpretation related to factor analysis is his work on subtest scatter (Kaufman, 1976a) and V-P differences (Kaufman, 1976b).

Given the far greater experts in this book on cognitive testing, I would not revisit the details or benefits of Kaufman's intelligence testing system. Instead, I have been intrigued by how well it related to current tenants of CFA even though it was developed (Kaufman, 1979) years before CFA was

---

[1] Some differences were found among latent means, indicating the known differences between ethnic groups on some of the subtests. These effects were small, and did not impact the interpretation of the CFA models, which do not use latent means.

even whispered in the IQ literature. From a factor analytic perspective, one of the main tenants of the intelligent testing system is to affirm that lower-order interpretations are appropriate before moving on to higher order interpretation. In latent modeling, this same approach is undertaken with examination of the measurement model (Schumacker & Lomax, 2004). Both intelligent testing and measurement model examination require that scores are sufficiently fit to the scoring system before one can interpret larger constructs. If you try to move to interpretation of a higher-order construct (e.g., VIQ) without examination of the components within VIQ and how well they fit together, the validity of the VIQ score has been inexplicably assumed to be appropriate when tests to measure the validity exist. Whereas the Kaufman intelligent testing system provides a means for examining the validity on the individual level, CFA provides a means for determining the validity of interpretation for group-level data. Moreover, results are the same when the data do not fit the model: interpretation of the factors leads to an ever-increasing likelihood of misinterpretation of the data with greater violations of fit. Despite developing his system years before confirmatory latent modeling was part of the applied IQ literature, Kaufman's intelligent design was insisting on the same kind of data checks at the ideographic level that CFA requires at the nomothetic level.

The factor name Freedom from Distractibility in the WISC-R and WISC-III is often ascribed to Kaufman, even recently (e.g., Niklasson, Rasmussen, Óskarsdóttir, & Gillberg, 2005). Unfortunately, ascribing this factor name to Alan is not quite accurate. The eminent psychometrician Jacob Cohen had named such influences as a Freedom from Distractibility construct in previous work (Cohen, 1952, 1957) on the Wechsler scales. As Kaufman has noted (1979, 1994), Kaufman also labeled the third factor on the WISC-R as Freedom from Distractibility (Kaufman, 1975) for historical reasons based on Cohen's work, and also because he was afraid to break with tradition. However, to be clear, Kaufman has observed: "In truth, that label should have been trashed years ago. I cringe whenever I read 'Kaufman's Freedom from Distractibility factor.' It's not mine, and I don't want it" (Kaufman, 1994, p. 212). Indeed, Alan discussed with me (personal communication, December 27, 2006) that the factor should have been given a cognitive name (e.g., symbolic processing, numerical reasoning, or short-term memory) rather than a behavioral name given its use on a measure of cognitive ability. As he has noted elsewhere (Kaufman, 1994), if Freedom from Distractibility is appropriate for the third WISC-III factor then Freedom from Bad Attitude should be an appropriate label for Processing Speed (the fourth WISC-III factor), given its sensitivity to low motivation. Summarily, the label Freedom from Distractibility should not be ascribed to Kaufman, but to Cohen. Alan prefers much more appropriate titles that aid in the interpretation of this factor.

Last, but definitely not least in Alan's eyes, analysis of subtest scatter and V-P differences have helped progression interpretation in IQ. Prior to Kaufman's seminal work on these important matters, it was assumed that children with learning disabilities had a lot of test scatter. Moreover, clinical problems and brain damage were assumed to be virtually the only cause of differences between Verbal and Performance IQ (V-P differences). However, Kaufman's two papers in 1976 (Kaufman, 1976a, b) provided the first empirical investigation of significant scatter and V-P differences. Not only did this research help provide boundaries on when scatter and V-P differences should be considered significant and how frequently such patterns occurred in the general normal population, it also provided the stepping stones for the development of intelligent testing. If significant scatter was found in a profile, it soon came to reason that the construct such subtests reflected could not be considered a singular reliable entity for an individual. Conversely, when limited scatter was found, higher-order constructs were encouraged to be interpreted because they are virtually always appropriately psychometrically efficacious and thus more interpretatively beneficial (Kaufman & Lichtenberger, 2006).

ADVANCES TO PSYCHOMETRICS FROM ALAN KAUFMAN

Although Alan somewhat scoffed at the idea that he has had influence on factor analysis itself (personal communication, December 27, 2006), I believe his influence in the use of factor analysis in cognitive assessment is substantial. Kaufman (1975) provided guidelines on interpreting sufficiency of subtests loadings on g as .70 and above are good measures of g, .51 to .69 are fair, and .50 and below are poor; guidelines which are still often used today during factor analysis studies involving g influence. However, most of Kaufman's influence on the field of cognitive assessment has been through his criticism on what not to do with factor analysis.

Prior to the first book on intelligent testing, Cohen had a lot of influence on the field of cognitive assessment. Although Cohen is one of the most regarded statisticians to have published in psychology, he has been critiqued as applying overly analytic interpretations to cognitive factor analyses without regard to theory or clinical utility (Kaufman, 1979, 1994). Indeed, Cohen's factor analysis of the WISC-R was once declared as the most extreme instance of over-factor analyzing ever conducted.

With Alan's ever-growing readership of his intelligent testing system in the 1980s and 1990s came with it more regard for the synergy between psychometric efficacy and theory. Alan has made it clear that one cannot rely on psychometrics alone to interpret results; the psychometrics must themselves be guided by theory, and interpretations of results conducted similarly (personal communication, December 27, 2006). Once again, Alan had posited a stance that eventually became a mandate from the confirmatory latent modeling literature: theory must guide the development of a latent model and not the other way around (Cole et al., 2005; Schumacker & Lomax, 2004). With EFA, it was too easy to rely strictly on the psychometric results without care for theory, even when it came to interpretation. However, with the development and omnipresent availability of CFA techniques, a clear distinction between EFA and CFA was presented (Floyd & Widaman, 1995). EFA was only appropriate for variable reduction from a set of variables (i.e., items from a subtest, or subtests from a general construct), and perhaps in rare cases when no theory was available it could be used to initially examine the latent factors of a set of variables. Whenever one had an appropriate theory (and hopefully competing theories), then confirmatory modeling is to be enacted, allowing for a test and comparison of the efficacy of how well one's data fit the theoretical model. Essentially, Alan has been arguing for the tenants of CFA over EFA several years before CFA was used in applied cognitive research.

Finally, Alan has also had his influence on factor analysis use in cognitive assessment through his prolific work as a reviewer for many of the top journals in cognitive assessment. This influence of his has come out in three ways, including limiting "knee-jerk" principal component analysis (PCA), correcting methods for how many factors to include, and critiquing the use of poorly executed CFA as a means to boondoggle the reviewers into believing poor results.

Alan conveyed to me that (personal communication, December 27, 2006), especially back in the 1980s and 1990s, he frequently had to reject papers based on the "knee-jerk" execution of PCA. PCA was once considered to be a very-near cousin of general EFA, except that it explained 100 percent of each test within the latent structure (Comrey & Lee, 1992). This was once considered to be desirable, as we often hope to explain as much of the variance as possible. Nevertheless, PCA conducted the complete explanation of variance by employing formative latent models. Without getting too technical, formative latent models assume that (a) one's external variables are 100 percent reliable and (b) that it is the combination of such variables that creates a latent factor (Kline, 2006) (these issues are mathematically related, but discussed separately for conceptual issues). A great example of where this works well is with socioeconomic status (SES). Consider education level, annual income, and parent's highest educational level as components for the creation of SES. Each of these three variables could be measured without flaw, thereby allowing them to be considered (at least theoretically) as 100 percent reliable. Moreover, we would not consider the latent construct of one's current SES to influence one's educational status, annual income, and especially not one's parent's highest educational level. Therefore, considering the combination of these three variables to have an influence on SES makes theoretical sense. Unfortunately, the formative model does not work in cognitive assessment. First, we know that the subtests are never perfectly reliable, and this is partially so because we are measuring complex tasks that sometimes involve chance. More importantly, we do not think of one's score on block design as influencing their PIQ. Instead, scores on PIQ reflect (or are influenced by) PIQ. Hence, cognitive assessment should almost always be interpreted from a reflective measurement model (Kline, 2006, provides more discussion on formative and reflective models).

Alan also had to critique researchers' determination of how many factors to interpret. According to Alan (personal communication, December 27, 2006), the most frequent problem he encountered from authors determining how many factors to keep was the use of the Kaiser–Guttman criterion (see Gorsuch, 1983) when examining factor analysis (and not PCA) results (i.e., applying the rule to interpret eigenvalues of 1.0 or more). Indeed, I still see this problem in the papers I review today. The problem with the Kaiser–Guttman criterion is that it is only appropriate for PCA (which, as noted, has its own problems for us in cognitive assessment). Alan has tried to encourage researchers to use a combination of statistical techniques that are appropriate (such as Scree plots, and so forth; see Preacher & MacCallum, 2003) along with theoretical rational.

Finally, Alan has been a critic of misuse of CFA in cognitive research. Specifically, he is concerned that CFA can be used to show support for whatever factor structure is desired by conducting an incomplete analysis (personal communication, December 27, 2006). Unfortunately, such incomplete analyses are not hard to conduct for a few reasons. First, with the popularity of easy-to-use CFA programs such as AMOS (Arbuckle, 2006),[2] it is easy for

---

[2] For which I believe is excellent, and I have served as a technical reviewer for the AMOS author on the last two versions. My concern is use of any program without proper instruction.

researchers without a complete understanding of latent modeling to run a few models and show a few favorable results without understanding all of the technical minutia, which must be addressed for proper interpretation. Second, and perhaps more nefarious, interpretation of model results can be misinformed in a few important ways. For example, a plethora of fit statistics are now available, many of which have complimentary functions to one another (Hu & Bentler, 1999). Interpreting only one or two of the primary fit statistics should raise concern that the model may be misfit in other ways not shown by the authors. Schumacker and Lomax (2004) recommended presenting several fit statistics so the reader can determine how the model does, and perhaps does not, fit the data. As another example, CFA is most powerful when used to compare competing models to one another (Vandenberg & Lance, 2000). Yet this can be poorly portrayed by either comparing the "ideal" model to a model doomed to fail or by not comparing it at all.

SUMMARY

When I entered graduate school, I was certain the life ahead of me was as a therapist and I wanted little to do with research, especially mathematical models of human cognition. I went to a very empirically based under-graduate program and, in my "well-versed" opinion back then, felt that mathematical models of human cognition were missing the essence of the person. Twelve years later, I head a statistical consulting company and work with industry to develop psychometrically sound models of human cognition and experience. What happened in between was one of the richest experiences of my life – working under the tutelage of Alan Kaufman.

I view my own transition similar to that of what many graduate students go through when learning the Kaufman intelligent testing system. We began by believing that just our being with a person was enough to fully understand them. Then, after exposure to such works as *clinical versus actuarial judgment* (Dawes, Faust, & Meehl, 1989), we made a major shift to thinking that our clinical skills were useless in the face of empirical data. Finally, we met Dr. Kaufman (or at least his text). When we entered our assessment course, we felt that this was the pinnacle of empirical over clinical, reason over empathy, numbers over people. However, the zeitgeist of the intelligent testing era took us into new areas: finally, we had synergy between empirical validation and theory, between clinical efficacy and psychometric efficacy, and between the number and the person.

Kaufman's work in improving the field of cognitive assessment with factor analysis is not impressive because of its methodological sophistication (for which he was often ahead of his times). Instead, Kaufman's use of factor analysis is so impressive because we often do not notice the sophistication behind it. One need not know about oblique rotation or root mean square error of approximation in order to understand that too much scatter means we do not interpret high-order constructs. One does not need to analyze polychoric correlation matrices with multigroup structural equation modeling to use two different scoring systems in the KABC-II. Alan has made these benefits available to researchers in order to better understand the person without putting the umbrage of latent modeling particulars in every person we assess. That is what makes Alan's work with and on factor analysis in cognitive assessment an act of a master.

REFERENCES

Arbuckle, J.L. (2006). AMOS (Version 7.0). Chicago, IL: Small Waters.

Cohen, J. (1952). A factor-analytically based rationale for the Wechsler–Bellevue. *Journal of Consulting Psychology*, 16, 272–277.

Cohen, J. (1957). A factor-analytically based rationale for the Wechsler Adult Intelligence Scale. *Journal of Consulting Psychology*, 21, 451–457.

Cohen, J.C., Kaufman, J.C., & Dang, J. (in press). Ethnic and gender invariance on the KABC-II: A multigroup structural validation for ages 7–18 years. *International Journal of Testing*.

Cole, J.C., Motivala, S.J., Khanna, D., Lee, J.Y., Paulus, H.E., & Irwin, M.R. (2005). Validation of a single-factor structure and the scoring protocol for the Health Assessment Questionnaire-Disability Index (HAQ-DI). *Arthritis Care and Research*, 53, 536–542.

Comrey, A.L., & Lee, H.B. (1992). *A First Course in Factor Analysis* (2nd ed.). Hillsdale, NJ: Lawrence Erlbaum.

Daleo, D.V., Lopez, B.R., Cole, J.C., Kaufman, A.S., Kaufman, N.L., Newcomer, B.L., et al. (1999). K-ABC simultaneous processing, DAS non-verbal reasoning, and Horn's expanded fluid-crystallized theory. *Psychological Reports*, 84, 563–574.

Dawes, R.M., Faust, D., & Meehl, P.E. (1989). Clinical versus actuarial judgment. *Science*, 243, 1668–1673.

Floyd, F.J., & Widaman, K.F. (1995). Factor analysis in the development of clinical assessment instruments. *Psychological Assessment*, 7, 286–299.

Gorsuch, R.L. (1983). *Factor Analysis*. Hillsdale, NJ: Lawrence Erlbaum.

Groth-Marnat, G. (1997). *Handbook of Psychological Assessment* (3rd ed.). New York: Wiley.

Horn, J.L. (1991). Measurement of intellectual capabilities: A review of theory. In K.S. McGrew, J.K. Werder & R.W. Woodcock (Eds.), *Woodcock-Johnson Technical Manual: A Reference on Theory and Current Research* (pp. 197–246). Allen, TX: DLM Teaching Resources.

Horn, J.L., & Cattell, R.B. (1966). Refinement and test of the theory of fluid and crystallized intelligence. *Journal of Educational Psychology, 57,* 253–270.

Hu, L.-t., &Bentler, P.M. (1999). Cutoff criteria for fit indexes in covariance structure analysis: Conventional criteria versus new alternatives. *Structural Equation Modeling, 6,* 1–55.

Kaufman, A.S. (1975). Factor analysis of the WISC-R at 11 age levels between 6 1/2 years and 16 1/2 years. *Journal of Consulting and Clinical Psychology, 43,* 135–147.

Kaufman, A.S. (1976a). A new approach to the interpretation of test scatter on the WISC-R. *Journal of Learning Disabilities, 9,* 160–168.

Kaufman, A.S. (1976b). Verbal-Performance IQ discrepancies on the WISC-R. *Journal of Consulting and Clinical Psychology, 44* (739–744).

Kaufman, A.S. (1979). *Intelligent Testing with the WISC-R.* New York: Wiley.

Kaufman, A.S. (1990). *Assessing Adolescent and Adult Intelligence.* Boston, MA: Allyn and Bacon.

Kaufman, A.S. (1993). Joint exploratory factor analysis of the Kaufman Assessment Battery for Children and the Kaufman Adolescent and Adult Intelligence Test for 11- and 12-year olds. *Journal of Clinical Child Psychology, 22,* 355–364.

Kaufman, A.S. (1994). *Intelligent Testing with the WISC-III.* New York: Wiley.

Kaufman, A.S., Ishikuma, T., & Kaufman, N.L. (1994a). A horn analysis of the factors measured by the WAIS-R, Kaufman adolescent and adult intelligence test (KAIT), and two new brief cognitive measures for normal adolescents and adults. *Assessment, 1,* 353–366.

Kaufman, A.S., Ishikuma, T., & Kaufman, N.L. (1994b). Joint factor structure of the WISC-R and K-ABC for referred school children. *Assessment, 1,* 353–366.

Kaufman, A.S., & Kaufman, N.L. (1983). *Kaufman Assessment Battery for Children (K-ABC) Interpretive Manual.* Circle Pines, MN: American Guidance Service.

Kaufman, A.S., & Kaufman, N.L. (2004). *Kaufman Assessment Battery for Children – Second Edition (KABC-II) Administration and Scoring Manual.* Circle Pines, MN: American Guidance Service.

Kaufman, A.S., & Lichtenberger, E.O. (2006). *Assessing Adolescent and Adult Intelligence* (3rd ed.). New York: Wiley.

Kaufman, A.S., & McLean, J.E. (1986). K-ABC/WISC-R factor analysis for a learning disabled population. *Journal of Learning Disabilities, 19,* 145–153.

Kaufman, A.S., & McLean, J.E. (1987). Joint factor analysis of the K-ABC and WISC-R with normal children. *Journal of School Psychology, 25,* 105–118.

Kaufman, A.S., & O'Neil, M. (1988). Analysis of the cognitive, achievement, and general factors underlying the Woodcock-Johnson Psycho-Educational Battery. *Journal of Clinical Child Psychology, 17,* 143–151.

Keith, T.Z., & Novak, C.G. (1987). Joint factor structure of the WISC-R and K-ABC for referred school children. *Journal of Psychoeducational Assessment, 5,* 370–386.

Kline, R.B. (2006). Formative measurement and feedback loops. In G.R. Hancock & R.O. Mueller (Eds.), *Structural Equation Modeling: A Second Course* (pp. 43–68). Greenwich, CT: Information Age Publishing.

Lezak, M.D. (1988). IQ: R.I.P. *Journal of Clinical and Experimental Neuropsychology, 10,* 351–361.

Lichtenberger, E.O., Broadbooks, D.A., & Kaufman, A.S. (2000). *Essentials of Cognitive Assessment with KAIT and Other Kaufman Measures.* New York: Wiley.

Luria, A.R. (1966). *Higher Cortical Functions in Man.* New York: Harper & Row.

Luria, A.R. (1970). The functional organization of the brain. *Scientific American,* 222, 66–78.

Luria, A.R. (1973). *The Working Brain: An Introduction to Neuropsychology.* New York: Basic Books.

Naglieri, J.A., & Jensen, A.R. (1987). Comparison of black-white differences on the WISC-R and the K-ABC: Spearman's hypothesis. *Intelligence,* 11, 21–43.

Niklasson, L., Rasmussen, P., Óskarsdóttir, S., & Gillberg, C. (2005). Attention deficits in children with 22q.11 deletion syndrome. *Developmental Medicine & Child Neurology,* 47, 803–807.

Preacher, K.J., & MacCallum, R.C. (2003). Repairing Tom Swift's electric factor analysis machine. *Understanding Statistics,* 2, 13–43.

Reynolds, M.R., Keith, T.Z., Fine, G.J., Fisher, M.E., & Low, J. (in press). Confirmatory factor structure of the Kaufman Assessment Battery for Children - Second Edition: Consistency with Cattell-Horn-Carroll theory. *School Psychology Review.*

Schumacker, R.E., & Lomax, R.G. (2004). *A Beginner's Guide to Structural Equation Modeling* (2nd ed.). Mahwah, NJ: Lawrence Erlbaum.

Sperry, R.W. (1968). Hemispheric deconnection and unity in conscious awareness. *American Psychologist,* 23, 723–733.

Vandenberg, R.J., & Lance, C.E. (2000). A review and synthesis of the measurement invariance literature: Suggestions, practices, and recommendations for organizational research. *Organizational Research Methods,* 3, 4–70.

Wechsler, D. (1974). *Manual for the Wechsler Intelligence Scale for Children - Revised (WISC-R).* San Antonio, TX: Psychological Corporation.

Woodcock, R.W. (1990). Theoretical foundations of the WJ-R measures of cognitive ability. *Journal of Psychoeducational Assessment,* 8, 231–258.

PART 4

KAUFMAN ACROSS THE WORLD

12

The K-ABC in France

CLAIRE ÉNÉA-DRAPEAU
Aix Marseille University and CNRS
University Institute of France

MICHÈLE CARLIER
Aix Marseille University, CNRS, and University

The K-ABC was introduced in France by three researchers (Christiane Capron, Michèle Carlier, and Michel Duyme) who wanted to use a new assessment of cognitive performance for an extensive study of children in France. They decided to translate the mental processing part only. At almost the same time, the publishing house *Editions du Centre de Psychologie Appliquée* obtained the rights to translate and publish the test. The adaptation of the test was a long process and the researchers and the publisher's research manager Mireille Simon developed an excellent working relationship with M. Carlier and M. Duyme. Moreover M. Carlier and Rose-Marie Bourgault translated the two American manuals. The K-ABC was published in France in 1993, and since then has been used extensively by both practitioners and researchers. The first part of this chapter presents a general report on the use of the French version of the K-ABC by researchers, and reviews studies conducted in France (and probably unknown in North America as many of them were published in French only). The second part contains information on training to use the K-ABC in psychology programs in French universities, and also on the use of the K-ABC by French practitioners.

FRENCH STUDIES USING THE K-ABC

After the French version of the K-ABC was launched, one of the first publications was a book devoted solely to the K-ABC: Kaufman et al., 1994, *K-ABC Pratique et fondements théoriques* [*K-ABC, Practice and Theoretical Foundations*]. Robert Voyazopoulos was behind the initiative, and reported on the first research projects using the K-ABC conducted in France (the first two chapters of the book were written by Alan S. Kaufman and Randy W. Kamphaus). It is interesting to see that the book covered most of the key topics developed subsequently, e.g., the advantages of the K-ABC over other intelligence tests (Lemmel, Meljac, and Gillet), a study of the factorial and external validities of the scales used (Spitz), a qualitative analysis (Lemmel), the use of the test for atypical populations (Petot; Adrien et al.; Douet and Brabant), and its application to studies of specific cognitive disorders (Tribhou).

Papers Published in Journals

We have found six papers in English written by French teams reporting on the French version of the K-ABC. Billard, Livet, Motte, Vallee, Gillet (2002) validated a neuropsychological test battery with the K-ABC as one of the external criteria. Grégoire (1995) published a shortened version of his original French paper on the Mantel-Haenszel procedure as a means of analysing the differential item functioning comparing girls and boys in the French adaptation of the K-ABC. Planche (2002) described the performance of autistic children on the basis of the K-ABC.

Carlier used the K-ABC in three research programs. Spitz et al. studied populations of twins (1996) and selected the K-ABC because of the focus on information processing. For the other two studies, the K-ABC was used to assess the cognitive functioning of children with autism (Tordjman et al., 2001) and of patients with a genetic disease – *OPHN* 1 mutations. In the third study, the K-ABC gave a better description of strengths and weaknesses in cognitive functioning compared to the Wechsler scales where a floor effect was observed for some patients (Chabrol et al., 2005).

Further papers published in French and found in data bases are listed in Table 12.1. There are not many (31 publications in 18 journals; see Table 12.1). Perhaps our search of data bases was not sufficiently thorough, but a more likely explanation would be that there are fewer papers on the K-ABC than on the Wechsler scales. This was particularly the case of research projects on cohorts of normally developing subjects. Most of the papers listed in Table 12.1 are on children with a disability (motor, sensory, or intellectual). Other studies of nondisabled groups include comparisons of the K-ABC and Wechsler scales and assessments of the internal or external validity of the French version.

Chapters and Books

Many French textbooks on psychological assessments, for both undergraduate and graduate students, present the K-ABC [e.g., Huteau & Lautrey (2003, 2006), Lautrey (2001), Petot (2003), and Tourrette (2006)]. The

TABLE 12.1. *Papers published in french using the french version of the K-ABC (Alphabetical order of journals. Full references are listed under "References")*

Journal	Date	Author(s)	Subject
ANAE – Approche neuropsychologique des apprentissages chez l'enfant	2000	Gomot, Blanc, Barthelemy, Isingrini, Adrien	Children with developmental disorders
	2003	Pry, Guillain, LeDesert	North African immigrant children
	2004	Deforge, Toniolo	Preterm children
Annales médico psychologiques	2002	Planche. Lemonnier., Moalic, Labous, Lazarigues	Children with autism
Archives de pédiatrie	2003	Blondet al.	Preterm children
	2006	Deforge	Preterm children
Bulletin de Psychologie	2002	Planche	Effect of bilingualism on cognitive performance
Bulletin de Psychologie Scolaire et d'Orientation	1993	Stassen	Description of the new French K-ABC
	1995	Grégoire	Critical review of the utility of the K-ABC in intelligence testing and diagnosis of learning disabilities in children
Enfance	1996	Pry, Guillain, Foxonet	Socio-cognitive skills in young children
	1999	Petot	Weakness of sequential processes among hyperactive children and attention disorder
	2005	Frenkel, Lagneau, Vandromme	Attempt to adapt the K-ABC to individuals with Trisomy 21 to avoid leveling effect
European Review of Applied Psychology/Revue Européenne de Psychologie Appliquée	2001	Bernoussi, Khomsi, Florin	Longitudinal study of the factorial structure of the K-ABC.

(continued)

TABLE 12.1 (continued)

Journal	Date	Author(s)	Subject
Handicap Revue De Sciences Humaines Et Sociales	1999	Vergniaux, Deret, Jamet	Adaptation of matrix analogies for children with visual impairment
	2001	Heyndrickx, Jamet, Deret	Test of efficiency of learning spatial localisation using 3 subtests of the K-ABC (Triangles, Gestalt closure and Spatial memory) in children with cerebral palsy
Journal de thérapie comportementale et cognitive	2006	Gattegno, Abenhaim, Kremer, Castro, Adrien	Longitudinal study of cognitive and social development of an child with autism enrolled in a home coaching program
Neuropsychiatrie de l'enfance et de l'adolescence	1997	Pry	K-ABC and mental retardation
	1998	Lemmel, Bailly, Meljac	Abilities and personality of 18 children with Williams-Beuren syndrome
Perspectives Psychiatriques	1994	Meljac, Bailly, Du Pasquier	Cognitive processes in children with Williams-Beuren Syndrome
Psychologie & éducation	1997	Florin, Bernoussi, Capponi, Giraudeau, Khomsi	Effects of early schooling on cognitive and language performance and school behavior
	1997	Pry, Guillain	Longitudinal study of migrant children compared to a standard cohort
	2001	Laffaiteur, Casali, Gualbert, Madeline	Comparison of WICS-III and K-ABC
	2003	Zanga	Comparison of WICS-III and K-ABC
Psychologie clinique et projective	2000	Weismann-Arcache.	Use of the K-ABC in a psychoanalytical case study

176

	Year	Authors	Title
Psychologie et psychométrie	1998	Pry, Guillain	Socio-cognitive skills among children
Psychologie Française	2004	Lemmel	Study of under-achievement in school children using the Rorschach comprehensive system. The K-ABC as used to assess general cognitive level
	2006	Pochon, Brun, Mellier	Emotional recognition in children with trisomy 21 matched using the K-ABC, non-verbal scale to the developmental age of other mentally disabled children and typically developing children
Revue européenne du handicap mental	2003	Wierzbicki	Children with Trisomy 21
Revue neurologique	2002	Billard et al.	Validation of a clinical scale for cognitive function in preschool and school-age children. The K-ABC is a external criterion
	2005	Coste-Zeitoun et al.	Evaluation of children with severe, specific language and/or reading disorders over an academic year, after specific remedial therapy
Revue francophone de la déficience intellectuelle	1999	Bonnaud, Jamet, Deret, Neyt-Dumesnil	Performance on Face Recognition subtest in adults with severe intellectual disability

proceedings of some meetings also include brief descriptions of research done using the K-ABC, e.g., the proceedings of the *Journées de Psychologie Differentielle* (a conference held every two years, with the proceedings published by Presse Universitaire de Rennes). Bailleux et al. (2006) assessed cognitive skill in 400 preschoolers tested on 24 cognitive tasks including one K-ABC subtest (Reading/Understanding). Petot (2002) analyzed the Rorschach results of depressive children with suicidal ideation and measured their cognitive level with both the Weschler and K-ABC scales.

POSITION OF THE K-ABC IN THE PRACTICE OF PSYCHOLOGY IN FRANCE

Three years after the publication of the French K-ABC, an extensive survey showed that it was one of the top ten tests most used by French practitioners (Castro, Meljac, & Joubert, 1996). It is widely used in French schools where school psychologists are involved in the detection of learning disorders. On some official Web sites of the French National education authority, the K-ABC is recommended for general cognitive assessment or to evaluate learning levels (see, for example, http://www.ia53.ac-nantes.fr). Some clinical psychologists remain disappointed and have called for more research into cognitive remediation programs for children whose weak and/or strong points were diagnosed with the K-ABC (Cognet, 2001).

In 2007, the French National Health Institute (Institut National de la Santé et de la Recherche Médicale – Inserm) published a critical analysis of the literature on dyslexia, innumeracy and dysorthography. In the section on prevention and support, the authors noted that the K-ABC and the Wechsler scales did not accurately identify children likely to have learning impairments. However, they accepted as valid subtests for Reading/Decoding, Reading/Understanding, and Arithmetic when assessing current levels of literacy and numeracy.

K-ABC TRAINING IN PSYCHOLOGY PROGRAMS IN FRENCH UNIVERSITIES

A small-scale survey of psychology courses in university departments of psychology in France shows that these courses can include training in the K-ABC in the third (i.e. final) year of a bachelor's degree, but in most cases it is done in first or second year of a master's degree when specializing in clinical or developmental psychology. Most departments have a library of tests which includes the K-ABC.

CONCLUSION

It can be concluded that in France the K-ABC is widely used by researchers studying specific populations of disabled subjects, but is even more widely used by practitioners wishing to have a valid instrument to assess children before programming cognitive remediation. The second edition of the French K-ABC has been released in June 2008 (ECPA 2008). It is interesting to add that a new computerized test has been recently developed by Nadeen and Alan Kaufman specifically for French-speaking countries: the K-CLASSIC (ECPA 2007).

REFERENCES

Bailleux, C., Piolat, M., Paour, J.-L., Cèbe, S., Goigoux, R., Pellenq, C., & Blaye, A. (2006). Évaluer les processus cognitifs généraux en GS pour prévenir les difficultés d'apprentissage en CP: l'utilisation du Cognitive Assessment System (C.A.S.) de Das & Naglieri. In: Houssemand, C., Martin, R., & Dickes, P. (sous la direction de) *Perspectives de psychologie différentielle* (pp. 53–57). Rennes: PUR.

Bernoussi M., Khomsi A., & Florin A. (2001). La structure factorielle du K. ABC: Une étude longitudinale [The factorial structure of the K-ABC Battery: a longitudinal study]. *European Review of Applied Psychology/Revue Européenne de Psychologie Appliquée*, 51(3), 169–177.

Billard C., Vol S., Livet M.O., Motte J., Vallee L., Gillet P., & Marquet T. (2002). BREV: une batterie rapide clinique d'évaluation des fonctions cognitives chez les enfants d'âge scolaire et préscolaire: Etalonnage chez 500 enfants de référence et validation chez 202 enfants épileptiques [BREV: a rapid clinical scale for cognitive function in preschool and school-age children]. *Revue neurologique Paris*, 158(2), 167–175.

Billard C., Livet M.O., Motte J., Vallee L., & Gillet P. (2002). The BREV neuropsychological test: Part I. Results from 500 normally developing children. *Developmental Medicine and Child Neurology*, 44(6): 391–7.

Blond M.H., Castello-Herbreteau B., Ajam E., Lecuyer A.I. Fradet A., Patat F., Dupin R., Deletang N., Laugier J., Gold F. Saliba E., & Bremond M. (2003). Devenir médical, cognitif et affectif à l'âge de quatre ans des prématurés indemnes de handicap sévère. Étude prospective cas-témoins [Medical, cognitive and affective status of four-year-old very premature babies without severe disability. A case–control study]. *Archives de pédiatrie Paris*, 10(2), 117–125.

Bonnaud C., Jamet F., Deret D., & Neyt-Dumesnil C. (1999). La reconnaissance de visages chez des adultes présentant un retard mental profond [Recognition of human faces by adults with severe mental retardation]. *Revue francophone de la déficience intellectuelle*, 10(1), 5–17.

Chabrol B., Girard N., N'Guyen K., Gérard A., Carlier M., Villard L., & Philip N. (2005). Delineation of the clinical phenotype associated with OPHN-1 mutations based on the clinical and neuropsychological evaluation of three families. *American Journal of Medical Genetics. A.* 138, 314–317.

Cognet G. (2001, Avril). La pratique des tests d'intelligence. *Le journal des psychologues,* 181, 30–33.

Coste-Zeitoun D., Pinton F., Barondiot C., Ducot B., Warszawski J., & Billard C. (2005). Évaluation ouverte de l'efficacité de la prise en charge en milieu spécialisé de 31 enfants avec un trouble spécifique sévère du langage oral/écrit [Specific remedial therapy in a specialist unit: evaluation of 31 children with severe, specific language or reading disorders over an academic year]. *Revue neurologique Paris,* 161(3), 299–310.

Dalens H., Sole M., Neyrial M., Villedieu K., & Coulangeon L.M. (2003). La reconnaissance visuelle d'images chez l'enfant normal de 3 à 8 ans: étude de 100 cas [Visual face recognition in normal children from 3 to 8 years of age: A study with 100 cases]. *Revue de neuropsychologie Marseille,* 13(4), 411–425.

Deforge H., Andre M., Hascoet J.M., Toniolo A.M., Demange V., & Fresson J. (2006). Développement cognitif et performances attentionnelles de l'ancien prématuré "normal" à l'âge scolaire [Cognitive development and attention performance at school age of "normal" prematurely born children]. *Archives de pédiatrie Paris,* 13(9), 1195–1201.

Deforge H., & Toniolo A.M. (2004) Un outil précieux pour l'évaluation du fonctionnement cognitif des enfants anciens prématurés: Le K-ABC [A precious aid for the assessment of preterm children's cognitive functioning: K-ABC]. *A.N.A.E. Approche Neuropsychologique des Apprentissages chez l'Enfant,* 16, (1–2), [76–77], 153–161.

Florin A., Bernoussi M., Capponi I., Giraudeau C., & Khomsi A. (1997). Scolarisation précoce et autres modes de garde. *Psychologie & Education,* 28, 67–83.

Frenkel S., Lagneau F., & Vandromme L. (2005). Essai d'adaptation du K-ABC à une population d'enfants avec trisomie 21 [K-ABC: an adaptation for children with Trisomy 21]. *Enfance,* 4, 317–334.

Gattegno M.P., Abenhaim N., Kremer A., Castro C., & Adrien J.L. (2006). Étude longitudinale du développement cognitif et social d'un enfant autiste bénéficiant du programme IDDEES [Longitudinal study of cognitive and social development of an autistic child enrolled in a home coaching program (IDHSFC)]. *Journal de thérapie comportementale et cognitive,* 16(4), 157–168.

Gomot M., Blanc R., Barthelemy C., Isingrini M., & Adrien J.L. (2000). Psychopathologie des processus cognitifs et attentionnels chez des enfants présentant des troubles du développement [Attentional processes in children with developmental disorders]. *A.N.A.E. Approche Neuropsychologique des Apprentissages chez l'Enfant.* 11(1) [56], 7–12.

Grégoire J. (1995). La Kaufman Assessment Battery for Children (K-ABC). Un progrès pour l'évaluation diagnostique? [The Kaufman Assessment Battery for Children (K-ABC): an advance in diagnostic evaluation?] *Bulletin de Psychologie Scolaire et d'Orientation.* 44(2), 65–85.

Grégoire J. (*1995*). Application de la méthode de Mantel-Haenszel à l'analyse du fonctionnement différentiel des items du K-ABC entre filles et garçons [Application of the Mantel-Haenszel procedure to analyse the differential item functioning between girls and boys in the French adaptation of the K-ABC]. *European Review of Applied Psychology,* 45(2), 111–119.

Heyndrickx I., Jamet F., & Deret D. (2001). La représentation de l'espace chez des enfants IMC: rôle de l'image mentale. *Handicap Revue De Sciences Humaines Et Sociales*, 91, 51–63.

Huteau M., & Lautrey J. (2003). Evaluer l'intelligence: Psychométrie cognitive. Paris: Presse Universitaire de France.

Huteau M., & Lautrey J. (2006). Les tests d'intelligence. Paris, France: Editions La découverte.

Kaufman A. (1993). K-ABC Pratique et fondements théoriques [K-ABC, Practice and theoretical foundations]. Grenoble, France: Editions La Pensée Sauvage.

Kaufman A.S, & Kaufman, N.L. (1993). K-ABC Batterie pour l'examen psychologique de l'enfant. Paris, France: ECPA.

Kaufman A.S., & Kaufman, N.L. (2007). K-CLASSIC Evaluation informatisée des capacités cognitives et attentionnelle. Paris, France: ECPA.

Kaufman A.S, & Kaufman, N.L. (2008). K-ABC II Batterie pour l'examen psychologique de l'enfant. Deuxième édition. Paris, France: ECPA.

Laffaiteur J.P., Casali M., Gualbert J.M., & Madeline C. (2001). Étude comparative du WISC-III et du K. ABC. *Psychologie & Education*, 46, 115–131.

Lautrey, J. (2001). L'évaluation de l'intelligence: état actuel et tentatives de renouvellemet. In M. Huteau, Les figures de l'intelligence (pp. 19–42). Paris, France: Editions et Applications Psychologiques.

Lemmel G. (2004). Penser autrement les difficultés scolaires: les apports du Rorschach en système intégré [Rethinking academic difficulties: the contributions of the Rorschach comprehensive system]. *Psychologie Française*, 49, 51–62.

Lemmel L.G, Bailly L, & Meljac C. (1998). Aptitudes et personnalité d'enfants atteints du syndrome de Williams-Beuren: Nouvelles perspectives. *Neuropsychiatrie de l'enfance et de l'adolescence*, 46(12), 605–617

Meljac C., Bailly L., & Du Pasquier Y. (1994). Le syndrome de Williams-Beuren: une recherche sur les particularités des processus de pensée. Du secteur à la recherche en psychiatrie infanto-juvénile. *Perspectives-Psychiatriques*, 33(41),50–52.

Petot D. (1999). Enfants hyperactifs: troubles cognitifs spécifiques et troubles de l'attention [Specific cognitive disturbances among hyperactive children and attention disorder]. *Enfance*, 2, 137–156.

Petot D. (2002). Rorschach characteristics of depressive children with suicidal ideation. In A. Andronikof (Ed). *Rorschachiana XXV: Yearbook of the International Rorschach Society* (pp. 163–174). Ashland, OH, US: Hogrefe & Huber Publishers.

Petot D. (2003). *L'évaluation clinique en psychopathologie de l'enfant*. Paris: Dunod.

Planche P., Lemonnier E., Moalic K., Labous C., & Lazarigues A. (2002). Les modalités du traitement de l'information chez les enfants autistes [Modalities of information processing in autistic children]. *Annales médico psychologiques*, 160, 559–564.

Planche P. (2002). L'apprentissage d'une seconde langue dès l'école maternelle: quelle influence sur le raisonnement de l'enfant? *Bulletin de Psychologie*, 55(5)/461, 535–842.

Pochon R., Brun P., & Mellier D. (2006). Développement de la reconnaissance des émotions chez l'enfant avec trisomie 21 [Emotional recognition in children with Trisomy 21: Developmental approach]. *Psychologie Française*, 51, 381–390.

Pry R., Guillain A. (1998). Adaptation sociale et adaptation scolaire: évaluation des compétences socio-cognitives chez l'enfant de 3 à 6 ans [Social and school adaptation: assessment of socio-cognitive skills of children aged 3–6]. *Psychologie et psychométrie*, 19, 5–16.

Pry R. (1997). K-ABC et retard mental. Cognition et développement [K-ABC and mental retardation. Cognition and development]. *Neuropsychiatrie de l'enfance et de l'adolescence*, 45, 396–398.

Pry R., & Guillain A. (1997). Comportements adaptatifs, compétences cognitives et devenir scolaire d'enfants entre 4 et 7 ans [Adaptive behavior, cognitive skills and school outcomes in 4 to 7 year-old children]. *Psychologie & Education*, 29, 63–75.

Pry R., Guillain A., & Foxonet C. (1996). Adaptation sociale et compétences socio-cognitives chez l'enfant de 4–5 ans [Social adaptation and socio-cognitive skills in children 4–5 years of age]. *Enfance*, 3, 315–329.

Pry R., Guillain A., & LeDesert B. (2003). Anxiété et performances cognitives chez des enfants de 9 à 11 ans issus de l'immigration [Anxiety and cognitive performance in 9 to 11 year old children from immigrant families]. *A.N.A.E. Approche Neuropsychologique des Apprentissages chez l'Enfant*, 15(1) [71], 43–47.

Spitz E., Carlier M., Vacher-Lavenu M.-C., Reed T., Moutier R., Busnel M.-C., & Roubertoux P.L. (1996). [Long-term effect of prenatal heterogeneity among monozygotes]. *CPC Cahiers de Psychology Cognitive Current Psychology of Cognition*, 15, 283–308.

Stassen M. (1993). Un nouveau test individuel d'intelligence: le K-ABC [A new individual intelligence test: the Kaufman Assessment Battery for Children (K-ABC)]. *Bulletin de Psychologie Scolaire et d'Orientation*, 42(4), 169–175.

Tordjman S., Gutknecht L., Carlier M., Spitz E., Antoine C, Slama F., Carsalade V., Cohen D.J., Ferrari P., Roubertoux P.L., & Anderson G.M. (2001). Role of the serotonin transporter gene in the behavioral expression of autism. *Molecular Psychiatry*, 6, 434–439.

Tourrette C. (2006). Évaluer les enfants avec déficiences ou troubles du développement. Dunod.

Vergniaux C., Deret D., & Jamet F. (1999). Déficience visuelle et raisonnement analogique. *Handicap Revue De Sciences Humaines Et Sociales*, 84: 43–59.

Weismann-Arcache C. (2000). Les enjeux de l'examen psychologique du jeune enfant: Organisation et désorganisation psychiques chez l'enfant [The stakes involved in the psychological appraisal of the young child: Psychic organization and disorganization in the child]. *Psychologie clinique et projective*, 6, 85–99.

Wierzbicki C. (2003). Utilisation du K-ABC pour l'évaluation d'enfants porteurs de trisomie 21. *Revue européenne du handicap mental*, 27, 3–15.

Zanga A. (2003). WISC-III et K-ABC: Comparaison des concepts sous-jacents et des aptitudes mesurées [A theoretical and practical comparison of WICS-III and K-ABC showing similarities between the two tools]. *Psychologie & Education*, 55, 69–82.

13

Dr. Alan Kaufman's Contribution to Japan: K-ABC, Intelligent Testing, and School Psychology

TOSHINORI ISHIKUMA
University of Tsukuba

In my thirties I studied and worked in the United States from 1981 to 1990. Starting with the Alabama Language Institute, I went on to pursue a psychology major at the University of Montevallo, and finally finished a PhD in school psychology with Dr. Alan S. Kaufman as my thesis supervisor and mentor. I was able to conclude my journey from ABC (English lessons at Alabama Language Institute) to PhD and start school psychology services in Japan thanks to Drs. Alan and Nadeen Kaufman.

I first came to know about Kaufman in 1985 through *Kaufman Assessment Battery for Children* (K-ABC) (Kaufman & Kaufman, 1983), which was the textbook for psychological testing at the University of Montevallo. I was very interested in the K-ABC, which consisted of subtests that can be used for Japanese children because of the low loading of language and cultural factors. Immediately, I strongly felt that I should translate the K-ABC into Japanese even when I was still an undergraduate student (though I was 34 years old!). Dr. Julia Rogers, professor of psychology at the University of Montevallo, was so kind that she introduced me to Dr. Alan Kaufman at the University of Alabama. I was brave enough to talk to Dr. Kaufman about "the Japanese K-ABC." Dr. Kaufman treated me as a psychologist from Japan without measuring my intelligence or achievement and expressed a strong interest in the Japanese version of K-ABC. Dr. Kaufman showed his respect for Japanese culture (now I know that Alan and Nadeen love Japanese food) and his willingness for K-ABC to be used in other countries. In the fall of 1985, I became a graduate student at the University of Alabama and started to work with Dr. Kaufman. Before the end of 1985, Dr. Kaufman wrote a letter to Mohachi Motegi, who at that time was the president of Nihon Bunka Kagakusha, a publishing company for psychological tests and books such as the Japanese WISC-R (Kodama,

Shinagawa & Motegi, 1978), WISC-III (Azuma, Ueno, Fujita, Maekawa, Ishikuma & Sato, 1998), recommending that I develop the Japanese version of the K-ABC for Nihon Bunka Kagakusha. Thanks to Dr. Kaufman's recommendation, Nihon Bunka Kagakusha supported me as I began work on the Japanese K-ABC. We started translating K-ABC for Nihon Bunka Kagakusha, which planned to publish the Japanese K-ABC but decided not to do so. Then Maruzen Mates took over the project and finally published the K-ABC in 1993.

The goal of this chapter is to describe how Dr. Alan Kaufman has contributed to education and psychology practices in Japan through the K-ABC, intelligent testing, and school psychology.

DEVELOPMENT OF THE JAPANESE K-ABC

Before the Japanese K-ABC was published, Dr. Kaufman was known among Japanese psychologists and teachers as the author of the book, *Intelligent Testing with the WISC-R*, translated into Japanese by Motegi, Tagawa, and Nakatsuka (1983). The Japanese K-ABC team was built in 1987 by Nihon Bunka Kagakusha. The team consisted of Professors Tatsuya Matubara, Kazuhiko Fujita, Hisao Maekawa, a great practitioner with learning disabilities, and myself. Mr. Matsubara, a leader in school counseling, had the experience of developing the Japanese WIPPSI, while Mr. Fujita, an expert in special support education, had developed the Japanese Columbia Mental Maturity Scale. Dr. Maekawa, a practitioner with disabilities, was interested in Luria's model and had already "founded the K-ABC" in Japan. All of three authors were from the faculty of the University of Tsukuba, which I joined in 1990.

In 1980s, developing the Japanese K-ABC, a very new test, was a risky project for the publisher partially because in Japan, psychological tests were rather negatively received as discriminating the people with disabilities and also because the Japanese WISC-R and Binet Scales were already in use. However, the Japanese K-ABC team's belief in Kaufmans' idea of testing to create better ways of teaching and helping children, coupled with Kaufman's high reputation, enabled the start of the Japanese K-ABC project, and in 1990, Maruzen Mates succeeded in publishing the project, deciding that contribution to education was important to the company.

The Japanese K-ABC consists of all American subtests excluding Photo Series and Faces & Places (Matsubara et al., 1993). Faces & Places was not included in the Japanese version partially because it was difficult to find "famous individuals" whom children are expected to know because Japanese history is known to children as a story of what happened rather than who did what. Almost all items were kept in the subtests on Mental Processing Scale, whereas some items were modified and new items were written in the Achievement Scale. The Japanese K-ABC was standardized on 1680 children from the age of 2 years and 6 months to 12 years and 11 months, sampling by age, sex, and it included 21 children with intellectual disabilities or who were receiving educational counseling. For school age children older than 6 years, Split half reliability were from .69 (Gestalt Closure) to .81 (Matrix Analogy) in subtests on the Mental Processing Scale, and from .82 (Riddles) to .95 (Reading Decoding) in those on the Achievement Scale.

Exploring Factor Analysis (Principal factor analysis and Valimax Rotation) of 1680 children's data supported the Mental Processing Scale consisting of Sequential Processing and Simultaneous Processing. For children older than 6 years, Exploring Factor Analysis supported the K-ABC consisting of Sequential Processing, Simultaneous Processing, and Achievement. Interestingly Hand Movement was loaded .57 in Sequential Processing and .42 in Simultaneous Processing. For 51 children aged between 7 years and 6 months and 12 years and 9 months, the correlations were .68 between the Mental Processing Index on the K-ABC and the FIQ on the WISC-R, .75 between Simultaneous Processing Score and Performance IQ, and .79 between Achievement Scale and Verbal IQ. Interestingly, these results were very similar to the American data (Kaufman and Kaufman, 1983). The knowledge on factors of children's intelligence that Drs. Kaufman had accumulated over the years had finally crossed the Pacific Ocean.

Today "the Big Three" in individualized intelligence tests in Japan are the WISC-III, K-ABC, and Tanaka–Binet V (Sugihara et al., 2003). The WISC-III and K-ABC are most frequently used for making educational plans for children with learning difficulties (LD), attention-deficit hyperactivity disorder (ADHD), and other developmental disabilities.

It is important to add that the Japanese Association of the K-ABC Assessment has enrolled more than 600 members including teachers and psychologists and Professor Kazuhiro Fujita is its president. Thirteen local associations of the K-ABC Assessment have also been established. Why are there so many associations only for one intelligent test? Of course, because the K-ABC is so powerful a tool for practitioners. Also because practitioners in education are motivated to find opportunities for learning to understand the child's strengths and weakness in abilities and achievement, and use the test results to create teaching methods and a learning environment better responding to the child's unique needs. The national association conducts workshops, case study meetings, an annual conference, and publishes newsletters and an academic journal, *The Japanese Journal of K-ABC Assessment*. The KABC-II is now being developed.

INTELLIGENT TESTING IN JAPAN

As part of my PhD program at the University of Alabama, in which a course on "Individual Intelligence Test and Case Report" was included, I received training on intelligent testing (Kaufman, 1979, 1994) from my thesis supervisors, Drs. Alan and Nadeen Kaufman. It is impossible to express how much I was influenced by Drs. Kaufman in this course. I distinctly remember three episodes.

The first episode is about role play between Dr. Alan and students. Yes, the most difficult part in learning to administer psychological tests was to establish a trusting relationship with a child who takes the test. So role play took place several times in which Dr. Kaufman wore a baseball cap and played the role of a child with whom establishing rapport was difficult, while his students took the role of a tester and tried to administer a test to him. We learned to imagine how the child feels when tested and how best to inform the child about what we were doing by testing. Fortunately, I have never met a child more difficult to establish rapport with than "Alan," the child.

The second one is about stopping the test. In the course, Dr. Kaufman asked the students: "What you would do if the child tested started talking about his sisters he lost last month? Would you keep testing or stop testing to listen to him?" The decision may depend on the referral reasons. However, Dr. Kaufman taught us that tester may stop testing to listen to the child because the tester must try to understand the child and registering the test score is not the goal of the tester.

The third one is about the case report writing. The students handed over a case report, 5 to 7 pages in length, based on the test scores. Then, Dr. Kaufman gave them back the report with detailed comments. The comments on the report were demanding and comprehensive. When I wrote in the case report, based solely on the profile analysis of the WISC-R, that the boy had a poor educational environment in his early childhood, Dr. Kaufman asked me: "Did you see his early days? How can you explain the hypotheses to his parents?" I learned that the tester builds hypothesis about the child based not only on the tests but on the basis of additional information through classroom observation, interview with teachers and parents, and reading the records. Also I learned that that we, testers, always should think how the readers, especially parents and teachers, of the case report would feel. These rich experiences in intelligent testing in Drs. Kaufmans' course gave me a firm foundation to be a school psychologist.

In 1989, I moved from Alabama to California, enjoying a trip from South to South-West. I did my field internship in Solana Beach School District while working as a lecturer in the School Psychology as part of an academic internship at the San Diego State University (SDSU). At SDSU, my supervisors were Drs. Valerie Cook-Moles and Carol Robinson-Zanartu. I learned multicultural psychology and felt that Japanese culture was well respected by my supervisors in SDSU as much as it was by Drs. Kaufman. They emphasized that for children in multicultural situations, ecological assessment is the key to helping Culturally and Linguistically Different children (Cook-Moles, Robinson-Zanartu, & Green, 2006). I realized that my model of school psychology services were on the transition from "child as an individual with strengths and weakness," which I learned from Drs. Kaufman, to "child in the environment," which I was learning in California. My transition was very smooth. Why? Because my transition was really an expansion of intelligent testing! The intelligent testing paradigm emphasizes an interaction between a child and the environment in which the child lives (Kaufman, 1979, 1994). I know that Dr. Kaufman respects cultures and minorities. The K-ABC was carefully developed to be sensitive to minority groups and lowered language and cultural loading on the Mental Processing Scale to reduce disadvantages to minority group children. As a result, the difference of the standard scores on Mental Processing Scale between African American children and Anglo-Saxon children was half (−7.0) that of the FIQ on the WISC-R (−15.9) (Kaufman & Kaufman, 1983). Drs. Kaufman lowered language and cultural loading on the Mental Processing Scale to reduce disadvantages to the minority group children, whereas in a multicultural and ecological assessment, cultural and language factors are respected and observed to understand the child in the environment. Reducing cultural factors and focusing cultural factors are both essential in the assessment of a child's abilities, especially when the child is in problem situations concerning language, cultural, and developmental factors. In Japan, I have introduced Kaufman's paradigm of assessment of "Intelligent Testing" with basic principles (Kaufman, 1994) and discussed about "Wise Assessment" in psychoeducational services to children focusing on the child, the environment, and interaction between the child and the environment (Ishikuma, 1999, 2004).

Dr. Kaufman said: "We test the child NOT for sitting in the chair and waiting to see if the child will fail as the test predicts, BUT for helping the child to succeed and kill the prediction!" This became my basic philosophy as a school psychologist and as a human being.

SCHOOL PSYCHOLOGISTS

A formal system of school psychology has not been established and presently school psychologist is not an established profession in Japan. However, school psychology services, such as assessment and consultation for children with difficulties in the schools, are offered by teachers and counselors in Japanese schools (Ishikuma, Shinohara, & Nakao, 2006). In Japan, school psychology is assumed to be a team effort for school psychology services rather than that of school psychologists. School psychology is defined as "a field integrating education and psychology, where the practices and research regarding psycho-educational services to students are discussed and integrated to improve services helping each student deal with academic, psychosocial, health, and career problems, and promote student development" (Ishikuma, 1999). School psychology services include primary intervention for all children in the classroom and secondary and tertiary interventions for children with special educational needs (Ishikuma, Shinohara, & Nakao, 2006). So school psychology services in Japan might include the services offered by school psychologists and school counselors in the United States.

It 1990, the Japanese Association of Educational Psychology established the School Psychology Executive Committee, which prepared the criteria for school psychology certification and in 1997, the Japanese Association of Educational Psychology began to certify school psychologists to promote psychoeducational services to children. I joined the School Psychology Executive Committee and am a member of the Japanese Board for Certifying School Psychologists. In 2002, a collaborative effort of the Japanese Association of Educational Psychology, the Japanese Association of Special Education, the Japanese Association of Developmental Disabilities, the Japanese Association of Developmental Psychology, and the Japanese Academy of Learning Disabilities established the Japanese Organization of Certifying and Managing School Psychologists. Since 2002, the Japanese Organization of Certifying and Managing School Psychologists has certified school psychologists. In 2007, the organization was expanded to accommodate four more associations: Japanese Association of School Psychology, Japanese Association of Applied Educational Psychology,

Japanese Association of School Counseling, and Japanese Association for The Study of Guidance and Counseling. The eligible candidates for school psychology certification include (a) graduates from an MA course fulfilling the seven school psychology subjects, with one year of experience in psychoeducational services, and (b) teachers, special support teachers, or health teachers with five years of experience in psychoeducational services. The seven subjects in graduate programs are Educational Psychology, Developmental Psychology, Clinical Psychology with psychology as the base, Education and Psychology for children with disabilities, Student Guidance and Career Guidance with education as the base, and Evaluation and Psychological Testing and School Counseling as part of psychoeducational service practices. Applicants are required to complete a multiple choice test on the seven school psychology subjects as well as an essay test on a topic in school psychology. All applicants also need to submit a report on a supervised case (Japanese Organization for Certifying and Managing School Psychologist, 2008). As of April 2008, there were more than 3,700 teachers, counselors, teacher consultants at the Board of Education, and university professors certified as school psychologists who offer psychoeducational services as part of their profession.

Ishikuma et al. (2006) states that the school psychology movement has been influenced mainly by (a) the increasing difficulty in solving school education problems such as nonattendance, bullying, juvenile delinquency; (b) the need to improve special support education, especially for children with Learning Disabilities, Attention Deficit Hyperactivity Disorder, and high-functioning autism (e.g., Ministry of Education, Culture, Sports, Science and Technology: Survey and Study Committee on Special Support Education, 2003; Ueno, 1984,); and (c) the introduction of school psychology practices followed in the United States in Japan, including intelligent assessment (e.g., Ishikuma, 1994, 1999). Dr. Alan Kaufman has influenced school psychology movement through frequent use of the K-ABC in special support education and school psychology practices based on wise assessment in Japan.

CONCLUSION

I would like to show my great appreciation to my supervisors, onshi (Japanese word for a teacher to whom you owe a great deal and whom you respect highly), research partners, Drs. Alan and Nadeen Kaufman. Drs. Kaufman taught me the significant role of intelligent helpers in understanding the child and changing their school life. I have learned that becoming a school psychologist is very tough but valuable. Knowing Drs. Kaufman had great impact on my career and my life. School psychology services in Japan will continue to be influenced by Drs. Kaufman through the K-ABC(II) and wise assessment by the Japanese school psychologists.

REFERENCES

Azuma, H., Ueno, K., Fujita, K., Maekawa, H., Ishikuma, T., & Sano, H. (1998). *The Japanese Version of Wechsler Intelligence Scale for Children-III*. Tokyo, Japan: Nihon Bunka Kagakusha.

Cook-Morales, V.J., Robinson-Zañartu, C.A. & Duren Green, T. (2006). When part of the problem becomes part of the solution: Moving from evaluation to assessment. *SpecialEDge*, 20, 3–4, 14.

Ishikuma, T. (1994). School psychologists and school psychology: New perspective on school education. *The Annual Report of Educational Psychology in Japan*, 33, 144–154.

Ishikuma, T. (1999). *School Psychology: Psycho-educational Services by a Team of Teachers, School Counselors, and Parents*. Tokyo, Japan: Seishinshobo.

Ishikuma, T. (2004). Research and practices in school psychology in Japan: Moving toward to a system of psycho-educational services. *Japanese Psychological Review*, 3, 332–347.

Ishikuma, T., Shinohara, Y, & Nakao, T. (2006). School psychology in Japan. In S. Jimerson, T. Oakland., & F. Peter (Eds.), *Handbook of International School Psychology*. New York: Sage Publishing, pp. 217–227.

Japanese Organization for Certifying and Managing School Psychologist (2008). For applicants for the school psychologist: manual and application forms 2008.

Kaufman, A.S. (1979). *Intelligent Testing with the WISC-R*. New York: John Wiley & Sons, Inc. [Motegi, Tagawa, & Nakatsuka (1983). *Intelligent Testing with the WISC-R* (Japanese Translation.) Tokyo, Japan: Nihon Bunka Kagakusha.]

Kaufman, A.S. (1994). *Intelligent Testing with the WISC-III*. New York: Wiley.

Kodama, S., Shinagawa, F., Motegi, M. (1978). *The Japanese Version of WISC-R*. Tokyo, Japan: Nihon Bunka Kagakusha.

Ministry of Education, Culture, Sports, Science and Technology: Survey and Study Committee on Special Support Education (2003). Final Report on Future of Special Support Education. Ministry of Education, Culture, Sports, Science and Technology.

Sugihara, K., Sugihara, T., Nakamura, J., Okawa, I., Nohara, R., & Serizawa N. (Eds.) (2003). *Tanaka Binet Intelligence Scale V*. Tokyo, Japan: Taken Shuppan.

Ueno, K. (1984). *Learning Disabilities in Classroom*. Tokyo, Japan: Yuhikaku

14

Alan Kaufman's Deep Influence in Sweden

JAN ALM

Uppsala University, Sweden

It took a long time before Swedish psychologists got the good news from the United States. By good luck I got hold of a copy of *Assessing Adolescent and Adult Intelligence* at Dillons bookstore in London in 1994. In the same year, I found *Intelligent Testing with the WISC-III* at Barnes & Nobles in New York. A new world opened for me in my professional life. I suddenly got the knowledge of how to professionally evaluate the only important test batteries translated into Swedish, the Wechsler scales. I looked around in Sweden and I found the books nowhere.

At first I was filled with the feeling that I found a goldmine and I was the only owner. I started to dive deep into it and my self-confidence was peaking. I then started courses in the proposed methods of interpretation and the Swedish psychologists were eager to listen. Alan later on came to Uppsala University and gathered crowds of interested psychologists. I informed one of the staff at the Swedish Psychological Corporation about the event and she exclaimed: "But he is almost a legend you know." We later also got the opportunity to listen to Dr Nadeen Kaufman in Uppsala. Her influence has continuously been very crucial both for the development of their own test instruments as well as for the development of the interpretation approach. Alan was also the first invited speaker at the Policy on Dyslexia Conference held by Uppsala University and European Dyslexia Academy for Research and Training, August 14–16, 2002 in Uppsala. The conference was opened by and held in the presence of Her Majesty Queen Silvia of Sweden, who also got the opportunity to personally meet with him and Nadeen.

How sad and strange that existing professional knowledge in one of the most central areas of clinical work, i.e., doing diagnostic assessments and giving recommendations, took 15 years to reach Europe. At that time Swedish psychologists used the WISC and WAIS-R and there was no information in the test manual on interpreting the test results, except for computing the three IQs. The assessment process was then both boring and frustrating. You did a WISC because you had to. Many children and adults with learning disabilities (LD)/dyslexia were misdiagnosed as mental retarded or borderline just because we did not know better. No recommendations were generally written. That was not in our tradition and we did not know how to do it.

In the history of psychology there are different outlooks. Are changes due to certain individuals like Pavlov, Skinner, Bandura, and Freud, or is it just that the time is ripe for the knowledge to burst out? As usual, there is probably a combination. The first outlook is however more obvious and when it comes to Alan Kaufman, I feel that through his books, his deep interest for good tests and intelligent interpretations he has saved a generation of psychologists from doing bad work. Today the knowledge is on our bookshelves. Our self-confidence has increased tremendously. To be an expert, a real professional is rewarding by itself, is essential for your clients, and helps raising the self image of psychologists to a level where it should have been a long time ago. It also helps raising our wages!

15

Intelligent Testing of Underserved Populations

R. STEVE MCCALLUM
University of Tennessee, Knoxville

BRUCE A. BRACKEN
The College of William and Mary

INTELLIGENT TESTING OF UNDERSERVED POPULATIONS

The imperative for nonverbal assessment in the United States is obvious and growing. According to U.S. Census data reported in 2000, more than 31 million people 5 years and older spoke a language other than English in the home and almost 2,000,000 had no English-speaking ability (U.S. Bureau of the Census). By 2005 the number of individuals who speak a language other than English in their homes had increased to nearly 60 million (approximately 20 percent of the U.S. population). In the United States, 12 individual states report that 20 percent or more of their respective populations speak a language other than English. California was the state that reported the largest percentage of non-English speakers (42.3 percent); Puerto Rico was the American territory reporting the largest incidence of non-English speakers (95.4 percent) (http://factfinder.census.gov/home/saff/main.html).

Minority children and children from non-White racial or ethnic backgrounds comprise an increasingly larger percentage of public school children, particularly in many large metropolitan areas. For example, minority students comprise an overwhelming percentage of the school population in Miami (approximately 84 percent), Chicago (89 percent), and Houston (88 percent) (Bracken & McCallum, in press) Many of these minority children speak languages other than English, with the Limited English Proficient (LEP) population representing the fastest growing segment of the population in the United States. As examples of the high incidence of languages other than English spoken in the schools, there are more than

200 languages spoken in the schools in the Greater Chicago area (Pasko, 1994), 150 in California schools (Unz, 1997), and 61 in the Knoxville, Tennessee public schools (Forester, 2000). Many of these LEP students will receive cognitive assessments but they will not be well served by the traditional verbally laden instruments typically used in the schools (e.g., Wechsler Scales, Stanford-Binet). Similar assessment-related disadvantages exist for children with limited hearing abilities or receptive and expressive language disabilities who would be distinctly disadvantaged if administered a verbally oriented ability test.

Examinees with severe language-related disabilities are at a unique disadvantage when assessed by means of spoken language. According to the United States Office of Education, Department of Special Education 1,127,551 students with speech and language problems were served in 2005; 483,805 of whom were served with emotional disturbance, 140,920 with autism, and 71,903 with hearing impairments. Collectively, these individuals comprise an enormous segment of the U.S. school population. Many of these individuals will be evaluated during their educational careers in an effort to (a) determine eligibility for school and mental health services and (b) evaluate cognitive strengths and weaknesses, which may be directly or indirectly targeted for remediation.

If heavily verbally laden tests will be inappropriate for many, in not most, of these individuals with diverse racial, ethnic, or disability backgrounds and characteristics, what is the alternative? Over the past couple decades and especially the last few years, many psychometrically sound assessment options have appeared. Importantly, Alan Kaufman has been involved, either directly or indirectly, in the development of the great majority of those instruments, as we describe below. In fact, Alan and his wife and partner, Nadeen L. Kaufman, developed one of the first dual purpose (i.e., verbal *and* nonverbal) individualized cognitive tests more than two decades ago, the *Kaufman Assessment Battery for Children* (K-ABC; Kaufman & Kaufman, 1983). The K-ABC has been revised recently, but imbedded in the original battery as well as the most recent battery is a performance-based, language-reduced nonverbal scale.

NONVERBAL COGNITIVE ASSESSMENT OF UNDERSERVED POPULATIONS

When Kaufman and Kaufman (1983) published the K-ABC, there were very few good multidimensional nonverbal cognitive instruments available. In fact, the *Leiter International Performance Scale* (LIP; Leiter, 1979) was the test of choice at the time, but its standardization sample was aging and increasingly questionable in terms of its utility. Consequently, many school-based practitioners used either the LIP or the Performance Scales of one of the *Wechsler Intelligence Scale for Children – Revised* (WISC-R; Wechsler, 1974) for nonverbal assessments, even though the latter measure employed Performance subtests laden with verbal directions. Although the K-ABC Nonverbal Scale was not truly or totally nonverbal, it represented a significant advancement over the WICS-R because it de-emphasized verbal directions and responses. For this reason and many others, the K-ABC was a welcome addition to the field. The K-ABC was model based, user friendly, attractive to young children, and importantly it reduced White–non-White mean score differences.

To include a "nonverbal scale" into a multidimensional cognitive test battery was a valued contribution for the K-ABC. When the K-ABC was developed the term *nonverbal,* as applied to cognitive assessment, had generally referred to visual-spatial tasks that did not require a verbal response from the examiner, as was generally the case with the WISC-R. Kaufman and Kaufman adopted this meaning to characterize the administration of the K-ABC Nonverbal Scale, though they took the concept further and deemphasized significantly verbal demands on the examinee. Historically, Kaufman (1979) recognized the important and detrimental effects of using test directions that were verbally laden with basic language concepts in early childhood cognitive assessments. This awareness, in part, led Alan and Nadeen to shorten and simplify the verbal directions on the K-ABC, thus helping to make the test a better cognitive measure rather than a verbal ability measure.

Most comprehensive intelligence or cognitive ability tests today still use this convention of employing performance tests and calling them "nonverbal" (e.g., see the Stanford-Binet Intelligence Scale – Fifth Edition; SB5, Roid, 2003). Other test authors have recommended that the term "nonverbal" be applied in a more accurate and restrictive manner, wherein nonverbal means testing in which "no verbal directions are spoken or read by the examiner and no verbal responses are spoken or written by the examinee" (Bracken & McCallum, 1998). Currently, the term is often used to characterize either traditional performance-based testing with verbal directions or the more accurate and restrictive application where the test is administered in a 100 percent nonverbal manner. Practitioners, often confused by the different applications of the term nonverbal are required to read the administration directions for any particular test to determine whether the test is truly nonverbal or only nonverbal in name.

The K-ABC and its successor, the K-ABC-II, are individually administered clinical instruments, and are used to provide in depth cognitive assessment. The K-ABC, like other individual tests that assess a wide variety of cognitive skills employing a variety of administration formats, is considered a multidimensional measure of cognitive/intellectual abilities (as opposed to tests whose content and administration format is singularly focused, thus providing a more narrow assessment of cognitive functioning). Results from multidimensional tests provide broader assessments and more readily contribute to special education eligibility decisions and identifying examinees' cognitive strengths and weaknesses presumed to underlie academic and occupational success. Multidimensional tests of cognitive ability are useful when a broad survey of abilities is need, but not all examinees are in need of such an intensive evaluation. In fact, many examinees are best suited to brief intellectual screening. Screening tests may be of two basic administration types, group administered and individually administered. Currently, there are several sound individually administered unidimensional and multidimensional tests for examiners to choose from. Similarly, there are several high quality screening tests available as well. In the sections that follow, we discuss several instruments across these broad categories (i.e., multidimensional, unidimensional, individually administered, group administered) that have been directly or indirectly influenced by Alan Kaufman.

INTELLIGENT TESTING OF UNDERSERVED POPULATIONS USING INDIVIDUALLY ADMINISTERED, MULTIDIMENSIONAL INSTRUMENTS

As coauthor of the K-ABC and K-ABC-II, Alan Kaufman has contributed significantly to the creation and use of multidimensional tests for the assessment of underserved populations. Additionally, as Project Director of the McCarthy Scales of Children's Abilities (MSCA; McCarthy, 1972), Alan sought to reduce mean score differences between White and African American children (Kaufman, 1994). His influence can also been seen in the development of another major multidimensional, individually administered nonverbal test, the Universal Nonverbal Intelligence Test (UNIT; Bracken & McCallum, 1998), through his substantial influence on the authors of that test.

We describe some of the innovative elements of the K-ABC, K-ABC-II, UNIT, and other tests in this chapter. As coauthors of the UNIT, we are intimately connected to the history of the test and its development, as well as the recent research that has defined and extolled its utility. In the sections that follow, we describe aspects of UNIT development and research to illustrate how Alan Kaufman's influence was felt. Also, when describing other tests, Alan's influence on the filed of testing of underserved populations will be highlighted.

K-ABC AND K-ABC-II

As many readers are aware, Alan worked as a young psychologist at the Psychological Corporation with David Wechsler on the revision and restandardization of the WISC in the early 1970s. Because of his work on the WISC-R and his extensive knowledge of the Wechsler scales, Alan has contributed significantly to the literature on the use and interpretation of those scales. For example, he applied the four component information processing model of Silver (1993) and the channels of communication approach found in the *Illinois Test of Psycholinguistic Abilities* (Kirk, McCarthy, & Kirk, 1968) to the interpretation of the WISC-R. This information processing approach led to consideration of how aspects of the models might contribute to a thoughtful examination of examinees' strengths and weaknesses, as well as (potential) test bias. Information processing models include consideration of (a) input, or how information from the sense organs enter the brain; (b) integration, or how the information is interpreted and processed; (c) storage, how the information is contained within the organism and made available for later retrieval; and (d) output, how the information is expressed through language, gesture, or other muscular activity.

Drawing on the work of Jensen and Reynolds (1982) and Naglieri and Jensen (1987), and using his knowledge of Silver's model, Kaufman noticed that input and output demands seemed to significantly influence race differences in assessed abilities, particularly Black–White differences on the Wechsler Scales. In particular, he contrasted the highly verbal task demands on the *Information* subtest from the Wechsler scales, a subtest that typically produced large Black–White differences, with a highly visual information-related subtest from the K-ABC, Faces and Places. Both subtests are highly culturally laden, yet Faces and Places reduced the magnitude of the race difference by nearly one-half (Kaufman, 1994). What was responsible for the reduction in the Black–White score differences on *Faces and Places*? In part, the reduced score discrepancy seems to be related to the modality change in the input–output aspects of the tasks. While Information relies on auditory channel of communication for input and vocal channel of communication for output (i.e., oral–aural), the Faces and Places subtest is dependent on a visual–vocal combination of channels of communication.

The Kaufmans developed one of the first comprehensive achievement batteries conormed with a cognitive battery. The K-ABC Achievement Battery included another unique feature, a reading subtest that also took greater advantage of the visual modality of some minority children. The *Reading Understanding* subtest requires examinees to read items and then to act out the requests embedded in the items, thus using visual-motor channels of communication. The K-ABC Examiner's Manual reports that the Reading Understanding subtest produced reduced Black–White differences as compared to the Black–White achievement discrepancies found on other traditional reading comprehension measures. It should be recognized, however, that some of this reduced Black–White difference may have been a result in part of a limited floor to the test and other nonintellective factors (Bracken, 1985). However, as with Faces and Places, the input–output modality differences in Reading Understanding may have contributed to reducing this traditional race-based discrepancy. Kaufman (1994) concluded that the validity of these findings may be supported by claims of some African-American psychologists who stress the central role of nonverbal and gestural communication within the African-American community (Abrahams, 1973; Carter, 1977; Torrance, 1982).

A number of innovative K-ABC characteristics contributed to the perception among practicing psychologists that the K-ABC represented a "fairer" test, buttressed of course by the reduction of overall Black–White differences in K-ABC composite scores, relative to the differences found on extant traditional ability measures (e.g., Wechsler Scales, Stanford–Binet). Some of the K-ABC (and K-ABC-II) innovations include: (a) availability of a nonverbal scale; (b) colorful and interesting stimuli for young examinees; (c) briefer administration time, particularly for younger examinees; (d) a unique theoretical model underpinning the constructs assessed (i.e., the K-ABC-II reflects components of both the Luria-based neuropsychological model and the Cattell-Horn-Carroll, CHC, theory of cognitive abilities); (e) inclusion of "teaching" items; and (f) conormed cognitive and achievement tests.

Many of these aforementioned innovations are related to the goal of creating better, more refined, fairer intelligence testing for underserved populations, and many of these features and psychometric principles have been adopted by and incorporated into instruments created by Alan Kaufman's students. One test is particular has earned a reputation of being an equitable and highly sensitive assessment for underserved populations, the UNIT. The coauthors of the UNIT (and this chapter) were doctoral students of Alan Kaufman at the University of Georgia, and both have followed his work (and the Kaufman family) closely over the years. As we describe the UNIT below, Alan's influence in our work will become apparent.

UNIVERSAL NONVERBAL INTELLIGENCE TEST (UNIT)

Every year tens of thousands of cognitive tests are administered in the public schools. Most of these test administrations will include what has become considered "traditional" verbally laden tests of intelligence, cognitive functioning or ability. Because language often can provide an excellent window on the intellect, these traditional measures frequently provide insightful views of students' intellectual skills and abilities. However, for many students, especially those who speak English as a second language or who come from nontraditional cultural backgrounds or who are limited in their communication skills (e.g., deaf/hard of hearing, autism, language-related learning disabilities, speech/language disabilities) traditional, language-loaded intelligence tests create an unfair disadvantage. In many such instances, construct irrelevant variance (i.e., test bias) is created in the psychologists assessment of intelligence, which is confounded by the sometimes nonintellective aspects of language. Just as all achievement tests are first and foremost reading tests for reading disabled students, all verbally loaded intelligence tests are first and foremost language tests for student with language-related disorders or who speak a native language other than English.

What are the options for assessing students with linguistic or culturally different backgrounds? The options are "culture fair" tests, translated tests, or language-reduced performance (or nonverbal) tests. It is not possible to translate and norm each of the available popular and widely adopted traditional tests; even if the tests could be translated and normed, multilingual psychologists would be needed to administer the tests to the students who speak the 200 or so languages found in Chicago alone. State-of-the-art test translation, adaptation, and validation is difficult, costly, and time-consuming, with many issues that must be addressed (e.g., Bracken & Barona, 1991; Bracken, Barona, Bauermeister, Howell, Poggioli, & Puente, 1990; Bracken & Fouad, 1987; Fouad & Bracken, 1986). As a result of these difficulties, costs, and issues, it is not feasible to translate tests to meet the needs of every student, and the use of nonverbal tests of intelligence is the most viable and realistic solution for the assessment of culturally and linguistically diverse students. Consistent with this observation, IDEA (2004) admonishes educators to select and administer technically sound tests that will *not* result in discriminatory practices based on racial or cultural bias. Consequently, children with communication limitations or impairments can be more equitably assessed with comprehensive, truly nonverbal intelligence tests, such as the UNIT.

Theory and Structure of the UNIT

The UNIT comprehensive test battery includes six subtests designed to assess cognitive functioning according to a two-tiered model of intelligence (i.e., two primary intellectual factors: memory and reasoning), which incorporates two organizational strategies (i.e., two means by which information might be organized: symbolic and nonsymbolic). Figure 15.1, a graphical display of the UNIT two-by-two theoretical model, reveals that three memory subtests are included on the Memory Scale: Object Memory (OM), Spatial Memory (Spa M), and Symbolic Memory (Sym M). Similarly, the figure identifies three subtests available to assess reasoning: Cube Design (CD), Mazes (M), and Analogic Reasoning (AR). In terms of task demands, all subtests are visually oriented; one subtest (AR) requires a pointing response and the remaining five require minor motoric manipulation. With two exceptions (CD, M)

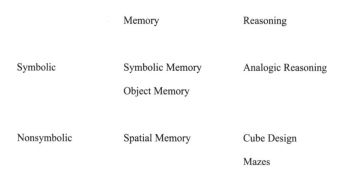

	Memory	Reasoning
Symbolic	Symbolic Memory	Analogic Reasoning
	Object Memory	
Nonsymbolic	Spatial Memory	Cube Design
		Mazes

FIGURE 15.1. Conceptual model of the UNIT.

the subtests that require motoric manipulation can be adapted to allow for a pointing response only.

Symbolic organization strategies represent the use of concrete and abstract symbols to conceptualize the environment; typically these symbols are language-related (i.e., words) although symbols may take on other forms (e.g., numbers, flags, dice, objects). Once symbols are internalized, they automatically label, mediate, and make meaningful our experiences; that is, they stand for or generalize to the concept being represented (e.g., an open hand held with fingers together and pointed upward is a hand gesture that universally symbolizes "stop"). In contrast, nonsymbolic strategies require individuals to perceive and make sense of novel depictions without the use of or representation by accepted symbols. Making meaningful judgments about the physical relationships of such novel depictions within our environment in a symbol-free manner is frequently characterized as a "fluid" intellectual skill.

Within each of the two fundamental organizational categories included in the UNIT (i.e., nonsymbolic and symbolic), problem solution requires either memory or reasoning. Some memory items require primarily symbolic organization (e.g., recalling the sequential order of black and green symbols representing man, woman, boy, girl, and baby). Other items require considerable symbolic organization and reasoning skills (e.g., visual analogies employing concrete objects to symbolic convey a concept – hand, glove; foot...?). Yet other items on the UNIT require nonsymbolic organization strategies and memory primarily (e.g., items that show the placement of green and black circles on a 4 × 3 grid). Finally, others may require nonsymbolic organization and reasoning (e.g., reproducing a three-dimensional cube design represented in an artist's depiction).

The underpinning organization of the UNIT is consistent with a number of theoretical orientations within the cognitive literature, including Wechsler's (1939) emphasis on the importance of distinguishing between highly symbolic (verbal) and nonsymbolic (perceptual-performance) means of expressing intelligence. Similarly, Jensen (1980) provides rationale for a two-tiered hierarchical conceptualization of intelligence consisting of the two subconstructs of memory (Level I) and reasoning (Level II). The UNIT can be interpreted from perspectives of more recently developed models, such as the Cattell-Horn-Carroll (CHC) model as described by Woodcock, McGrew, and Mather (2001). The UNIT subtests tap stratum I and II components within the CHC model, including fluid reasoning, general sequential reasoning, visual processing, visual memory, spatial scanning, spatial scanning, spatial relations, and induction. Using aspects of the various models, the UNIT can primarily be considered a nonverbal measure of general intelligence (i.e., *g*); the UNIT should not be confused as a measure of nonverbal intelligence, which is a construct that is different from general intelligence.

Description of the UNIT Scales and Subtests

On the UNIT, several scores can be calculated, including a Full Scale Intelligence Quotient (FSIQ), Memory Quotient (MQ), Reasoning Quotient (RQ), Symbolic Quotient (SQ), and Nonsymbolic Quotient (NSQ). Each of the UNIT quotients has a mean of 100 and standard deviations of 15. The six UNIT subtests contribute to three quotients (i.e., FSIQ, MQ or RQ, and SQ or NSQ) and each subtest can be considered individually with its own subtest score, with a mean of 10 and standard deviation of 3.

Memory Scale. Three UNIT subtests assess memory and either symbolic or nonsymbolic processing, as follows:

1. Symbolic Memory (Symbolic Scale): the examinee recalls and recreates sequences of visually presented universal symbols (e.g., green boy, Black woman).
2. Spatial Memory (Nonsymbolic Scale): the examinee must remember and recreate the placement of black and/or green round chips on a 3×3 or 4×4 grid.
3. Object Memory (Symbolic Scale): the examinee is shown a visual array of common objects (e.g., shoe, telephone, tree) for five seconds, after which the examinee identifies the pictured objects from a larger array of pictured objects.

Memory Scale. Three UNIT subtests assess memory and either symbolic or nonsymbolic processing, as follows:

4. Cube Design (Nonsymbolic Scale): the examinee completes a three-dimensional block design task using between one and nine green and white blocks.
5. Analogic Reasoning (Symbolic Scale): the examinee completes a matrix analogies task using common objects (e.g., hand/glove, foot/...?) and novel geometric figures.
6. Mazes (Nonsymbolic Scale): the examinee completes a maze task by tracing a path from the center starting point to the exit.

Administration and Scoring

UNIT administration time varies according to which battery option the examiner selects. The complete, six-subtest Extended Battery requires about 45 minutes; the four-subtest Standard Battery required approximately 30 minutes; and the two-subtest Abbreviated Battery requires approximately 15 minutes. Although the UNIT is administered in a 100 percent nonverbal manner, the examiner may communicate for purposes of rapport and general conversation with the examinee if they share a common language.

UNIT stimuli and accompanying task demands are presented to the examinee nonverbally, using eight universal nonverbal gestures as described in the Examiner's Manual (and on a training video or CD available from the publisher). In addition to these gestures, the examiner is instructed to present demonstration items, sample items, and "checkpoint" items to ensure examinees' understanding of task demands. Demonstration items, as the name implies, demonstrate how the examinee should approach the task and how stimuli will be presented. Sample items are nonscored items that allow examinees to attempt the task without errors being counted against them and require the examiner to provide feedback on the accuracy/inaccuracy of an examinee's response. Checkpoint items allow the examiner to provide feedback on failed items only, but those item failures are scored.

All UNIT visual stimuli are presented on two easels, except Mazes, which is in separate test booklet. Some manipulatives accompany the easel-bound visual stimuli, such as green and white cubes, small round green and black round chips, and small square chips with either green or black human figures. All subtests, except Analogic Reasoning are timed in terms of either exposure (i.e., Memory subtests) or response time (i.e., Mazes, Cube Design), but all response time requirements are liberal to be fair to cultures that do not value speeded responses. UNIT scoring is quite simple and straightforward. Raw scores are easily determined and transformed to standard scores using either the tables provided in the UNIT Manual (1998) or by UNIT Compuscore software (Bracken & McCallum, 2001).

UNIT Psychometric Properties

As reported in the UNIT Examiner's Manual, standardization data were collected from a representative sample of children and adolescents ranging in age from 5 years, 0 months to 17 years, 11 months. In all, 2100 children and adolescents were carefully selected to represent the U.S. population based on age, sex, race, parent educational attainment, community size, geographic region, and ethnicity and special education categories. More than 1,700 additional students were tested for various reliability, validity, or special studies. Traditional psychometric data are reported in the manual, along with extensive data for a variety of populations (e.g., internal consistency reported by race/ethnicity, gender, exceptionality, important decision-making IQ levels). Reliability data are strong; the average composite scale reliability coefficients range from .86 to .96 for the typical and clinical/exceptional samples across all batteries. Subsample FSIQ internal consistency coefficients range from .91 to .93; stability coefficients (corrected for restriction in range) ranged from .79 to .84. The average test–retest practice effects (over an approximate three week interval) are 7.2 IQ points for the Abbreviated Battery, 5.0 for the Standard Battery, and 4.8 for the Extended Battery.

Validity data support the UNIT theoretical model. In terms of developmental growth from a cross-sectional analysis, the average raw scores for Cube Design progress from 13 to 19, 26, and 33 for the 5–7, 8–10, 11–13, and 14–17-year-old groups, respectively. Exploratory factor analysis yielded a large first eigen value, 2.33; others were below 1.0, suggesting the presence of a strong first factor (read g factor), commensurate with the interpretation of the FSIQ as a good overall index of global intellectual ability. Confirmatory factor analyses support a one factor model, two-factor (i.e., memory and reasoning model, and a four-factor model (i.e., memory and reasoning; symbolic and nonsymbolic).

Strong evidence supporting concurrent validity of the UNIT is reported in the Examiner's Manual for typical students and special student groups. For example, data from a sample of children with learning disabilities yielded correlation coefficients (corrected for restriction in range) between the FSIQs from each of the three UNIT batteries and the WISC-III FSIQ ranging from .78 to .84. Slightly higher correlations (i.e., .84 to .88) were found between the UNIT and WISC III for a sample of children with Mental Retardation. Strong coefficients also were obtained between the UNIT and a variety of other instruments for various populations (e.g., Native Americans).

Additional evidence of construct validity can be seen in a qualitative analysis of the differential correlation pattern between the UNIT Symbolic Quotient and measures of language-based achievement (e.g., reading subtests); coefficients are often higher between the Symbolic Quotient and these language loaded measures than between the UNIT Nonsymbolic

Quotient and these same measures. In fact, this differential pattern is found in 21 of 36 comparisons, which would be predicted from the nature of the symbolic versus nonsymbolic distinction. Even in those instances where this pattern did not hold up, one must consider that all UNIT subtests, except Mazes, have strong g-loadings at or above .70; g is a strong predictor of academic achievement whether its origin is symbolic or nonsymbolic. In general, predictive validity coefficients between the UNIT and various achievement tests are strong, especially when it is considered that a nonverbal variable is used to predict a verbal outcome. UNIT-achievement correlations are comparable to those reported traditional between language-loaded tests and achievement measures.

Since publication of the UNIT, results from several independent studies have been made available and continue to provide strong support for the UNIT. For example, a recent study explored the relationship between the Leiter International Performance Scale-Revised (Roid & Miller, 1997) for 100 elementary and middle school students. Hooper and Bell (2006) reported statistically significant correlations (p < .01) that ranged from .33 (discriminant correlation) between the UNIT Memory Quotient/Leiter-R Fluid Reasoning comparison to .72 (convergent correlation) between the UNIT FSIQ and the Leiter-R FSIQ. Importantly, global scale mean scores for the two tests are generally similar, although the UNIT FSIQ was approximately 5 points higher than the Leiter-R FSIQ. Hooper and Bell (2006) also reported correlation coefficients ranging from .49 to .72 between the four UNIT global scores and end of the year scores from the Total Reading, Total Math, and Total Language scores of the Comprehensive Test of Basic Skills (CTBS/McGraw-Hill, 1996). Using stepwise multiple regression analyses Hooper (2002) reported that the UNIT FSIQ predicted three academic subjects from the CTBS better than the Leiter-R FSIQ; the UNIT FSIQ entered the multiple regression equation first and accounted for from 39 to 55 percent of the variance in the three criterion scores and the Leiter-R contributed an additional 1 to 2 percent for each.

UNIT and Leiter-R scores were also compared by Ferrell and Phelps (2000) for school children with severe language disorders. Correlation coefficients between the UNIT quotients and Leiter-R Fluid Reasoning Scale scores range from .65 to .67; the coefficients between UNIT quotients and Leiter-R Visualization Reasoning Full Scale scores range from .73 to .80. Means were similar in magnitude. The Leiter-R mean scale scores were 65.07 and 66.33, for the Fluid Reasoning and Visualization/Reasoning FSIQ, respectively, and the UNIT global scale scores ranged from 66.71 (FSIQ) to 70 (Symbolic Quotient). The authors concluded that these two instruments should be considered superior to conventional language-loaded tests for use with this population.

Other researchers have contributed to the literature showing the utility of the UNIT by examining relationships between the UNIT and important external criteria. For example, Scardapane, Egan, Torres-Gallegos, Levine, and Owens (2002) investigated the relationship between the UNIT, the Wide Range Intelligence Test (WRIT; Glutting, Adams, & Sheslow, 2000), and the Gifted and Talented Evaluation Scales (GATES; Gilliam, Carpenter, & Christensen, 1996) for English-speaking children and English Language Learners (ELL). The correlation coefficient between the WRIT Visual and the UNIT FSIQ of .59 can be compared to the coefficient between the UNIT FSIQ and the WRIT Verbal scale of .11. Contrary to the authors' predictions, the coefficients between the GATES scores and the WRIT Verbal IQ were not higher than the coefficients between the UNIT FSIQ and the four GATES scores. The coefficients between the UNIT FSIQ and the GATES scales of Intellectual Ability, Academic Skills, Creativity, Leadership, and Artistic Talent ranges from .50 to .57 ($p < .05$); the coefficients between the WRIT Verbal IQ and these GATES scores ranged from .004 to .10 ($p = .05$). According to these authors the data support the use of the UNIT as a nonverbal measure of intelligence.

UNIT Fairness

Alan Kaufman has contributed significantly to the testing literature, and due to his strong social conscience, has addressed the notion of fairness in numerous publications (e.g., Kaufman, 1994; Kaufman & Kaufman, 1983, 2004). His students have carried this tradition forward into their work. For example, Kaufman's influence can be seen in the many developmental characteristics built into the UNIT to ensure fairer assessment. In fact, the UNIT Manual includes an entire chapter entitled "Fairness," and describes extensive efforts to ensure that the test is appropriate for use for all children in the U.S. (i.e., construct irrelevant variance is minimized for all relevant populations). According to the Examiner's Manual, the UNIT was formulated based on five core concepts of fairness and equity: (a) a language-free test is less susceptible to bias than a language-loaded test, (b) a multidimensional measures of cognition are fairer than unidimensional measures because of the breath of constructs assessed; (c) a test that minimizes the influence of acquired knowledge (i.e., crystallized ability) is fairer than one that does not; (d) a test that minimizes speeded performance is better than one with greater emphases on speed; and (e) a test that relies on a variety of response modes is more motivating and thereby "fairer" than those relying on a unidimensional response mode.

In addition to these guiding principles, several other steps were taken to ensure assessment fairness in the UNIT. For example, in the initial item development phase all items were submitted to a panel of "bias experts"; that is, individuals who would be sensitive to items that might be offensive to or more difficult for individuals within certain populations (e.g., Native Americans, Hispanics). Items identified by these individual as problematic, and those identified via statistical item bias analyses, were removed from the test.

A number of statistical procedures were conducted to help demonstrate fairness, including calculation of separate reliabilities, factor structure statistics, and mean-difference analyses. For example, reliabilities were calculated using FSIQs for females, males, African Americans, and Hispanic Americans separately, and all were greater than .91, uncorrected, and .94, corrected for the Abbreviated Battery, and greater than .95 for the Standard and Extended Battery. Separate confirmatory factor analyses for these subpopulations provide convincing evidence to support a single general intelligence factor, for both primary and secondary scales, and for the construct validity of the UNIT across sex, race, and ethnic groups (Bracken & McCallum, 1998).

Mean IQ difference analyses using matched groups from the UNIT standardization data also provide evidence of fairness, especially support for favorable consequential validity for groups typically disadvantaged by traditional, language-loaded intelligence tests. The mean IQs for males and females matched on age, parent educational level, and ethnicity are nearly identical, with effect sizes ranging from .02 to .03 across the three batteries. Samples matched on age, gender, and parent educational levels resulted in mean FSIQ differences, as shown through resulting effect sizes, in the small to moderate range (e.g., .22 to .43) for Native Americans as compared to Whites (the largest mean difference was 6.50, favoring Whites on the Standard Battery); small effect sizes were obtained for Hispanic/non-Hispanic comparisons (i.e., .10 to.14), with the largest FSIQ difference of 2.13 favoring non-Hispanics on the Standard Battery. Effect sizes for African Americans matched with Whites were moderate and ranged from .51 to .65; a mean FSIQ difference of 8.63 was the largest discrepancy between African Americans and Whites, which was obtained on the Standard Battery.

Further reduction in mean differences was obtained using a more refined matching strategy, which also added community size and the educational level of both parents, rather than just the parent with the highest educational level (Upson, 2003). Although Hispanic–non-Hispanic differences were minor to begin with (i.e., < 2.2 IQ points), the more refined matching reduced the mean differences between Hispanic Americans and Whites considerably to only 0.47 IQ point. That is less than one IQ point separated the two samples of matched Hispanic and non-Hispanic individuals. Refined sample matching reduced African American and White mean differences on the Standard Battery FSIQ only slightly to 8.51 (as compared to 8.63). Additional mean difference analyses are provided in the UNIT Manual and provide favorable consequential validity evidence for deaf and hard of hearing examinees (e.g., a mean FSIQ Standard Battery difference of 6.20) and for culturally and linguistically different examinees (e.g., a Standard Battery FSIQ mean difference of 5.33 was found for a sample of students living in Ecuador matched with a non-Ecuadorian sample living in the United States).

Predictive validity bias was examined for gender and race/ethnicity by using the regression slope as a measure of the strength of the relationships between UNIT and achievement scores on the Woodcock-Johnson-Revised Achievement Battery. Neither race nor gender contributed significantly to the prediction ($p = .05$) (see Bracken & McCallum, 1998 and McCallum, 1999 for a more detailed description of all these efforts to investigate UNIT fairness).

UNIT fairness studies conducted after the test was published have also produced encouraging findings. For example, Maller (2000) relied on the Mantel–Haenszel (MH) and Item Response Theory (IRT) to evaluate differential item functioning (DIF) for deaf children and adolescents. She concluded that *no items* on the UNIT exhibited gender or ethnicity-based DIF using either the MH or IRT; that is, the probability of a correct response on UNIT items was not affected by students' hearing status. Additional evidence for this conclusion is provided by Krivitski (2000), who conducted profile analyses which revealed that children who are deaf display similar profile patterns on UNIT subtests as compared to a matched sample of nondeaf children. Krivitski concluded that the data support the use of the UNIT for children classified as deaf.

In a review of five nonverbal instruments, Athanasiou (2000) concluded that all have unique strengths and weaknesses. Although she notes that the UNIT fails to meet Bracken's (1987) criterion for test–retest stability (.90) at all ages, her assessment of the UNIT is otherwise quite favorable. For example, she commented that the UNIT's reliance on only nonverbal directions likely reduced the potential for cultural bias in administration; the use of checkpoint items allows for periodic assessment of understanding during the administration; presentation of psychometric properties of subpopulations enhance the confidence users can have that the test is appropriate for a variety of examinees; and the floors, ceilings, and item gradients for UNIT Standard and Extended batteries exceed minimum recommendations; and so on. Perhaps the most important observation Athanasiou offered regarding the UNIT was the extent to which the Examiner's Manual provides thorough evidence of test fairness. She noted that although all the tests reviewed were generally impressive in terms of their technical adequacy, the other test authors presented much less statistical evidence of test fairness than did the UNIT authors.

Similar to Athanasiou's review, Fives and Flanagan (2002) concluded that the UNIT is well constructed, theoretically driven, psychometrically sound, highly useful, and that its use will permit more effective assessment of some traditionally difficult to assess populations. Additional reviews by Bandalos (2001), Kamphaus (2001), and Sattler (2001) also are generally positive, particularly regarding basic technical properties (e.g., reliability, floors, ceilings). Bandalos concluded a UNIT review in the Buros Mental Measurement Yearbook by noting that the UNIT provides a much needed means of obtaining reliable and valid assessments of intelligence for children with a wide array of disabilities who cannot be tested accurately with existing instruments. Bandalos also characterized the test as a carefully developed instrument with excellent reliability and impressive evidence of validity for use as supplement to or substitute for more traditional measures such as the WISC-III.

Interpreting the UNIT

Multidimensional test interpretation is complicated, partly because it requires that examiners engage in a number of interpretative steps, consult numerous tables, consider a variety of cognitive models, consider carefully the limitations of the instruments they use, and finally and most importantly, make the test results relevant for real-world application. In addition, there are at least three relatively unique interpretive models available to guide examiners' test interpretation (i.e., traditional ipsative strategies, subtest profile base-rate analyses, and cross-battery assessment (CBA) techniques). Citations are provided for specific guidelines for the ipsative, base rate, and CBA methods, and details are available in Bracken (1992), McCallum and Bracken (2005), McCallum, Bracken & Wasserman (2001), and McCallum (2003).

Traditional ipsative interpretation is controversial, but is used by practitioners who want to glean more information from instruments than the powerful, but limiting, predictive capabilities of a FSIQ. The goal of ipsative interpretation is to uncover relationships between individual cognitive strengths and weaknesses and important academic and work-related skills. Stability of ipsatively derived strengths and weaknesses is modest at best for a variety of cognitive ability tests (Bracken, Howell, Harrison, Stanford, & Zahn, 1991; Bracken & Lamprecht, 2002).

Using the UNIT for Intelligent Testing of Underserved Populations

The authors of the UNIT included several innovation features that contribute to intelligent testing of underserved populations, and consequently, follow in the tradition of their mentor, Alan Kaufman. For example, the UNIT is administered solely through examiner demonstrations and gestures, with liberal use of demonstration, sample, and (unique) checkpoint items. Second, subtests task demands provide the opportunity for both motoric and motor-reduced (i.e., pointing) responses, and administration can be modified to allow a pointing response when needed on four of the six subtests. The use of motoric and motor-reduced subtests facilitates administration by optimizing student motivation and rapport and may be indicated for children with limited motor skills. Third, subtests contain items which are culturally fair as possible (e.g., line drawings and objects that are recognizable to individuals from all cultures). Fourth, the test is model-based, assessing reasoning and memory, both symbolically and non-symbollically. Fifth, samples of non-English-speaking individuals and students with special education diagnoses were included in UNIT validation studies and norming. Sixth, battery length and administration time can be controlled by the examiner, depending on the number of subtests selected for administration. Seventh, reliability estimates were calculated for critical cutpoints (i.e., FSIQs of 70 $\pm$ 10 points and FSIQs of 130 $\pm$ 10 points). Finally, the UNIT authors provide important support resources, including a training video, a university training kit and materials, and a computerized scoring and interpretation software program. Two new UNIT-based instruments are currently in development, both with strong application for testing underserved populations, as described in the following section.

USING GROUP-ADMINISTERED INSTRUMENTS FOR INTELLIGENCE TESTING OF UNDERSERVED POPULATIONS

In addition to his influence on assessment using individualized cognitive instruments, Alan Kaufman has indirectly influenced the development of a number of group-administered measures by mentoring the authors of these tests. In this section, we describe briefly a few of these group-administered instruments.

General Ability Measure for Adults

The General Ability Measure for Adults (GAMA; Naglieri & Bardos, 1997) is coauthored by Jack Naglieri, a student of Alan Kaufman's, whose influence is obvious in this test. Naglieri and his coauthor use abstract figures to provide a fair assessment of general cognitive ability, and more specifically the application of reasoning and logic to solve problems. Evidence that the items are not biased based on race, ethnicity, and gender is provided in the manual.

The GAMA is a self- or group-administered multiple-choice test that assesses overall general ability for adults 18 years and older. Four subtests can be administered in about 25 minutes. The subtests include Matching (requires the examinee to determine which option is the same as the stimulus option based on shape and color), Sequences (requires the examinee to complete a sequence based on interrelationships of designs as they move through space), Analogies (requires the examinee to discover the relationships in a pair of abstract figures and then recognize a similar conceptual relationship in a difference pair of figures), and Construction (requires the examinee to "construct" a new figure based on analysis, synthesis, and rotation of spatial designs).

Naglieri Nonverbal Ability Test

Jack Naglieri also authored the Naglieri Nonverbal Ability Test (NNAT; Naglieri, 1997), a group- or individually administered matrix reasoning test for students in kindergarten through grade 12. The NNAT takes about 45 minutes to administer. The NNAT is a test of general cognitive reasoning via four matrices-based items types: Pattern Completion (requires the examinee to recognize a missing part by selecting one of four or five choices that contains the same pattern of the missing part or is continuous with the spatial orientation of the lines in a pattern around a missing part); Reasoning by Analogy (requires the examinee to recognize a logical relationship between several geometric shapes based on changes in the object across rows or columns); Serial Reasoning (requires the examinee to identify a sequential pattern); and Spatial Visualization (requires the examinee to recognize how two or more designs might look if combined or transformed in some manner, e.g., rotated in space).

Studies of test bias and fairness are described in the Manual, including DIF studies. Items showing potential bias were removed in the developmental process. Additional studies addressing test fairness are reported in the literature (e.g., Naglieri & Ronning, 2000a, b). These studies have produced impressive results and generally reveal no evidence of bias. In fact, the NNAT predicted reading better for African-Americans than for Whites and most of the correlation and mean-difference analyses revealed favorable results.

UNIT-Group Ability Test

The UNIT Group Ability Test (UNIT GAT; Bracken & McCallum, 2007) provides a group-administered assessment of intelligence based on the theoretical model of the UNIT. That is, the UNIT-GAT assesses (and provides scores for) memory and reasoning, symbolic processing and non-symbolic processing, and provides a composite-cognitive ability score as well. In a 45-minute administration, the UNIT-GAT can be administered in individual or group formats using gestures; as with the UNIT administration, examiners may talk during the test for rapport, classroom management, and directives (e.g., "stop," "look"). UNIT-GAT is currently in standardization, and preliminary evidence from pilot and field testing suggest that it will provide a strong screening assessment of all children, but, like the UNIT, the group-administered version will be particularly sensitive to those students who have difficulty using the English language. Because the UNIT-GAT is based on the UNIT theoretical model and builds on its developmental innovations, it exhibits many of the same characteristics of fairness. As the test continues through the developmental stages, data will be gathered to further examine its utility and fairness.

One useful feature of UNIT-GAT allows it to be used in conjunction with a teacher rating scale of gifted characteristics, the UNIT-Gifted Screening Scale (UNIT GSS; McCallum & Bracken, in press). That is, the UNIT-GAT and UNIT-GSS are being conormed, and are intended to be combined for screening students who may be gifted. Salient characteristics of the UNIT-GSS are described in the following section.

Universal Nonverbal Intelligence Test-Gifted Screening Scale

The Universal Nonverbal Intelligence Test – Gifted Screening Scale (UNIT-GSS) is a comprehensive teacher rating scale designed to evaluate student's aptitude in a variety of cognitive, social, and academic areas.

Like the UNIT and the UNIT-GAT, the UNIT GSS is developed to be particularly sensitive to those students who do not have strong English language skills, but for whom teachers may identify behaviors associated with giftedness. Teachers are instructed to evaluate examinees based on the effectiveness of the particular communication system the student possesses or uses (e.g., American Sign Language, Spanish, Mong, gestures). Consequently, examinees should not be penalized for immature or nonstandard use of English; obviously, language skills are evaluated in the context of academic work, but these skills and aptitude may be displayed using any language system.

Specific aptitudes assessed by the examinee's teacher include: Cognitive, Creative Arts, Emotional, Leadership, Language Arts, Math, Reading, and Science. Scores will be provided in each of these areas; in addition, the first four scales can be summed to provide a General Cognitive/Social Aptitude Score, and the second four scales will provide a General Academic Aptitude score. Finally, all the scales may be summed to provide an overall General Aptitude score. Because of the manner in which the UNIT-GSS is being standardized, it is particularly sensitive to local student performance levels. Teachers are instructed to evaluate (and rate) each student based on how well the student performs compared to same-age peers in the local environment. As the UNIT-GSS is developed, data will be collected to determine its utility and fairness.

SUMMARY

As is obvious from the description of the tests in this chapter, Alan Kaufman has influenced tremendously the field of cognitive testing; his direct and indirect influence have been extensive and overwhelmingly positive on the field in general and on the collection of students he has mentored. Alan and the cohort of University of Georgia doctoral students who obtained their doctorates in 1978 and 1979 under his supervision have been incredibly productive, producing literally scores of innovative tests and an enormous corpus of assessment literature in subfields of psychology and education. For example, his students have authored or coauthored several verbally oriented multidimensional cognitive tests, including the Adaptive Behavior Assessment System – II (ABAS; Harrison & Oakland, 2000), Bracken Basic Concept Scale (Bracken, 1984, 1998, 2006a, b), Cognitive Assessment System (CAS; Naglieri & Das, 1997), and the Reynolds Intellectual Assessment Scales (RIAS; Reynolds & Kamphaus, 2005). Also, his students have developed a considerable number of personality and/or behavioral scales, such as the

Behavior Assessment System for Children-II (BASC-II; Reynolds & Kamphaus, 1994), Clinical Assessment of Behavior (CAB; Bracken & Keith, 2004), Clinical Assessment of Depression (CAD; Bracken & Howell, 2004), Clinical Assessment of Attention Deficit (CAT; Bracken & Boatwright, 2005a, b), Clinical Assessment of Interpersonal Relations (CAIR; Bracken, 2006c), Draw A Person (Naglieri, McNeish, & Bardos, 1991), the Devereaux Scales of Mental Disorders (Naglieri, LeBuffe, & Pfeiffer, 1994), and Multidimensional Self Concept Scale (MSCS; Bracken, 1992), among others. Alan Kaufman's influence on psychological measurement in general and cognitive assessment in particular is perhaps as significant as any psychologist in history, living or dead. And, as we have indicated in this chapter, his influence on the intelligent assessment of underserved populations has been extensive. His influence on his several assessment-oriented students from a single cluster at the University of Georgia (1978–1979) has been tremendous. We salute his work and his legacy.

REFERENCES

Abrahams, R.D. (1973). The advantages of Black English. In J.S. De Stephano (Ed.) *Language, Society, and Education: A profile of Black English.* Worthington, OH: Charles A. Jones.

Athanasiou, M.S. (2000). Current nonverbal assessment instruments: A comparison of psychometric integrity and test fairness. *Journal of Psychoeducational Assessment,* 18, 211–299.

Bandalos, D.L. (2001). Review of the Universal Nonverbal Intelligence Test, in B.S. Plake & J.C. Impara (Eds.). *Fourteenth Mental Measurments Yearbook* (pp. 1296–1298). Lincoln, NE: Buros Institute.

Bracken, B.A. (1984). *Bracken Basic Concept Scale.* San Antonio, TX: The Psychological Corporation.

Bracken, B.A. (1985). Critical review of the Kaufman Assessment Battery for Children (K-ABC). *School Psychology Review,* 14, 21–36.

Bracken, B.A. (1987). Limitations of preschool instruments and standards for minimal levels of technical adequacy. *Journal of Psychoeducational Assessment,* 5, 313–326.

Bracken, B.A. (1992). *Multidimensional Self Concept Scale.* Austin, TX: PRO-ED.

Bracken, B.A. (1992). The interpretation of psychological tests. In R. Most and M. Zeidner (Eds.), *Psychological Testing: An Inside View* (pp. 119–158). Palo Alto, CA: Consulting Psychologists Press.

Bracken, B.A. (1998). *Bracken Basic Concept Scale – Revised.* San Antonio, TX: The Psychological Corporation.

Bracken, B.A. (2006a). *Bracken Basic Concept Scale – Receptive Third Edition.* San Antonio, TX: Harcourt Assessment.

Bracken, B.A. (2006b). *Bracken Basic Concept Scale: Expressive.* San Antonio, TX: Harcourt Assessment.

Bracken, B.A. (2006c). *Clinical Assessment of Interpersonal Relations*. Odessa, FL: Psychological Assessment Resources.

Bracken, B.A., & Barona, A. (1991). State-of-the-art Procedures for Translating, Validating, and Using Psychoeducational Tests for Cross-Cultural Assessment. *School Psychology International*, 12, 119–132.

Bracken, B.A., & Boatwright, B.S. (2005a). *Clinical Assessment of Attention Deficit – Child*. Odessa, FL: Psychological Assessment Resources.

Bracken, B.A., & Boatwright, B.S. (2005b). *Clinical Assessment of Attention Deficit – Adult*. Odessa, FL: Psychological Assessment Resources.

Bracken, B.A., & Fouad, N.A. (1987). Spanish translation and validation of the Bracken Basic Concept Scale. *School Psychology Review*, 15, 94–102.

Bracken, B.A., & Howell, K.K. (2004). *Clinical Assessment of Depression*. Odessa, FL: Psychological Assessment Resources.

Bracken, B.A., & Lamprecht, S. (2002). Ipsative subtest stability of the Universal Nonverbal Intelligence Test. Paper presented at the International Congress of Applied Psychology (Division 2), Singapore, July 2002.

Bracken, B.A., & McCallum, R.S. (1998). *The Universal Nonverbal Intelligence Test*. Chicago, IL: Riverside Publishing Company.

Bracken, B.A., & McCallum, R.S. (2001). *UNIT Compuscore*. Chicago, IL: Riverside Publishing Company.

Bracken, B.A., & McCallum, R.S. (2007). *UNIT Group Ability Test*. Itasca, IL: Riverside Publishing, Test in Progress.

Bracken, B.A., Barona, A., Bauermeister, J.J., Howell, K.K., Poggioli, L., & Puente, A. (1990). Multinational validation of the Bracken Basic Concept Scale. *Journal of School Psychology*, 28, 325–341.

Bracken, B.A., Howell, K.K., Harrison, T.E., Stanford, L.D., & Zahn, B.H. (1991). Ipsative subtest pattern stability of the Bracken Basic Concept Scale and the Kaufman Assessment Battery for Children in a preschool sample. *School Psychology Review*, 20, 309–324.

Bracken, B.A., Keith, L.K. (2004). *Clinical Assessment of Behavior*. Odessa, FL: Psychological Assessment Resources.

Brown, L., Sherbenou, R.J., & Johnson, S.K. (1990). *Test of Nonverbal Intelligence-2*. Austin, TX:Pro-Ed.

Carroll, J.B. (1993). *Human Cognitive Abilities: A Survey of Factor-Analytic Studies*. Cambridge, England: Cambridge University Press.

Carter, C. (1977). Prospectus on black communications. *School Psychology Digest*, 6, 23–30.

Cattell, R.B. (1963). Theory for fluid and crystallized intelligence: A critical experiment. *Journal of Educational Psychology*, 54, 1–22.

CTBS/McGraw-Hill (1996). *Comprehensive Test of Basic Skills*. Monterrey, CA: CTB/McGraw-Hill.

Farrell, M.M., & Phelps, L. (2000). A comparison of the Leiter-R and the Universal Nonverbal Intelligence Test (UNIT) with children classified as language impaired. *Journal of Psychoeducational Assessment*, 18, 268–274.

Fives, C.J., & Flanagan, R. (2002). A review of the Universal Nonverbal Intelligence Test (UNIT): An advance for evaluating youngsters with diverse needs. *School Psychology International*, 23, 425–448.

Fouad, N.A., & Bracken, B.A. (1986). Cross-cultural translation and validation of two psychoeducational assessment instruments. *School Psychology International,* 7, 167–172.

Forester, S. (2000). *Personal communication.*

Gilliam, J.E., Carpenter, B.O., & Christensen, J.R. (1996). *Gifted and Talented Evaluation Scales: A Norm Referenced Procedure for Identifying Gifted and Talented Students.* Austin, TX: PRO:ED.

Glutting, J., Adams, W., & Sheslow, D. (2002). *WRIT: Wide Range Intelligence Test Manual.* Wilmington, DE: Wide Range, Inc.

Glutting, J., McDermott, P.A., & Konold, T.R. (1997). Ontology, structure, and diagnosis benefits of a normative subtest taxonomy from the WISC-III standardization sample. In D.P. Flanagan, J.L. Genshaft, & P.L. Harrison (Eds.), *Contemporary Intellectual Assessment* (pp. 349–372). New York: Guilford.

Harrison, P.L., & Oakland, T. (2000). *Adaptive Behavior Assessment System.* San Antonio, TX: The Psychological Corporation.

Hooper, V.S. (2002). Concurrent and predictive validity of the Universal Nonverbal Intelligence Test and the Leiter International Performance Scale-Revised. Unpublished doctoral dissertation, University of Tennessee, Knoxville, TN.

Hooper, V.S., & Bell, S.M. (2006). Concurrent validity of the Universal Nonverbal Intelligence Test and the Leiter International Performance Scale-Revised. *Psychology in the Schools,* 43(2), 143–148.

Horn, J.L. (1968). Organization of abilities and the development of intelligence. *Psychological Review,* 75, 242–259.

Horn, J.L. (1994a). Theory of fluid and crystallized intelligence. In R.J. Sternberg (Ed.), *Encyclopedia of human intelligence* (pp. 443–451). New York: Macmillan.

Individuals with Disabilities Education Act, Pub. L. No. 101-476, 1400 et seq., 104 Stat. 1142 (1991).

Individuals with Disabilities Education Act Amendments (IDEA) of 2004, 20 U.S.C.

Jensen, A.R. (1980). *Bias in Mental Testing.* New York: The Free Press.

Jensen, A.R., & Reynolds, C.R. (1982). Race, social class and ability patterns on the WISC-R. *Personality and Individual Differences,* 3, 423–438.

Jimenez, S. (2001). An analysis of the reliability and validity of the Universal Nonverbal Intelligence Test (UNIT) with Puerto Rican children (Doctoral dissertation, Texas A&M University, 2001). *Dissertation Abstracts International,* 62, 5424.

Kamphaus, R.W. (2001). *Clinical Assessment of Child and Adolescent Intelligence* (2nd ed.). Boston: Allyn and Bacon.

Kaufman, A.S. (1979). *Intelligent Testing with the WISC-R.* New York: Wiley.

Kaufman, A.S. (1994). *Intelligent Testing with the WISC-III.* New York: Wiley.

Kaufman, A.S., & Kaufman, N.L. (1973). Black–white differences at age 2 ½–8 ½ on the McCarthy Scales of Children's Abilities. *Journal of School Psychology,* 11(3), 196–206.

Kaufman, A.S., & Kaufman, N.L. (1983). *Kaufman Assessment Battery for Children (K-ABC).* Circle Pines, MN: American Guidance Service.

Kaufman, A.S., & Kaufman, N.L. (2004). *Kaufman Assessment Battery for Children-II (K-ABC-II).* Circle Pines, MN: American Guidance Service.

Kirk, S.A., McCarthy, J.J., & Kirk, W.D. (1968). *Examiner's Manual: Illinois Test of Psycholinguistic Abilities*. Urbana, IL: Illinois University Press.

Krivitski, E.C. (2000). Profile analysis of deaf children using the Universal Nonverbal Intelligence Test (Doctoral dissertation, State University of New York at Albany, 2000). *Dissertation Abstracts International*, 61, 2593.

Leiter, R.G. (1979). *Intruction manual for the Leiter International Performance Scale*. Wood Dale, IL: Stoelting.

Maller, S.J. (2000). Item invariance in four subtests of the Universal Nonverbal Intelligence Test (UNIT) across groups of deaf and hearing children. *Journal of Psychoeducational Assessment*, 18, 240–254.

Markwardt, F.C. (1989). *Peabody Individual Achievement Test – Revised: Manual*. Circle Pines, MN: American Guidance Service.

McCallum, R.S. (1991). Using the Stanford-Binet: FE to assess preschool children. In B.A. Bracken (Ed.), *The Psychoeducational Assessment of Preschool Children* (2nd ed.). Boston, MA: Allyn Bacon.

McCallum, R.S. (1999). A 'baker's dozen criteria for evaluating fairness in nonverbal testing. *The School Psychologist*, 53, 40–43.

McCallum, R.S. (Ed.). (2003). *Handbook of Nonverbal Assessment*. New York: Kluwer Academic/Plenum Press.

McCallum, R.S., & Bracken, B.A. (In press). *UNIT Gifted Screening Scales*. Itasca, IL: Riverside Publishing.

McCallum, R.S., Bracken, B.A., & Wasserman, J. (2001). *Essentials of Nonverbal Assessment*. New York: Wiley.

McCarthy, D. (1972). *McCarthy Scales of Children's Abilities*. New York: Psychological Corporation.

McGrew. K.S., & Flanagan, D.P. (1998). *The Intelligence Test Desk Reference (ITDR): Gf-Gc Cross-Battery Assessment*. Boston, MA: Allyn & Bacon.

Naglieri, J.A. (1985). *Matrix Analogies Test Expanded Form: Examiner's Manual*. San Antonio, Tx: Psychological Corporation.

Naglieri, J.A, & Jensen, A.R. (1987). Comparison of black-white differences on the WISC-R and the K-ABC: Spearmen's hypothesis. *Intelligence*, 11, 21–43.

Naglieri, J.A., (1997). *Naglieri Nonverbal Ability Test 3/4 Multilevel Form Technical Manual*. San Antonio, TX: Harcourt Brace Educational Measurement.

Naglieri, J.A., McNeish, T.J., & Bardos, A.N. (1991). *Draw A Person: Screening Procedure for Emotional Disturbance*. Austin, TX: Proed.

Naglieri, J.A., LeBuffe, P.A., Pfeiffer, S.I. (1994). *Devereux Scales of Mental Disorders*. San Antonio, TX: The Psychological Corporation.

Naglieri, J.A., & Bardos, A.N. (1997). *General Ability Measure for Adults*. Minneapolis, MN: NCS Assessments.

Naglieri, J.A., & Das, J.P. (1997). *Cognitive Assessment System*. Itasca, IL: Riverside.

Naglieri, J., & Ronning, M.E. (2000a). The relationship between general ability using the NNAT and SAT reading achievement. *Journal of Psychoeducational Assessment*, 18, 230–239.

Naglieri, J., & Ronning, M.E. (2000b). Comparison of White, African-American, Hispanic, and Asian Children on the Naglieri Nonverbal Ability Test. *Psychological Assessment*, 12, 328–334.

Pasko, J.R. (1994). Chicago – don't miss it. *Communique*, 23, 2.

Raven, J.C. (1960). *Guide to Standard Progressive Matrices*. London, England: Lewis.

Reed, M.T., & McCallum, R.S. (1994). Construct validity of the Universal Nonverbal Intelligence Test (UNIT). Manuscript submitted for publication.

Reynolds, C.R., & Kamphaus, R.W. (1994). *Behavior Assessment System for Children. Second Edition*. Circle Pines, MN: AGS Publishing.

Reynolds, C.R., & Kamphaus, R.W. (2005). *Reynolds Intellectual Assessment System*. Lutz, FL: Psychological Assessment Resources.

Roid, G.H., & Miller, L.J. (1997). *Leiter International Performance Scale – Revised*. Wooddale, IL: Stoelting.

Roid, G.H. (2003). *Stanford-Binet Intelligence Scales, Fifth Edition*. Itasca, IL: Riverside Publishing.

Sattler, J.M. (2001). *Assessment of Children: Cognitive Applications*. (4th ed.). San Diego, CA: Jerome M. Sattler.

Scardapane, J.R., Egan, A., Torres-Gallegos, M., Levine, N., & Owens, S. (2002, March). Relationships among WRIT, UNIT, and GATES scores and language proficiency. *Paper* presented at the Counsel for Exceptional Children, New York, NY.

Silver, L.B. (1993). Introduction and overview to the clinical concepts of learning disabilities. *Child and Adolescent Psychiatric Clinics of North America: Learning Disabilities*, 2, 181–192.

The Psychological Corporation (1992). *Wechsler Individual Achievement Test: Manual*. San Antonio, TX: Author.

Thorndike, R.L., Hagen, E.P., & Sattler, J.M. (1986). *The Stanford-Binet Intelligence Scale: Fourth Edition*. Chicago: Riverside Publishing Company.

Torrance, E.P. (1982). Identifying and capitalizing on the strengths of culturally different children. In C.R. Reynolds & T.B. Gutkin (Eds.), *The Handbook of School Psychology* (pp. 481–500). New York: Wiley.

Unz, R. (1997, October 19). Bilingual is a damaging myth. *Los Angeles Times*.

U.S. Bureau of the Census. (2000). Language use [Online]. Available: http://www.census.gov/population.www.socdemo/lang_use.html

Upson, L.M. (2003). Effects of an increasingly precise socioeconomic match on mean score differences in nonverbal intelligence test scores. Unpublished doctoral dissertation, University of Tennessee, Knoxville, TN.

Wechsler, D. (1939). *The Measurement of Adult Intelligence*. Baltimore, MD: Williams & Wilkins.

Wechsler, D. (1991). *Wechsler Intelligence Scale for Children – III*. San Antonio, TX: The Psychological Corporation.

Wechsler, D. (1974). *Wechsler Intelligence Scale for Children – Revised*. San Antonio, TX: The Psychological Corporation.

Wilhoit, B.E., & McCallum, R.S. (2002). Profile analysis of the Universal Nonverbal Intelligence Test standardized sample. *School Psychology Review*, 31, 263–281.

Wilhoit, B., & McCallum, R.S. (2003). Cross-battery analysis of the UNIT. In R.S. McCallum (Ed.), *Handbook of Nonverbal Assessment*. New York: Kluwer Academic/Plenum Press.

Woodcock, R.W. (1990). Theoretical foundations of the WJ-R measures of cognitive ability. *Journal of Psychoeducational Assessment*, 8, 231–258.

Woodcock, R.W. (1991). Woodcock Language Proficiency Battery-Revised: English and Spanish forms. *Journal of Psychoeducational Assessment,* 8, 231–258.

Woodcock, R.W., McGrew, K.S., & Mather, N. (2001). *Woodcock-Johnson III Tests of Cognitive Abilities.* Itasca, IL; Riverside Publishing.

Woodcock, R.W., & Munoz-Sandoval, A.F. (1996). *Bateria Woodcock-Munoz Pruebas de habilidad cognoscitiva – Revisada.* Chicago, IL: Riverside.

16

Alan S. Kaufman: The Effects of One Man's Extraordinary Vision

JAMES C. KAUFMAN
California State University at San Bernardino

JACK A. NAGLIERI
George Mason University

Anne Anastasi described the field of intelligence and intelligence tests as one of the most important contributions psychology has made to society. Whereas early leaders such as Alfred Binet and David Wechsler played a key role in the early development of intelligence tests used today, Alan S. Kaufman is an extraordinary and dynamic psychologist who extended their influence to have a profound influence on the field of psychological assessment and has subsequently distinguished himself as a world leader in the field. Whereas Binet and Wechsler were instrumental in initiating the field, Alan S. Kaufman's provided the field with a vision based upon a scientific approach to intelligence test development and interpretation that have contributed dramatically to the evolution of the field. In addition, Kaufman changed the direction of assessment by applying sound research-based theory to clinical practice via innovative methodology. His influence has been far-reaching and profound, as evidenced by the diverse chapters written by the contributors to this book.

Kaufman began his influence on the field of cognitive assessment in 1969, when he worked closely with Dorothea McCarthy to develop and standardize the *McCarthy Scales of Children's Abilities*, one of the leading tests for preschool children for more than two decades. In the early 1970s, Kaufman worked closely with David Wechsler and had a profound influence on the development and standardization of the Wechsler Intelligence Scales for Children – Revised. Kaufman significantly influenced the nature and characteristics of these two popular tests. Both McCarthy and Wechsler greatly affected Kaufman's life by providing him with a deep clinical understanding of psychological assessment. Additionally, Kaufman received outstanding psychometric mentorship through his work with Robert Thorndike at Columbia University during his graduate training. These important accomplishments set the stage for those students of Kaufman's that would follow in his tradition, particularly as Kaufman worked to merge sound science with application in the field of psychology.

Kaufman developed an innovative approach for interpreting Wechsler's IQ tests in the 1970s that systematically applied statistical rules and guidelines to help explain fluctuations among the scaled scores of a person's subtest profile. Previously, examiners interpreted very small, even trivial differences as important and often made critical decisions about children on the basis of these findings. In Chapter 8 Sternberg discusses his own trials to overcome the conservative college admissions testing conventions, which were also predicated on strict psychometric models of intelligence. In addition, Kaufman's understanding of the role factor analysis could play in test validation and interpretation dramatically changed the field. Kaufman's 1975 WISC-R factor analysis article is illustrative of his application of good science to test construction and interpretation. In that paper, he urged examiners to focus on interpreting the three major factors that formed the foundation of Wechsler's scales, rather than the Verbal and Performance IQs, because the two-dimensional model did not correspond well to the statistical structure of the test. His emphasis on factors helped align clinical interpretation with the statistical structure of the test and therefore emphasized reliable global scores.

Another aspect of Kaufman's innovative interpretive approach was to look for consistency among scores on the total profile to ensure that conclusions about the person's strengths and weaknesses were based on the examinee's entire set of scores. This new approach to test interpretation was first articulated in the 1979 book *Intelligent Testing with the WISC-R*, which was a landmark publication that changed the nature of test interpretation within the fields of school, clinical, and neuropsychology, as well as special education. Examining an individual within a broad context extends to other enduring traits that affect behavior as well (cognitive or interpersonal), and Kaufman's emphasis on viewing a child with many sources of distinct abilities is reflected in Chapter 6 by Bassett and Oakland: they encourage psychologists to "routinely assess children's temperament and thereby identify some of their strengths that, when properly utilized, have the potential to foster their academic, social, emotional, and vocational development."

As Elaine Fletcher-Janzen (Chapter 4) notes, Kaufman's *Intelligent Testing* model "became the gold standard for psychometric test interpretation and clinical assessment" and served to blend what she describes as the romantic and classical aspects of assessment. She emphasizes the role that

Kaufman's integrated approach to intellectual assessment played in the field of neuropsychology, just as Nancy Mather (Chapter 5) articulates the key role he played in the field of special education, most notably the identification of children with specific learning disabilities. Randy Kamphaus and Cecil Reynolds (Chapter 10) agree, stating, "We think that his most innovative work, and the contribution likely to have the most long-term impact, was his joining of the two disciplines of measurement science and clinical assessment practice. He did so by essentially creating a new methodology of intelligence test interpretation, a method that has spread to clinical assessment practice in general, and it may be characterized in today's terminology as a early form of 'evidence-based' test interpretive practice, one that emphasizes a psychometric approach to evaluating individual performance on a battery of tests as expressed as test scores." Jan Alm of Uppsala, Sweden (Chapter 14), writes: "In the history of psychology there are different outlooks. Are changes due to certain individuals like Pavlov, Skinner, Bandura and Freud or is it just that the time is ripe for the knowledge to burst out? As usual there is probably a combination. The first outlook is however more obvious and when it comes to Alan Kaufman I feel that through his books, his deep interest for good tests and intelligent interpretations he has saved a generation of psychologists from doing bad work."

Intelligent Testing with the WISC-R was immensely popular, as was its 1994 sequel (*Intelligent Testing with the WISC-III*), the 1999 text *Essentials of WAIS-III Assessment* (with Elizabeth Lichtenberger), and the 2004 book *Essentials of WISC-IV Assessment* (with Dawn Flanagan). These books became staples in graduate programs and were commonly found on the bookshelves of practitioners. Ultimately, virtually all of Kaufman authored or coauthored books on intelligence tests and testing, which have spanned the age range from early preschool to geriatrics, have been extremely popular and influential, and remain so decades after their initial publication. His work has greatly affected how generations of psychologists interpret intelligence tests, and how these tests continue to be interpreted. Sam Ortiz and Dawn Flanagan (Chapter 8) wrote in a Preface to one of their books that "Kaufman's 'intelligent' approach to Wechsler intelligence test interpretation is at the core of our teaching, writing, research, and practice" (Flanagan, McGrew, & Ortiz, 2000, p. xviii), and in their chapter, they each explain precisely how he impacted them personally and in the diverse aspects of their professional work, based on his research, and writing, and as a mentor and colleague.

Apart from his research and writing, Alan's personal mentorship has extended worldwide, as he and his wife, Nadeen Kaufman, have trained graduate students and psychologists from North and South America, Africa, Europe, and Asia. Toshinori Ishikuma (Chapter 13), from Tsukuba, Japan, writes, "I would like to show my great appreciation to my supervisors, onshi (Japanese word for a teacher to whom who you owe a great deal and you respect highly), and research partners, Drs. Alan and Nadeen Kaufman. Drs. Kaufman taught me the significant roles of intelligent helpers to understand the child and change their school life. I have learned that becoming a school psychologist is very tough but valuable. Knowing Drs. Kaufman had great impact on my career and my life." Alm (Chapter 14) wrote that after he discovered Kaufman's books, "At first I was filled with the feeling that I found a goldmine and I was the only owner. I started to dive deep into it and my self-confidence was peaking. I then started courses in the proposed methods of interpretation and the Swedish psychologists were eager to listen. Alan later on came to Uppsala University and gathered crowds of interested psychologists. . . . We later also got the opportunity to listen to Dr. Nadeen Kaufman in Uppsala. Her influence has continuously been very crucial."

At the time *Intelligent Testing* was published, not only was statistical significance typically ignored by clinicians when interpreting test profiles, but nonscientific approaches to test interpretation dominated. Freudian psychoanalytical interpretations abounded, as did overdiagnosis of brain damage from Verbal-Performance IQ (V-P IQ) differences. Kaufman's research on "normal scatter" among subtest scores (1976a) and "normal" V-P IQ differences (Kaufman, 1976b) gave clinicians useful and reliable yardsticks for evaluating whether the IQ discrepancies and range of subtest scores earned by their clients were common or rare within the general population. Prior to Kaufman's work, V-P IQ differences of 15 or more points were commonly considered to denote learning disabilities or brain damage when, in fact, Kaufman's research indicated that one child or adult out of four in the general population had V-P differences of 15 points or greater. Similarly, prior to Kaufman's contributions to test interpretation, children and adolescents were commonly diagnosed with learning disabilities because of "scatter" in the subtest profiles. His research indicated that the typical person in the general population had a range of 7 ($\pm$ 2) points in his or her scaled scores on the WISC-R, such that even ranges from 6 to 15 were "normal" and not sufficient reason for a diagnosis of any type of abnormality. Kaufman's research in this area had a powerful effect on the ways psychologists diagnosed brain damage, learning disabilities, and psychopathology by providing the field with data on what was truly normal and common in the general population. Kamphaus and Reynolds pronounce Kaufman the first person to introduce statistical guidelines to clinical and school psychologists. In those early days, clinicians and researchers lacked a realistic conception of the sizable fluctuations that characterize the test profiles of typical children and adults. Elaine Fletcher-Janzen explains, "Intelligent testing moved emphasis away from pure psychometric and reductionistic comparisons of test scores and demanded incorporation of a contextual analysis of the test subject and interventions that had ecological validity." It was, however, with a new test that one of Kaufman's most influential efforts would so greatly influence the field.

The 1983 *Kaufman Assessment Battery for Children* (K-ABC) developed with his wife and scholarly colleague, Nadeen, was a monumental contribution to the measurement of intelligence. The importance of the K-ABC cannot be fully described without also recognizing the enormity of the task and the contributions of both authors. Building a successful test requires an amalgam of skills and wide range of knowledge. The test must meet the needs and desires of research community as well as the clinician in the field. Tests must be built that take into consideration the nature of the subject and the tremendous variability among children and adolescents. Items must be written that engage and yet measure effectively. Directions must be crafted that will communicate effectively at different ages and ability levels. Documentation must be prepared that provides the sophistication of a research report and also addresses the interpretation and use issues faced by the test users. This diversity of tasks was eloquently managed by the team of Alan and Nadeen Kaufman, each playing a unique role, at the same time their combined efforts yielding more than the sum of the parts. Indeed, Nadeen's graduate degrees in psychology, reading and learning disabilities, and special education (neuroscience) from Columbia University form an outstanding base of knowledge for developing their tests; but when combined with her experiences as a teacher of learning-disabled children, school psychologist, learning disabilities specialist, and founder-director of several psychoeducational clinics, the quality of their work together is extraordinary. Clearly, the Kaufman tests would not have been written if not for *both* Kaufmans. We, therefore, recognize with great admiration the quantity and quality of the contributions made by Dr. Nadeen Kaufman to the two editions of the K-ABC.

The test was based uniquely on a blend of cognitive and neuropsychological theory at a time when intelligence tests were, and in many cases still are, based on a historical rather than theoretical foundation. Just as Kaufman's earlier research and interpretive approaches helped bridge the gap between psychometrics and the practice of psychology, the K-ABC helped bridge the gap between testing theory and practice. The most important aspect of the K-ABC was the shift from using verbal and nonverbal tests to ones based on process. That is, whereas traditional intelligence tests (e.g., Wechsler, Binet) were organized according to the *content* of the questions (verbal, quantitative, and nonverbal), tests on the K-ABC were organized on the basis of the *process needed to solve the question* (i.e., sequential and simultaneous processes). This shift in emphasis from test content to the process needed to solve the problem put more emphasis on the cognitive activities of the examinee and thereby a dramatic change of focus resulted. This test was developed to emphasize *how* children learn using an approach that is consistent with a variety of theories in cognitive psychology and neuropsychology. As Mather (Chapter 5) comments, the particular usefulness of a student's learning style can provide for the selection of remedial teaching interventions for the learning-disabled child: "For students with SLD, differential instruction that addresses the source of the problem is far more effective than global, generalized approaches that do not." In addition, she states the K-ABC's validity studies enabled more effective test interpretation: "The theoretical rationale provided by the K-ABC made it particularly appropriate for neuropsychological evaluations and the assessment of children suspected of having SLD."

Importantly, the K-ABC was developed with the goal of reducing the differences between the scores earned by European American children and minority children. This goal was addressed in several ways. Student interest was maintained by developing a variety of new tasks that were extremely interesting to children. Students from low socioeconomic backgrounds performed better on this test because the content of the questions did not rely as much on school learning, but favored tasks that rewarded new problem solving. The result was to reduce the typical European American–African American assessed cognitive ability difference in half (Naglieri, 1986) and to greatly reduce the differences between European American children and Hispanic American children (and also between European American children and Native American children) (Kaufman & Kaufman, 1983, Tables 4.35 to 4.37). That reduction in ethnic differences has been fully maintained on the KABC-II, underscoring the dramatic effect Kaufman has had on the movement for fair and nonbiased assessment of individuals from a diversity of ethnic backgrounds (Fletcher-Janzen, 2003; Kaufman & Kaufman, 2004; Tables 8.7 to 8.9; Kaufman, Lichtenberger, Fletcher-Janzen, & Kaufman, 2005).

One additional contribution of the original K-ABC was the Kaufmans' view of the content of test manuals. The K-ABC interpretive manual included extensive data to support the validity of the new test (i.e., more than 40 validity studies), a great step forward in test development; previously, test manuals for individual intelligence tests were virtually barren of validity data and interpretive guidelines. Alm (Chapter 14) refers to the dramatic effect of Kaufman's inclusion of interpretive information as part of test manuals: "How sad and strange that existing professional knowledge in one of the most central areas of clinical work, i.e. doing diagnostic assessments and giving recommendations, took 15 years to reach Europe. At that time Swedish psychologists used the WISC and WAIS-R and there was no information in the test manual on interpreting the test results, except for computing the three IQs." Additionally, the Kaufmans stressed the need to examine race and ethnic differences in their test. This innovative key contribution of the K-ABC and the reduction of ethnic differences has *not* been emulated by virtually any other comprehensive cognitive batteries, including the Wechsler scales, Stanford–Binet, and Woodcock–Johnson, the single exception among all of the major cognitive tests being the Cognitive Assessment System (Naglieri & Das, 1997), which has joined the K-ABC and KABC-II in greatly reducing ethnic differences. Ultimately, the innovations of the K-ABC – most notably the development of a test founded on theory, the shift from content to process, excellent manuals, and the inclusion of numerous validity studies in the test manual – have set a new standard for intelligence tests that have been developed or revised since the K-ABC's publication in 1983. This overarching "exception to the rule" status that the K-ABC achieved is addressed by Jack Naglieri: "The work [Alan] and Nadeen Kaufman did on the K-ABC was the best example of his conviction that the idea of an individual intelligence test could be reconceptualized."

Kaufman's dedication to the translation of theory to practice, to the development of fair test instruments, and to the application of psychometric principles to clinical assessment has been a career-long goal. His first publications in the early 1970s used psychometric approaches to relate theories of development and intelligence (Piaget, Gesell, Guilford) to assessment practice; these early research investigations also explored race differences on the McCarthy Scales and Wechsler Preschool and Primary Scale of Intelligence (WPPSI) with a focus on understanding the nature of these differences and ways to minimize them. Flanagan and Ortiz remark about Kaufman's attention to reduced discrepancies in test scores of different minority groups as a personal point of their professional growth: "Consistent with the intent of the K-ABC, our experiences with its use in evaluating culturally and linguistically diverse students provided a large part of the basis upon which our understanding of issues relative to non-discriminatory assessment evolved." He continued these lines of research throughout the 1970s and 1980s, though his theoretical interests had switched to the neuropsychological models associated with Sperry's cerebral specialization approach and the Luria-Das processing paradigm. The K-ABC reflected a highly successful merger of his passions for relating theory to practice, for developing assessment tools that are fair to diverse ethnic groups, and for using cutting-edge psychometric methodology (e.g., Rasch latent-trait modeling and Angoff-Ford item bias analyses) to develop his 1983 test. (Kamphaus and Reynolds note that he was the first person in test development to utilize factor analytical findings and present subtest specificity studies.) In the 1990s and extending to the present, Kaufman has refined his theoretical perspective (he currently favors an integration of Luria's three-block neuropsychological model [upon which Naglieri and Das' Cognitive Assessment System is based] with the Cattell–Horn–Carroll psychometric theory), while continuing to emphasize the best ways to translate theory to practice, to minimize ethnic differences, and to rely on state-of-the-art psychometric approaches for test construction (e.g., hierarchical confirmatory factor analysis, and differential item functioning analysis). Cole (Chapter 11) articulates the role of Kaufman's work in the use of factor-analytical studies to better understand any test: "These joint factor analysis findings not only provided further validation of the Wechsler scales, but they also fermented a rich allotment of enhanced interpretation based on theoretical models." Cole continues to describe the innovative ways Kaufman introduced psychometric methods in test development: "Despite developing his system years before confirmatory latent modeling was part of the applied IQ literature, Kaufman's intelligent design was insisting on the same kind of data checks at the ideographic level that CFA requires at the nomothetic level."

Internationally, Kaufman's interpretive approach and cognitive tests have had a dramatic influence on the testing and assessment practices throughout Canada, Europe, Africa, and Asia. Adaptations and translations of the K-ABC have been published throughout the world and are extremely popular in diverse countries, including France, Germany, Netherlands, Israel, Belgium, Switzerland, Korea, Japan, Egypt, Spain, Italy, Jordan, and Canada. Enea-Drapeau and Carlier devote part of their chapter to a "general report on the use of the French version of the K-ABC by researchers, and review studies conducted in France (and probably unknown in North America, as many of them were published in French only)." Ishikuma comments poetically about some statistical similarities to the United States version when he analyzed data from the Japanese K-ABC: "Knowledge on factors of children's intelligence that Drs. Kaufman accumulated over the years crossed over the Pacific Ocean!" The Japanese K-ABC's popularity is documented by the country's Japanese Association of K-ABC Assessment with 13 additional local associations of K-ABC assessment. It is seen as especially helpful, Ishikuma reports, for making educational plans for a child with learning disability (LD), attention deficit hyperactivity disorder (ADHD), and other developmental disabilities. Members of these K-ABC associations are mostly teachers and school psychologists who are "motivated to find opportunities for learning to understand the child's strengths and weakness in abilities and achievement and use the test results to create teaching methods and learning environment better responding to the child's unique needs." Ishikuma also notes: "The national association provides workshops, case study meetings, annual conference, and publishes newsletters and an academic journal, *The Japanese Journal of K-ABC Assessment.*"

Other Kaufman tests have also been published in Europe (i.e., K-BIT, K-SNAP, and KAIT, and the new computerized, cognitive processing-based K-CLASSIC). Currently in development is research in many different countries and imminent publication of the K-ABC II. In addition, his books on the intelligence of children, adolescents, and adults – as well as his frequent invited talks throughout the world – have provided strong international guidance and leadership. His books (both the English and translated versions), tests, and lectures have had groundbreaking worldwide impact on the interpretation of the Wechsler and Kaufman tests, and the diagnosis of learning disabilities, in France, Sweden, Germany, Brazil, Japan, Spain, Korea, Netherlands, Israel, Canada, England, Egypt, Russia, and numerous other countries. Among the many international doctoral students Kaufman has mentored, Toshinori Ishikuma (Chapter 13) has championed the development of the field of school psychology in Japan and has coauthored Japanese versions of various Wechsler and Kaufman scales; Jan Alm (Chapter 14) has played a prominent role in Sweden regarding the diagnosis and treatment of dyslexia; and Soo-Back Moon (Catholic University of Daegu) has coauthored the Korean K-ABC and is one of the leading psychologists in the Republic of Korea.

The Kaufmans' research and test development goals were applied to a variety of tests they have developed together, not just the measures of general cognitive ability. Most notable in this regard are the measures of academic achievement developed for the Achievement Scale on the original K-ABC, for the 1985 Kaufman Test of Educational Achievement (K-TEA), and for the 2004 KTEA-II. The Kaufmans developed novel tests of general information and reading comprehension for the K-ABC Achievement Scale that made use of pictorial stimuli (Faces & Places) and gestural responding (Reading Understanding). Both of these tasks produced ethnic differences that were substantially smaller than the differences consistently produced by traditional tests of general information and reading comprehension. McCallum and Bracken (Chapter 15) discuss the difficulties of testing children from linguistically and culturally different populations, as well as those who are hard-of-hearing or speech and language impaired, who therefore require different kinds of well-constructed cognitive instruments that were unavailable before Kaufman's research and attention to this topic. His 1978 publication about the high verbal load in then-current tests for preschool children focused on both young children's understanding of test directions spoken by the examiner, even on "nonverbal" tests, as well as the then-currents tests' emphasis on language required for the child to be successful. McCallum and Bracken describe Kaufman's contribution to this aspect of nonverbal assessment, starting with the original K-ABC's Nonverbal Scale: "The past couple of decades and especially the last few years, many psychometrically sound assessment options have appeared. Importantly, Alan Kaufman has been involved, either directly or indirectly, in the development of the great majority of those instruments . . ." McCallum and Bracken refer to their own research with Kaufman, early in their careers, as greatly affecting the development of their own major multidimensional, individually administered nonverbal test, the *Universal Nonverbal Intelligence Test* (UNIT; Bracken & McCallum, 1998). Of course, his influence has also led to other nonverbal tests such as the Naglieri Nonverbal Ability Test, now in its second edition (Naglieri, 2008), and the Wechsler Nonverbal Scale of Ability (Wechsler & Naglieri, 2006).

Furthermore, the very popular K-TEA and KTEA-II have made an important contribution to the current need for response to intervention by providing Error Analyses that identify each student's specific strong and weak areas of functioning within each academic area. The Error Analyses for reading, math, written expression, spelling, and oral expression were developed primarily from various theoretical perspectives within each academic area, consistent with Kaufman's goal of translating theory to practice. In addition, the KTEA-II was developed, in part, from the perspectives of both the Cattell–Horn–Carroll (CHC) theory and Luria's neuropsychological model. Indeed, the integration of the KTEA-II with the KABC-II from the vantage points of both CHC and Luria theory forms an important section of the 2005 book that the Kaufmans coauthored (*Essentials of KABC-II Assessment*).

Beginning in the late 1980s, and continuing to the present, Kaufman has authored or coauthored an important series of research studies that address the crucial issue of age changes in cognitive functioning across the adult life span. This research has featured various versions of Wechsler's adult scales and also several of his own scales, and he examined many of the controversies in the field about the nature of cognitive decline with increasing age. These studies have been of exceptional methodology; his cross-sectional investigations on the WAIS-R, with James McLean (University of Alabama) and Cecil Reynolds (Chapter 10), earned outstanding research awards from both the Mid-South Educational Research Association and the Mensa Education and Research Foundation. In addition, Kaufman used innovative methodology, a variant of Schaie's cohort-sequential approach that also employed cohort substitution, to conduct longitudinal investigations of the aging-IQ relationship based on data from the WAIS, WAIS-R, and WAIS-III standardization samples. These longitudinal studies have been reported in two articles, one devoted to the practical applications of the important findings (Kaufman, 2000) and another that explored the theoretical implications of the findings and helped resolve controversies about the degree of decline on diverse cognitive abilities that accompanies the normal aging process (Kaufman, 2001a).

Kaufman continues to be actively engaged in the area of aging research, currently investigating the changes in ability and academic achievement over the life span, using data from the recent standardizations of two Kaufman tests that included adults as old as 90 years – the Brief Form of the KTEA-II, and the KBIT-2 (Kaufman, Johnson, & Liu, in press). As has been true for all of the investigations he has conducted on aging, Kaufman continues to use state-of-the-art methodology to understand, not only the theoretical implications of the growth curves of maintained and vulnerable abilities, but especially the practical implications of the results for psychological assessment, for the societal impact of the aging process and for understanding whether the decline in certain vulnerable abilities can be delayed. Bassett and Oakland compare their important research on the lifelong construct of temperament with Kaufman's interest in cognitive abilities across child and adult development: "Temperament characterizes important and enduring qualities displayed by children, youth, and adults – a lifespan age range consistent with Dr. Kaufman's commitment to research-based scholarship that addresses important issues for persons of all ages (e.g., Kaufman, 1979, 1994)." The effect of an individual's temperament will continue through all interactions with one's environment, and study of it reflects, Bassett and Oakland argue, "Dr. Kaufman's commitment to a fundamental principle that professional services in psychology and education rest first and foremost on an accurate description of enduring traits."

Kaufman's dedication to the practical applications of research on cognitive, achievement, and neuropsychological tests has diversified in the past 10–15 years to other arenas. In 1992 he cofounded (with Jim McLean) the peer-reviewed journal *Research in the Schools*, whose mission was, precisely to bring psychological theory into the classroom via the application of sophisticated statistical and research methodology. Kaufman and McLean coedited the journal for 12 years, and it is still a well-respected journal. In addition, beginning in 1997, the Kaufmans coedited a book series for Wiley, *Essentials of Psychological Assessment*, that now includes more than 30 volumes. The Kaufmans are also the founding editors of two other book series: *Essentials of Mental Health Practice* and *Essentials of Behavioral Science*. All of these series have been extremely popular and have influenced greatly the way practitioners interpret cognitive, neuropsychological, vocational, personality, and achievement tests and apply the results in a clinically sound, systematic manner.

Throughout his career, Kaufman applied his training in psychometrics and research methodology under Robert Thorndike at Columbia University to the practical and societal applications of research findings, especially as they pertain to cognitive and neuropsychological tests. He critiqued the methodology of the studies that interpreted as fact a measurable IQ loss due to small amounts of bloodstream. His comprehensive article on this topic served as the centerpiece of a 2001 issue of *Archives of Clinical Neuropsychology* devoted to lead level and IQ loss (Kaufman, 2001b). With his colleagues at the Yale University School of Medicine, he coauthored a similar kind of methodological critique of the supposed neuropsychological and cognitive deficits attributed to another toxin – polychlorinated biphenyls (PCBs). That article also served as a centerpiece (of a 2004 issue of *Psychology in the Schools*) to encourage discussion and debate about the psychological and societal consequences of exposure to small amounts of toxins (Cicchetti, Kaufman, & Sparrow, 2004). By virtue of his continual work as an Editorial Board member (he has served on as many as ten at one time) and reviewer of many different psychology journals, Kaufman's knowledge affected new research publications. Cole points this out in the area of factor analysis: "Finally, Alan has also had his influence on factor analysis use in cognitive assessment through his prolific work as a reviewer for many of the top journals in cognitive assessment."

It is clear that the contributions Kaufman has made to the field and the numbers of practitioners who have benefited from his research and scientific approach to test use are profound. Considering the numbers of children served by generations of psychologists who have used his methods, benefited from his research, and applied the instruments he has produced, one can only conclude that he has dramatically changed the way psychologists have practiced. Kaufman's research and development efforts have led to substantial innovative applications in the area of psychological assessment. His efforts have significantly improved the application of psychological theory, and he has provided sophisticated solutions to some of the most difficult problems faced by practicing psychologists around the world. As summarized by Robert Sternberg (Chapter 9): "If one were to ask who are the people who most have influenced and impacted ability testing, almost certainly Alfred Binet would be #1. David Wechsler would probably be #2. In my mind, Alan Kaufman would be #3. And in terms of productivity, he surpassed Binet and Wechsler relatively early in his career."

REFERENCES

Bracken, B.A., & McCallum, R.S. (1998). *Universal Nonverbal Intelligence Test (UNIT)*. Chicago, IL: Riverside Publishing.

Cicchetti, D.V., Kaufman, A.S., & Sparrow, S.S. (2004). The Relationship between prenatal and postnatal exposure to polychlorinated biphenyls (PCBs) and cognitive, neuropsychological, and behavioral deficits: a critical appraisal. *Psychology in the Schools*, 41, 589–624.

Flanagan, D.P., & Kaufman, A.S. (2004). *Essentials of WISC-IV Assessment*. New York: Wiley.

Flanagan, D.P., McGrew, K.S. & Ortiz, S.O. (2000). *The Wechsler Intelligence Scales and Gf-Gc Theory: A Contemporary Interpretive Approach*. Boston, MA: Allyn & Bacon.

Fletcher-Janzen, E. (2003). *A Validity Study of the KABC-II and the KABC-II Pueblo Indian Children of New Mexico*. Bloomington, MN: Pearson Assessments.

Kaufman, A.S. (1976a). A new approach to the interpretation of test scatter on the WISC-R. *Journal of Learning Disabilities*, 9, 160–168.

Kaufman, A.S. (1976b). Verbal-performance IQ discrepancies on the WISC-R. *Journal of Consulting and Clinical Psychology*, 44, 739–744.

Kaufman, A.S. (1979). *Intelligent Testing with the WISC-R*. New York: Wiley.

Kaufman, A.S. (1994). *Intelligent Testing with the WISC-III*. New York: Wiley.

Kaufman, A.S. (2000). Seven questions about the WAIS-III regarding differences in abilities across the 16 to 89 year life span. *School Psychology Quarterly*, 15, 3–29.

Kaufman, A.S. (2001a). WAIS-III IQs, Horn's theory, and generational changes from young adulthood to old age. *Intelligence*, 29, 131–167.

Kaufman, A.S. (2001b). Do low levels of lead produce IQ loss in children? A careful examination of the literature. *Archives of Clinical Neuropsychology*, 16, 303–341.

Kaufman, A.S., Johnson, C.K., & Liu, X. (in press). A CHC theory-based analysis of age differences on cognitive abilities and academic skills at ages 22 to 90 years. *Journal of Psychoeducational Assessment*.

Kaufman, A.S. & Kaufman, N.L. (1983). *K-ABC Interpretive Manual*. Circle Pines, MN: American Guidance Service.

Kaufman, A.S. & Kaufman, N.L. (2004). *Kaufman Assessment Battery for Children – Second Edition (K-ABC-II)*. Circle Pines, MN: American Guidance Service.

Kaufman, A.S., & Lichtenberger, E.O. (1999). *Essentials of WAIS-III Assessment*. New York: Wiley.

Kaufman, A.S., Lichtenberger, E.O., Fletcher-Janzen, E., & Kaufman, N.L. (2005). *Essentials of KABC-II Assessment*. New York: Wiley.

Naglieri, J.A. (1986). WISC-R and K-ABC comparison for matched samples of Black and White children. *Journal of School Psychology*, 24, 81–88.

Naglieri, J.A. (2008). *Naglieri Nonverbal Ability Test, Second Edition*. San Antonio, TX: Pearson.

Naglieri, J.A., & Das, J.P. (1997a). *Cognitive Assessment System*. Itasca, IL: Riverside Publishing Company.

Wechsler, D., & Naglieri, J.A. (2006). *Wechsler Nonverbal Scale of Ability*. San Antonio, TX: Harcourt Assessments.

Author Index

A

Aaron, P. G. 32, 46, 49
Abrahams, R. D. 198, 214
Abenhaim, N. 180
Adams, W. 206, 216
Adrien, J. L. 180
Ahmadi, M. 133, 134, 144
Ajam, E. 179
Allen, M. 63, 69
Alfonso, V. C. 23, 27, 112
Alper, T. 23, 26
Ambert, A. M. 66, 67
Anastasi. A. 15, 26
Anderson, M. 49
Anderson, G. M. 174, 182
Andre, M. 180
Antoine, C. 174, 182
Aquilino, S. A. 87, 95
Arbuckle, J. L. 165, 167
Arend, R. 56, 70
Ashford, S. J. 145
Athanasiou, M. S. 214
Azuma, H. 184, 190

B

Bachmeier, R. J. 38, 51
Baddeley, A. D. 20, 26
Bailleux, C. 178, 179
Bailly L. 181
Baltes, M. M. 66, 67
Bandalos, D. L. 209, 215
Bandura, A. 63, 67

Banner, D. 55, 70
Bardos, A. N. 91, 94, 95, 211, 214, 217
Barona, A. 199, 215
Barnes, M. A. 27
Bauermeister, J. J. 199, 215
Barondiot, C. 180
Barthelemy, C. 180
Bassett, K. 61, 66, 67, 70
Bateman, B. 32, 49
Bayliss, D. 26
Baumrind, D. 66, 67
Bee, H. 67
Bell, L. 65, 67
Bell, S. M. 205, 216
Bem, S. L. 62, 67
Benson, N. 55, 67
Bentler, P. M. 166, 168
Berndt, T. J. 63, 66, 67
Berninger, V. W. 15, 21, 23, 26, 32, 49
Bernoussi, M. 179, 180
Berrios, M. 61, 69
Best, D. L. 63
Billard, C. 174, 179, 180
Binet, A. 17, 114, 115, 144
Birch, H. G. 54
Blanc, R. 180
Blaye, A. 178, 179
Blond, M. H. 179
Blumenthal, A. L 16, 28
Boies, S. J. 86, 95
Boatwright, B. S. 214, 215
Boudousquie, A. B. 27
Bonnaud, C. 179

235

Subject Index

A

B

C